OLD FACES OF 1976

OLD FACES OF 1976

A few thousand fairly well-chosen words on Jerry Ford, Nelson Rockefeller, Teddy Kennedy, George Wallace, Hubert Humphrey, Ronald Reagan, Ed Muskie, Scoop Jackson, George McGovern, Hugh Carey, Abe Beame, Jack Javits, Jerry Brown and some other men you probably wouldn't want your daughter to marry

RICHARD REEVES

HARPER & ROW, PUBLISHERS

NEW YORK, HAGERSTOWN, SAN FRANCISCO, LONDON

Portions of this work originally appeared in somewhat different form in *New York* magazine and *The New York Times Magazine.*

Lines of dialogue from the comic strip ''Lolly'' by Pete Hansen. © 1975 by The Chicago Tribune

FIRST EDITION

Designed by Sidney Feinberg

Library of Congress Cataloging in Publication Data

Reeves, Richard.
  Old faces of 1976.
  Includes index.
  1. United States—Politics and government—1974–
Anecdotes, facetiae, satire, etc. 2. United States—
Politics and government—1969–1974—Anecdotes, facetiae,
satire, etc. 3. Statesmen—United States—Anecdotes,
facetiae, satire, etc. I. Title.
E865.R4 1976   320.9'73'0925   75-30343
ISBN 0-06-013526-3

76 77 78 79 10 9 8 7 6 5 4 3 2 1

To Dorothy Forshay Reeves

Contents

Acknowledgments

Writing is not a solitary pursuit. There is editing, a process composed of about equal parts of slave-driving, inspiration, punctuation, lying, and common sense. I've benefited from almost all of it and I owe professional gratitude and personal appreciation to a great number of men and women who have changed my mind and words over the years, especially to Clay Felker, Shelley Zalaznick, Jack Nessel and Judy Daniels of *New York* magazine, and Lewis Bergman, Dan Schwartz and Harvey Shapiro of *The New York Times Magazine*. My work always looked a little better than it was because of the people responsible for the art and photography around it, Walter Bernard and Milton Glaser of *New York,* and Michael O'Keefe of *The New York Times.* On this book I am in debt to Jeannette Hopkins, Orren Alperstein and, as always, to my agent, Lynn Nesbit.

Preface

I have one of the best jobs in the world. Mainly, I follow politicians around and make fun of them. I get paid for it, usually by Clay Felker, the editor of *New York* magazine, or Lewis Bergman, the editor of *The New York Times Magazine.* I appreciate that, but, having some sense of perspective, I decided to dedicate this book to my mother.

Invariably, after I follow some pol around for a while, I am asked the same two questions: "Did you like so-and-so?" "What is he really like?" Well, I *like* them all—politicians are energetic, engaging people whose business is being liked. That doesn't mean I'd vote for all of them or that I wouldn't fight like hell to stop my daughter from marrying one of them. And I wrote what I thought each was really like. This was the best I could do in the first five years of the 1970s —I may not have been right, but I wasn't holding anything back.

What are politicians, in general, really like? I've always favored the answer of John Webster in his 1612 play *The White Devill:* "A Politician imitates the Devill, as the Devill imitates a cannon: wheresoever he comes to do mischiefe, he comes with his backside towardes you."

My own attitudes about my business, journalism, were pretty well summed up in the following piece which I wrote for *New York* magazine in November, 1973. Like all of the articles in this book, it has been slightly edited to remove or explain references that now seem dated.

I am a reporter. In twenty minutes, with a telephone and a typewriter, I can write a coherent and substantially accurate 700-word story of a subway accident or the fall of a government. With a rumor, two facts, and an inch-high stack of clippings, I can put together a scandalous account of what's being done with your tax dollars. I can fake my way through a probing conversation with a foreign minister or a mobster. I have knocked on strange doors at 4 A.M. to say, "I'm sorry your son was just killed, do you have a picture of him and could you tell me what kind of a kid he was?" I am, according to the New York Newspaper Guild, worth a minimum of $365 a week.

I love it, even if I know it's a kind of prolonged adolescence. That doesn't mean I don't take it seriously—I do, I think it's very, very important, but I'm glad it's fun. I have, I found today, 84 books about The Press on the shelves around my living room.

Looking at those books—and a few others with sections or chapters on The Press—I was struck by the fact that they seemed to progress chronologically from light-hearted biographies to serious studies of power, climaxing with "Power Struggle: President Versus Press," a chapter in *The Making of the President 1972,* by Theodore H. White:

> What lay at issue in 1972 between Richard Nixon, on the one hand, and the adversary press and media of America, on the other, was simple: it was power.
>
> The power of the press in America is a primordial one. It sets the agenda of public discussion . . . It determines what people will talk and think about —an authority that in other nations is reserved for tyrants, priests, parties, and mandarins . . .
>
> When the press seizes a great issue to thrust onto the agenda of talk, it moves action on its own—the cause of the environment, the cause of civil rights, the liquidation of the war in Vietnam, and, as the climax, the Watergate affair were all set on the agenda, in the first instance, by the press.

Huh? I don't remember The Press, in the first instance, putting civil rights or Vietnam on the agenda—or, for that matter, poverty, auto safety, Middle America, or China. We covered them and sometimes gave them priority, space, and time that probably helped speed things up. A real test of power would have been to try to ignore them.

The Power of The Press? I don't feel as powerful as David Brinkley, and he said: "There are numerous countries in the world where the politicians have seized absolute power and muzzled the press. There is no country in the world where the press has seized absolute power and muzzled the politicians."

Carrying that a large step further, Ithiel de Sola Pool, the political scientist from Massachusetts Institute of Technology, argued persuasively that if the American press really struggled with government there would be no free press. Speaking before the Aspen Institute Program on Communications and Society a year ago, Pool said:

> Unless one can prove that there are circumstances under which a free and critical press will help sustain national consensus and rally the nation in support of national goals, then no argument for a free press will save it in practice. No nation will indefinitely tolerate a freedom of the press that serves to divide the country and to open the floodgates of criticism against the freely chosen government that leads it . . . If the press is the government's enemy, it is the free press that will end up being destroyed.

Reporters love to quote professors—it takes the responsibility off us. Much of the business is about just that, avoiding responsibility. It might be going too far to say that The Press is essentially and inherently an irresponsible institution. Most reporters, however, and a hell of a lot of editors, are happily irreverent to the point of irresponsibility —and, among themselves, proud of it.

Power? It was one of Richard Nixon's many problems that he so misunderstood The Press that he believed, apparently to the point of mania, that we want to run his country. We don't want to run anything; that's the last thing we want. I don't presume to be "we," but I once ran something, a weekly newspaper in Phillipsburg, New Jersey, and I'm still running away from that. My God, I had to hire and *fire* people, deal with unions, suppliers, and advertisers, worry about bills and other kinds of money, answer to the town for noble editorials.

I just wanted to cover good stories, write them well, give the people kind enough to read them a sense of what's going on. I want to be

accurate, fair, perceptive and, when I'm lucky, incisive. If I'm interested in influence, it's influence with other reporters. More than anything I want the respect of the men and women in my peer group, the
"guys." When a journalism class I taught, rather badly, asked me
whom I write for, I found myself answering, "Other political reporters." I wish I had said history or something, but that's what I said.

I have met few editors and fewer reporters with ambitions greater
than getting better stories—getting stories, not Presidents.

I am not saying that the press is without real power, but I am
arguing that it is not an institution consciously and consistently dedicated to accumulating and exercising control over other institutions
or over people's lives. It is, in fact, rarely consistent and often uncon-
scious about the power it does have, not unlike a bunch of kids
throwing firecrackers in the Metropolitan Museum of Art. The major
thrust of journalism comes from the men and women who chose to
go into it, and most of that self-selected tribe, in my experience, don't
know or particularly care what effect they're having on the story of
the moment.

No one who has worked on the most powerful single medium in the
country, *The New York Times*—and I did for five years—can be
totally unaware of the power of that mighty Wurlitzer. It does, in
Teddy White's phrase, sometimes approach the status of "the public
agenda" of New York City, and its notes and tones are reflexively
broadcast and amplified by other journals and the electronic media.

But, among themselves, *Times*men live for, and glory in, the good
story. Of all the recent books about the press and politics lying around
here, the one I liked best was *The Boys on the Bus,* by Timothy
Crouse, not because I agreed with everything in it, but because it
captured a lot of the feel of what the business and reporters are like.
The book ends with the scene as George McGovern's campaign ended
on Election Day, 1972, in Washington:

> The reporters spilled out of the planes and stood on the tarmac, their
> hair blown about by violent gusts of wind. Suddenly everybody realized
> that it was all over, and their emotions flooded out. They wept, embraced,
> exchanged manful handshakes, cried on each other's shoulders, or simply

stood in a daze. It was like an orphanage being shut down . . . It would be a good while before any of them would again discover the same irresistible combination of camaraderie, hardship, and luxury. They now had to go back to paying the dues which would earn them another campaign in 1976.

The boys were thinking of themselves, not of McGovern or Nixon or the Republic. Of course, they didn't have to wait until 1976. A good story, a great story, and rarest of all, a new story—the collapse of an American government—was suddenly there for the getting. It was more than a big story, it was a big, breaking, running story—those are incendiary words in the business. Like a forest fire, big, running stories have a life of their own, lashing reporters and editors into frenzies, wildly sucking the best and the worst from them. It is then that James Naughton and four other *New York Times* reporters can smash together a striking narrative of the decline of Spiro Agnew; it is then that Jack Anderson can blurt a dangerous, prejudicial untruth into a radio microphone, that he has proof that Thomas Eagleton is a drunk.

I can't defend The Press in heat. That's when a professional makes a rumor and two facts look like the end of the world, whipping his sources for tidbits just big enough to support a three-column headline. (Protecting your sources, incidentally, is often a matter of keeping them secret from your editors—the mystery of where you get information is a base of the power reporters really want: power to manipulate editors.) If you know what you're doing, you don't need much to support a very large headline—compare the amount of information it took to produce millions of words about Spiro Agnew's Maryland maneuvering with the information in the 40-page Justice Department account of evidence against Agnew. All the headlines and stories added up to only a few sentences of the Justice document.

The techniques of the reporter are as old as . . . well, they're at least as old as Lincoln Steffens, whose autobiography includes a fascinating chapter about crime waves, in which he wrote:

> I enjoy crime waves. I made one once . . . many reporters joined in the uplift of the rising tide of crime . . . I feel that I know something the wise men do not know about crime waves and so get a certain sense of happy

superiority out of reading editorials, sermons, speeches, and learned theses on my specialty.

The police records of crimes . . . showed no increase at all; on the contrary the totals of crimes showed a diminution . . . It was only the newspaper reports of crimes that had increased.

That was 70 years ago, but the same thing still goes on—*The New York Times* makes a crime wave every couple of years, usually triggered by the burglary of an editor's apartment. I never said we were perfect; I just said we weren't after power. Crime waves are good stories, for a while. So were Agnew and Eagleton—we could savage them with equal glee. Same for a Nixon or a McGovern. We are jackals. We are reporters. They are meat. They are good stories.

(What is a good story? It's always important, almost always fun, and usually profitable. For a newspaperman that means page one by definition—and don't worry about the length. They don't yell "Stop the presses!" anymore, but they do react to your phone calls by calling across the desk, "Hold it. It's Reeves. He's got some more on . . ." It means they're not going to question your expense account, and when you get back to the city room, after three hours or three months, everyone is going to stand up, slowly, and come around with pats and smiles—the envy doesn't really show, but you know. There was the day Harrison Salisbury came back to *The Times* from Hanoi, and Phil Dougherty, a great man, started it by standing next to him at the urinals in the men's room off the city room and saying, "Hi, Harrison. Been away?")

Power? Did Harrison Salisbury go to Hanoi to end the war or to topple Lyndon Johnson? Or did he go because he's a great reporter and it was the best story in the world, and because he was going to come back and stand by the urinal and . . . ?

We see ourselves as the last angry men, stalking the truth wherever it leads. Richard Nixon probably believes that Salisbury was after Johnson. Nixon also believed that the way to tame the press was to put the screws to the principal owners of television networks and newspapers.

I was having dinner with a fairly prominent lawyer the other night, and he ruined my salad by saying, "I'll never have any respect for journalism after reading how the White House, how Chuck Colson made William Paley crawl."

"What the hell," I choked, "what the hell does Paley have to do with journalism? He's a rich man trying to protect his own interests. Why shouldn't he crawl? *I* wouldn't crawl. Do you think Walter Cronkite is crawling?"

Paley, of course, is the chairman of CBS, an entertainment conglomerate that also has a news division, and White House provocateur Colson had claimed in a 1969 memo that his threats had made Paley and other network chiefs "accommodating, cordial, and almost apologetic." The night after my dinner, Cronkite was on the air saying, "None of the pressure ever reached this desk"—and I believe him.

Paleys and publishers are men of power, but it must be frustrating for them to try to use that power over the cantankerous minions who collect and distribute the news for them. Arthur Ochs Sulzberger runs *The New York Times,* but he is sometimes just as unhappy as any other reader at what he sees there at breakfast. In one famous incident, Sulzberger was upset because all his critics—from architecture to opera—had panned everything about the brand-new Lincoln Center, and he sent a plaintive memo asking whether they couldn't find *anything* good to say about the center. The answer came back: "No." In an unfamous incident when I was *The Times*'s chief local political writer, I was told that Sulzberger was upset by my continuous ethnic analysis of election returns—particularly the emphasis on "Jewish voters"—and wondered whether I couldn't concentrate on economic or geographic analyses. My answer came back: "No"—and I never heard a word about it again.

All publishers, I have heard, are not Punch Sulzbergers or Katharine Grahams. A giant named Richard Mellon Scaife, who had a spare $1 million to donate to Nixon in 1972, fired a reporter from his Pennsylvania paper, the *Greensburg Tribune-Review,* because the reporter had been heard to say "One down and one to go," when Vice President Agnew resigned. But the *Greensburg Tribune-Review* also lost its managing editor and ten reporters, who quit in protest—it's easy to quit and get another job if you're not interested in becoming managing editor someday.

Most reporters are not interested in become managing anythings—that is a major point of this piece. Another is that The Press is a very disorganized and cranky thing. If a reporter has a good story, he's going to find someplace to get it out—even if it's Dispatch News Service, a third-string operation that Seymour Hersh had to go to to get his My Lai massacre story in print. If the Watergate media festival proved anything, it's that it's damn hard to cover up a good story in this country.

(I am not so naive as to believe that publishers and owners are controlled by two-fingered typists with press cards. In Jacksonville, the newspapers are owned by railroads, and the legend there is that trains never hit automobiles or people; rather, cars and people hit trains. But the press–government controversy is national, and I don't think disorganized and diverse owners can control disorganized and perverse editors and reporters.)

Whatever the internal politics of journalism, its external power seems to be increasing. But only *seems* to be, according to some of the sharper minds around the business. Richard Wald, the president of NBC News and one-time managing editor of the *New York Herald Tribune,* told me in a conversation one day:

> We, print and television, look powerful right now, but I think the power of the press is roughly a constant. It becomes impressive when things are happening in the society—and things are certainly happening right now—and when there are new developments in the technology of communication.
>
> Television is obviously the technological change, but its impact seems remarkably similar to the impact of the rotary press in the late nineteenth century. Circulation of news exploded, and there was a great outcry about the power of the "mass press." It was a time of change in society—the industrial revolution—it was not a happy event, having the problems of the day stated so widely; papers like the *New York Sun* were regularly accused of inflaming the masses.

It's entirely possible that television shapes the way you think, but television can't control the shaping. We simply wouldn't know enough about how to do it; television is run by people who were raised to be persuaded by written arguments. Maybe a new generation will be different, but I seriously doubt that television will be able to shape opinion in the way that, say, the *Chicago Tribune* used to for an awful lot of people.

The Power of The Press became an issue when the American consensus broke over civil rights, Vietnam, and the impact of technological revolution. The press didn't seem to be such a big deal when the nation was united around the American Way and against Nazis and Godless Communism. And it won't seem to be so important now that Nixon has been pushed down.

You see, we are good guys, a little hard to take these days because we're smarter and tougher than we used to be, but underneath we're still the same lovable, slightly disreputable band of opportunistic vagabonds that Stanley Walker, of the *Herald Tribune,* described in *City Editor* in 1934:

> What makes a good newspaperman? The answer is easy. He knows everything. He is aware not only of what goes on in the world today, but his brain is a repository of the accumulated wisdom of the ages . . . He is not only handsome, but he has the physical strength which enables him to perform great feats of energy. He can go for nights on end without sleep. He dresses well and talks with charm. Men admire him; women adore him; tycoons and statesmen are willing to share their secrets with him . . . He hates lies and meanness and sham, but keeps his temper. He is loyal to his paper and to what he looks upon as his profession; whether it is a profession, or merely a craft, he resents attempts to debase it. When he dies, a lot of people are sorry, and some of them remember him for several days.

Washington, D.C.
December, 1975

Prologue

"When the day of election nears, visit your constituents far and wide," said a former congressman visiting Little Rock, Arkansas, one day in 1835, "treat liberally and drink freely, in order to rise in their estimation, tho' you fall in your own."

The politician's name was Davy Crockett. He had served in the Tennessee legislature before being elected to two terms in Congress and he called the speech "How to Win an Election." He went on:

> Promise all that is asked and more if you can think of anything. Offer to build a bridge or a church, to divide a county, create a batch of new offices, make a turnpike, or anything they like. Promises cost nothing.
>
> Get up on all occasions, and sometimes on no occasions at all, and make long-winded speeches, though composed of nothing but wind. Rail against taxes of all kinds, and officeholders, and bad harvest weather; and wind up with a flourish about the heroes who fought and bled for our liberties in the times that tried men's souls.
>
> These few directions, properly attended to, will do your business; and when once elected, why a fig for the dirty children, the promises, the bridges, churches, the taxes, the offices and the subscriptions, for it is absolutely necessary to forget all these before you can be a thoroughgoing politician and patriot of the first water.

Never having met patriot Crockett—he ended up in the Alamo a few months later—I don't know whether he was kidding or perhaps had been drinking freely. I do know that he sounded as if he knew something about the 1976 election for President of the United States, an election complete with a dozen candidates who began running

1

almost two years before November 2, 1976. After a year of long-winded speeches, the campaign reached some kind of mini-climax on January 24, 1976, when an enthusiastic national radio reporter collared a rumpled black gentleman at a Democratic delegate selection caucus in Canton, Mississippi. How does it feel to be part of this great democratic process leading to the election of the most powerful man in the world? "Man," the black man answered, "they just got me out of bed. I don't understand any of this."

"I know what he means," said David Broder, the political editor of *The Washington Post.* Broder and a lot of us were out there trying to understand, in Iowa and Mississippi for caucuses in January and in New Hampshire for the country's first 1976 primary election on February 24 (the quadrennial rumor is that each breathing resident of that snowy little state must talk with 2.3 reporters and shake mittened hands with 3.2 candidates before primary day).

It is the way we select our President. Ah, Democracy! It is the best way men have conceived to govern themselves, but it sure can be a pain in the ass—and a lot of fun. Helen Thomas, the White House bureau chief of United Press International, once grumbled about the inhuman hours, the throwing of luggage and bodies onto planes and buses, and ended by saying: "The only thing worse than covering a campaign . . . is not covering a campaign."

For a reporter, the campaign trail is a mind-numbing gauntlet—the Dristan Express shuttling between icy New Hampshire and sunny Florida, a 99-degree difference on one of my swings. After two days, you find yourself downing bloody marys before breakfast, wondering about the guy in the next seat with a martini who's tapping out a story on an Olympia in his lap. When people mention San Antonio, you say, "Oh, yeah! I've been there," then remember that you haven't, you've only been at an airport and a hotel datelined San Antonio or Columbus or Pensacola or Sioux City.*

---

*The funniest story I have ever heard about the rigorous insanity of political traveling was told by Miles Benson of the Newhouse News Service. Benson was on a 1971 Edward Kennedy trip in Alaska and, as was prone to happen with the Kennedys, he was left behind in Point Barrow after being a few minutes late for the Kennedy charter plane. Having no way to get out for 24 hours, Benson decided to do something he would

For a candidate, it can only be worse. It is a miracle of adrenalin and ambition that they survive. Even in 1884, before jet planes made possible 27-hour days traveling west, fatigue could destroy a candidate. Republican James G. Blaine was apparently so tired after two months on the road that he did not hear, or did not understand, a Protestant minister praising him for standing up to "rum, Romanism, and rebellion." Those words, repeated by Democrats as Blaine's own, cost him enough Roman Catholic votes to deny him the Presidency of the United States.

Between January 26 and January 31, 1976, Democratic candidate Morris (Mo) Udall campaigned five days, making 62 separate appearances in 28 cities and towns in New Hampshire, Massachusetts, and New York. This was his schedule on January 27:

6:00 A.M.	Depart Hanover en route to Claremont, N.H.
6:30 A.M.	Greet workers, Joy Manufacturing Co.
8:10 A.M.	Meeting with editors, *Claremont Eagle Times*
8:45 A.M.	Press conference, Moody Hotel
9:20 A.M.	Reception, Pleasant Restaurant
10:00 A.M.	Remarks and Q&A, Stevens High School
10:45 A.M.	Depart Claremont en route to Charlestown
11:00 A.M.	Walk-through, Young's Diner
11:10 A.M.	Depart Charlestown en route to Keene
12:10 P.M.	Luncheon, Grace United Methodist Church
1:00 P.M.	Walking tour, downtown Keene
2:20 P.M.	Depart Keene, en route to Peterborough
3:10 P.M.	Walking tour, downtown Peterborough
3:30 P.M.	Depart Peterborough en route to Wilton
4:00 P.M.	Reception, home of Clarence and June Berger

---

probably never have a chance to do again—walk out on the frozen Arctic Ocean. He was about a half-mile from the shore when, 100 feet in front of him, a polar bear stepped out from behind an ice hill. Then another appeared, and another: Six bears stood in a row, wagging their great heads from side to side. Benson remembered reading that polar bears are the most vicious animals on earth and did the only thing he could think of—stood petrified with fear. Suddenly he heard someone screaming in Italian, and a man stepped from behind the hill and slapped one of the bears on the rear end. The guy was training the bears for a Walt Disney film.

4:15 P.M.   Depart Wilton en route to Nashua
4:45 P.M.   Walking tour, Main Street
5:15 P.M.   Depart Nashua, en route to Lawrence, Mass.
7:00 P.M.   Meeting with labor leaders, Joe Binett's Restaurant
7:40 P.M.   Meeting with Democratic leaders, Joe Binett's Restaurant
8:20 P.M.   Depart Lawrence en route to Lowell
8:35 P.M.   Reception, Speare House Restaurant
9:15 P.M.   Depart Lowell en route to Tewksbury, Mass.

What did Udall say at all those stops? About what Davy Crokett told candidates to say. What did he hear? Not a lot. At a reception the day before in Lebanon, New Hampshire, to which Udall volunteers had personally invited hundreds of people to "meet the candidate," twenty people showed up, 16 adults and four children.

Why do they do it? No one is quite sure. Professional politicians and their managers tend to agree that 90 percent of American campaigning is a waste of time and effort. Maybe 10 percent accomplishes something; but no one is sure which 10 percent. So they keep on doing the same things they've always done, many of the same things that Crockett did.

Much of what went on in New Hampshire and a dozen other early primary and caucus states in the first months of 1976 was done for the benefit of no one but the press. One of the things that seemed dated in Davy Crockett's speech was the phrase "when the day of election nears." By 1976, election campaigns tend to begin the day after the previous election. Part of the reason was that three-year-long campaigns for presidential nominations had succeeded recently—John Kennedy's in 1960, Barry Goldwater's in 1964, and George McGovern's in 1972—and part of the reason was the political nymphomania of the national press, specifically of national political reporters.

Reporters, both print and electronic, like long campaigns, despite the Dristan and bloody marys. It's fun—at least more fun than staying in the office under the eyes of bosses, covering murders and plane crashes or (God forbid!) covering the way the country is actually governed. One of the severest indictments of the American political press was its whining over the failure of Richard Nixon to leave the White House and campaign in 1972. Why should he or any other candidate have to pinball around the country? Let them run on their records if voters know them and what they've done. What the press should have done, and gave precious little consideration to doing, was to expand the manpower and money that would have gone into trailing a Nixon campaign on investigating what the Nixon administration had done in its first three years—to cover government instead of politics.

The relationship between the press and politics, it seems to me, has evolved into something like the relationship between network television and the National Football League. The game, or the campaign, becomes a spectacle used by television, newspapers, and magazines to meet their own internal needs and the needs of their constituent-viewers and readers. One event early in the 1976 campaign, the Iowa delegation selection caucuses on January 19, demonstrated how politics and the press have come to feed on each other. The Iowa State Democratic Committee charged citizens $10 each to visit their press headquarters and watch reporters work, advertising this as a chance to see, in the flesh, people like Roger Mudd of CBS and R.W. Apple, Jr., of *The New York Times*.

Most Americans have only the vaguest awareness of these shenanigans. A small percentage of the nation participates in the selection of the Republican and Democratic nominees for President. That's not as bad as it sounds; millions of people are involved—voting, caucusing, doing the spadework of politics. The party designation is still critical, despite disappearing voter loyalty to labels, because federal and state election laws, written by party-oriented legislators, institutionalize the two-party system on the ballots presented to those somewhat disinterested voters. And the printed press and television perpetuate the two-party framework of political communication—in part simply because they are used to it and follow a familiar routine. A network decision to stop televising and promoting the Republican and Democratic conventions could be the beginning of the end of the two-party system, just as the networks could kill the National Football League by withdrawing their electronic megaphone.

So, at least for the time being, the majority of Americans, when they focus on national politics, briefly, every four years, must choose between two candidates. Those candidates, however, are no longer defined so much by their institutional labels—Republican and Democratic—as by their cultural indentification: Is he one of us or one of them?

In 1972, after eleven months of candidates, airports, and hotels, I spent eleven days—October 11–21—in a single election district (precinct) in Bayside, Queens, ten blocks of America, thirteen miles east of Times Square. I wanted to look at a Presidential election from the bottom up, to try to determine how the millions of words, images, and dollars of the campaigns of Richard Nixon and George McGovern reached one group of Americans. I suppose I hoped to find "The Truth"—the Holy Grail hidden somewhere in Queens—but, of course, I didn't. I found as many truths as people I talked with.

The 39th E.D. of New York's 25th Assembly District is two thousand people living in neat, brick, attached and separate private homes and two- and three-story apartment buildings. For those who know New York City only through television it is quite near and not unlike the neighborhood used for the filming of the series, *All in the Family.* It is "Archie Bunker" country, but it is not a caricature. There are 620 enrolled voters in the district—369 enrolled Democrats, 144 Republicans, 20 members of New York's Conservative party, 18 Liberal party members, and 69 voters who did not enroll in any party. Local residents estimated that close to half the families in the district were Roman Catholic, mostly Italian and Irish, and the rest were about evenly divided between Protestants and Jews. Of the 620 names on the Board of Elections list for 1972, 112 were identifiably Italian, 111 Jewish, and 60 Irish. U.S. Census Bureau data for the area included these statistics: median income per family, $14,958; average value of a single home, $29,000; median education level, 12.5 years; self-employed heads of household, 7 percent; elementary school students in private or parochial schools, 30 percent.

In the 1968 presidential election, the 39th E.D. favored Hubert Humphrey over Richard Nixon, 55.9 percent to 39.6 percent, with George Wallace getting 4.5 percent. By the time I got there, it was pretty obvious that districts like the 39th, although nominally Democratic, would switch in 1972 and vote Republican, at least at the top of the ballot. And the 39th did. The people of Bayside walked over to Public School 31 on Bell Boulevard on November 7, 1972, and cast 56.7 percent of their votes for a man they did not like, Richard Nixon. Why? How do fairly disinterested, fairly well informed, but very rational and, I found, very decent Americans make their own sense out of the jumbled information and misinformation thrown at them in an election year?

"I don't understand politicians and I don't think they understand us," said Arthur Schmidt in his living room, a room with too little furniture that had been used too much. "I'm a Democrat. I'm middle-middle-right, I guess . . . But who would be interested in the philosophy of Artie Schmidt? Politicians, like actors, say what they think we like to hear."

Schmidt, in his middle forties, is doing better than most men in the 39th and, like most of them, he no longer works with his hands or his back—much of what is called "blue collar America" actually wears suits and ties to work these days. The G.I. Bill helped him become a nightschool lawyer after Korea, and he works in the legal department of a savings and loan association. His wife, Joan, works three days a week as a trucking company bookkeeper to keep ahead of the dental bills of their five children.

"I suppose I do think I'm being screwed by the system," he said, but his rhetoric turned out to be far more thoughtful and complex than that simple assertion. "I gripe about taxes and my salary compared to someone else's, but we're not doing all that bad . . . I support the war in Vietnam. At least I want an honorable peace . . . We pay $1,700 a year to keep the kids in parochial school, but I'm against aid to them. It's a matter of principle; the people who wrote the Constitution knew what they were doing . . . I'm for abortion. I personally believe it's murder, but I can't impose my standards on other people

. . . It's time to get people out of the ghettoes and into our schools —I'm not sure I have the guts to do it with my own kids, I'm already in a parochial school cycle—but if our children were in the same schools we'd make sure they were good."

His wife Joan, a Republican, said, "We're doing better than our parents did. We thought that was what America was all about, but the kids are asking other questions. I admire them . . . I'm against the war, but McGovern frightens me—all the contradictions. He should have been more prepared, he wanted the highest office. . . ."

For the Schmidts, the 39th was a pretty good place to bring up children. Kids and money were what people were talking about in Bayside, and crime, too, more and more, although none of the more than 100 voters I talked with had been a crime victim and the local 111th Precinct had just about the lowest crime rate in New York City (one felony for every 738 residents in 1971). It's a place of custom-made plastic slipcovers on the living room furniture and plastic flowers on the dining room table, four-year-old station wagons and bunk beds, crucifixes, and bearded rabbis holding the Torah on the walls, the boys' basketball trophies on the mantel. These were some of the impressions I got there:

• Nixon won by default. Few people volunteered that they thought the President was "good" or even "pretty good." From the perspective of one precinct, the key event of the 1972 campaign seems to have been the Democratic National Convention; the televised rhetoric of change and new politics simply drew a line across America and the Schmidts and other people of the 39th felt they were on the other side from McGovern, rich liberals, college professors, blacks, and Chicanos. The Democratic candidate, in the end, represented a minority of the nation—that's what democracy is. It seemed that the most significant event of the convention, probably of the campaign, was the Democrats' unseating of Chicago Mayor Richard Daley and his delegation of middle-aged, middle-American politicians—the argument could be made that McGovern lost the election at the moment television-America saw Jesse Jackson, a black leader of the substitute Illinois delegation, standing on Daley's chair with his fist in the air, chanting, "Freedom Now!" That incident, at least, was what I kept hearing about, much more than I heard about later events like the dumping of the first Democratic vice presidential nominee, Senator Thomas Eagleton. The later events, like McGovern's "flip-flops," I concluded, were merely rationales (or excuses) for decisions that voters made during convention week in July. "There isn't an individual on this block who didn't make up his mind a long time ago, no matter what they tell you," said Santo Frontario, a trade school principal who had been the 39th's Republican county committeeman for eighteen years. "I can tell because they're friendly this time; usually they avoid me around election time."

• People were turned off by—or at least barely tuned in to—politics, especially national politics, which voters of the 39th saw as only vaguely connected to the joys and troubles of their own lives. But reports of the "great American malaise" were probably exaggerated. The people I met were happy with their personal lives or at least found them tolerable and didn't blame the country for most of their own problems. Patricia Mulfall, a pretty woman aging too quickly, had problems that would stagger most of us: four young children in a four-room, $192-a-month apartment, a husband whose asthmatic condition had led to pneumonia four straight winters, no money for vacations, no car for day trips. She once spent an evening figuring out that the family would do better on welfare than on Bob Mulfall's $9,000 bank teller's salary. "It hasn't been a bad time for us," she said. "This is a wonderful neighborhood, we've been able to pay off a lot of bills, and Bob's advanced." (Her husband had gotten a $13,000 job as a branch nanager.) Then she added: "God help us if McGovern's elected."

• "America is Number One" was an important phrase to many people, and Nixon's use of "number one" rhetoric probably helped him a great deal in 1972. It was simply important to many in the 39th that the United States be first in war and peace, space and power, money and prestige—and most of them thought it was not important to the people behind McGovern.

• The mass media and advertising seemed more powerful and per-

vasive in a major campaign than I imagined (perhaps naively). Almost
every conversation I had was punctuated with lines that began: "CBS
said . . ." "I know all newspapers are slanted, but I read in *The Daily
News* . . ." "I saw in last night's *Long Island Press*, . . ." There was
no real political dialogue outside families in the 39th—"My neighbors
are lovely people," said Mrs. Claire Strauss, who telephone-canvassed
other districts for McGovern, "but I don't talk politics outside this
house"—and almost no original thought. Mrs. Salvatore Viccari, a
paperhanger's wife, said, "I vote for all Democrats . . . but there was
a TV special last night that said Nixon stopped pollution of the rivers
in some state. It was very good." The "TV special" she was talking
about was a paid political announcement by the Committee for the
Re-election of the President.

Some of that, I suppose, sounds discouraging, even dumb. But I
went away from Bayside elated. The people I met knew what they
were doing and why; they knew what they had to know, even if they
couldn't name the Secretary of Labor or some candidate's brilliant
manager. They had seen through a lot of the crap of American politics. I would gladly put the country in the hands of Joan and Artie
Schmidt or Patricia and Bob Mulfall—and I will return to that at the
end of this book—rather than in the tired hands of some of the old
faces running for president in 1976. Mrs. Schmidt has heard all the
arguments, from her mother who hates the United Nations and thinks
détente is part of a secret plan to crush the Russians and Chinese, and
from her daughter, a New Paltz State College student in 1972, "who's
into women's lib. "Mrs. Mulfall, who stays home with her four young
ones, said that "at least here we have something to say about what
goes on," then talked about her grandfather, who went to school with
Alfred E. Smith, and her father, John Higgins, who proudly escorted
each of his children, carrying their high school diplomas, to cast their
first vote years ago in Brooklyn.

One

Old Faces of 1976

1 | Ronald Reagan

Ronald Reagan, former actor and former governor of California, announced his candidacy for President on November 20, 1975, and Washington laughed. The capital's roundtable of conventional wisdom is a television show, *Agronsky & Company,* featuring five of the town's most celebrated journalists. On the night after Reagan said he would challenge President Ford for the Republican nomination, Martin Agronsky, the show's host, Peter Lisagor of the *Chicago Daily News* and columnist Carl Rowan quickly agreed that the Californian was "going nowhere"—the phrase was Lisagor's.

Everyone knew Ronald Reagan was a joke. One newspaper declared that "deep down Reagan is shallow," then went on to report a Reagan conversation the week before on his campaign plane: "Believe me, you must have credibility . . . Now you take my role in *Bedtime for Bonzo.* I was a scientist who raised a chimp as a child in my home. It was a huge money maker, terrific. People could believe in it. But then the studio decided to make a sequel called *Bonzo Goes to College.* I refused to play in it. It bombed. Who could believe a chimp could go to college and play on the football team? The whole thing lacked credibility."

One of the first men to laugh that hard at Ronald Reagan was Pat Brown, the first Edmund G. Brown to be governor of California. Brown was so sure that Reagan would be a pushover in 1966, a political joke, that he dug up some old dirt on Reagan's Republican primary opponent just to make sure that the ex-actor would be on the November ballot. "Remember, it was an actor who shot Lincoln," cracked Brown in a television commercial after Reagan had won the G.O.P. primary against his discredited opponent. Reagan beat Brown by 993,739 votes on November 8, 1966.

Nine years later, Bonzo's foster father was after the 38th President, Gerald Ford, who once said, "If Lincoln were alive today, he'd roll over in his grave." Ford had a way with words. The commander in chief named his election vehicle the President Ford Committee—PFC for those familiar with the ranks of the U.S. Army. Not only did Reagan have a stumbling enemy in Ford, but the challenger was in a position to make friends by exploiting *the* issue of 1976—Washington.

After Watergate, Vietnam, and a thousand smaller disasters, Washington was a bigger joke than even Reagan or Ford, the biggest joke in the country, but not a funny one. Just attacking Washington—and not being part of it—could keep a national campaign alive for Reagan, or for Democrats like George Wallace, Jimmy Carter, and Fred Harris.

Wallace, of course, has prospered since the early 1960s with attacks on "big thinkers in Washington" and "pointy-headed bureaucrats." In his announcement at the National Press Club three blocks from the White House, Reagan put it this way: "In my opinion, the root of these problems lies right here—in Washington, D.C. Our nation's capital has become the seat of a buddy system that functions for its own benefit—increasingly insensitive to the needs of the American worker who supports it with his taxes. Today it is difficult to find leaders who are independent of the forces which have brought us our problems—the Congress, the bureaucracy, the lobbyists, big business and big labor."

No matter how much truth one finds in that rhetoric—I find a lot —it is very salable, and Ronald Reagan is a hell of a salesman, for 20 Mule Team Borax, General Electric, conservatism, or himself. You cannot travel around the country without being struck—hard—by the disillusionment, even disgust, with politics in general and Washington politics in particular. The American people are not stupid, and they are not as isolated and insulated as Washingtonian Americans; people out there seem to have instinctively and fairly accurately calculated that about 80 percent of Washington's effort on issues like energy and the economy was being expended on trying to shift responsibility and blame to someone—anyone—else. The White House works long and hard to point fingers at Congress, the unions, and the dreaded bureaucracy; the Congress puts in as many hours and ergs yah-yah-hing at the White House, big business, and the Arabs. Jimmy Carter, the personable former governor of Georgia, made some surprising progress toward the Democratic presidential nomination by mocking Washington. He began many of his early speeches by saying that he would list his assets and liabilities, then said, well, his assets were all in his literature, so maybe he'd start with his liabilities: "I'm not from Washington." (There was laughter in the audience.) "I'm not a member of Congress." (More laughter.) "I've never been part of the national government." (There was often so much laughter that he couldn't continue.)

Carter learned some lessons as chairman of the Democratic National Committee's campaign group during the 1974 congressional elections. "It scared us in the beginning, not being from Washington," said Jody Powell, Carter's press secretary. "But in most of the campaigns we concentrated on, we were dealing with non-incumbents, and almost all of them benefited from being able to joke about Washington or take some licks at what was happening there."

To check his own perceptions and doubts, Carter commissioned national polling built around this question: People say a member of Congress should be preferred as a presidential candidate because of broad foreign policy experience. Others say a governor should be preferred because of experience running things. Which makes sense to you?

By 3-to-2, the respondents said they preferred a governor. Carter began talking about the "Washington mess" and using words like "loaded" . . . "confused" . . . "wasteful."

Fred Harris, another Democratic candidate and a former senator from Oklahoma, began by telling crowds that he used to be part of the mess and was now telling friends, "I spent five lousy years kissing their asses in Washington before I figured out it didn't mean anything, that I couldn't get anything done there anyway."

It's fun and probably productive for the Outs to bang away at the Washington issue. But what about the Ins? As much as they could, President Ford and a lot of other incumbent Washingtonians got ready for 1976 by trying to give the impression that they were not really part of the capital clutter—they just happened to be there trying to clean up the mess.

On the road, where he preferred to be, Ford did not talk about Washington as the place he had lived and worked most of his adult life. They were wasted years, to hear him tell it as he jetted around informing the folks about the awful Congress—he should know, he honored it and it honored him for 25 years—and the still worse bureaucracy. "Why don't you go back to Washington and do something about it instead of coming out here?" mumbled a San Francisco reporter as the President warned of bureaucratic menace during a West Coast tour.

Congressmen too, veterans and freshmen, geared up to run against the place where they worked. Thomas Rees, a five-term Democrat from Beverly Hills, said his most effective 1975 fund-raising letter was an attack on "the congressional establishment." "The money just poured in," Rees said, "I've never had anything like it . . . we're just so isolated in Washington."

Andrew Maguire, a young New Jersey Democrat who defeated a 25-year Republican congressman in 1974 by attacking Washington, came back for re-election with a variation on the theme: "I keep attacking weak leadership at the top, the congressional leadership."

There are, of course, no restrictions on Ronald Reagan's attacks on Washington, as there never have been any on George Wallace. The former actor probably began his campaign with an advantage—non-Washingtonness—at least as big as Ford's incumbency, the factor that seemed so awesome in Washington. In fact, any President looks bigger in Washington because the White House is the town's symbolic, social, and journalistic hub. But that doesn't make it the nation's political hub.

I doubt that the United States has a political hub at the moment. We are talking about a country in which only 32 percent of the people believe "you can trust the government in Washington to do what is right most of the time," in which 70 percent of the people believe that "government is pretty much run by a few big interests looking out for themselves," in which 47 percent of the people do not believe "the people running the government are smart people who usually know what they are doing." Those numbers are 1974 polling figures compiled by Market Opinion Research. Comparable figures compiled ten years earlier, in 1964, by the Center for Political Studies were strikingly different: 76 percent believed government usually did what was right; 29 percent believed government usually served big interests; only 27 percent did not believe government knew what it was doing.

The center was not holding particularly well in 1975 and it was possible that the advantages of Ford's incumbency did not go much beyond the young woman in the White House charged with the responsibility for deleting from the texts of his speeches the words that the president habitually mispronounced, like *judg-e-ment.*

So, Ford–Reagan began as a pretty fair fight. They are two of the thinnest men in the history of presidential politics—in the sense that Charles Coy, then Republican state chairman of Kentucky, spoke to me of Reagan in 1973: "We sure do like him down here. But as my daddy used to say, 'Some men are as thin as piss on a slate rock.' "

Reagan's campaign biography handed out at the National Press Club was so thin that by the fifth paragraph it was reduced to this: "Honorary degrees include—doctorate, humane letters, Eureka College, 1957; doctorate of laws, Pepperdine College, 1970; and doctorate of laws, Azusa Pacific College, 1973."

When Reagan ran in California the first time, he left blank the line on the state ballot marked "Occupation." Apparently he did not want to list "Actor." But, hell, it's honest work—he had made 50 movies —and an honest description of what many politicians really are. One of Reagan's great advantages in politics is that he's a real actor, trained and experienced. He knows what he's doing, as he wrote in his autobiography in 1965: "It has taken me many years to get used to seeing myself as others see me. Very few of us ever see ourselves except as we look directly at ourselves in a mirror. Thus we don't know how we look from behind, from the side, walking, standing, moving normally through a room."

That talent, knowing what impressions are being transmitted by voice and body, served Reagan well when his movie career began to fade in the 1950s. He connected with General Electric, serving as host on television's *GE Theater*—he later switched to *Death Valley Days* for 20 Mule Team Borax—and traveling the country meeting and speaking to GE employees at company pep rallies. He spoke to 250,000 employees in eight years, saying the same thing at each stop, The Speech, a sort of America is God's Country if *They* Don't Ruin It.

Reagan is still pretty much of a one speech man and his rhetoric, vague but inspiring, has not changed much from the original GE text:

> For almost two centuries, we have proved man's capacity for self-government, but today we are told we must choose between a left and a right, or, as others suggest, a third alternative, a kind of safe middle ground. I suggest to you there is no left or right, only an up or down. Up to the maximum of individual freedom consistent with law and order, or down to the antheap of totalitarianism . . . Already the hour is late, government has laid its hand on health, housing, farming, industry, commerce, education, and to an ever increasing degree interferes with the people's right to know.

Reagan emerged dramatically as a political force and a conservative hero when he gave The Speech on national television in 1964 to raise money for Barry Goldwater's presidential campaign. Within two years he was a candidate for governor, financed by a small group of Southern California millionaires and briefed by paid consultants from Behavior Science Corporation. What the consultants did was to persuade him to stop quoting *Reader's Digest.* "You should have seen those newspapermen jump when Ron first quoted Jefferson to them," said one of the BSC consultants, Dr. Kenneth Holden.

As the quality of Reagan's familiar quotations escalated, his rhetoric moderated somewhat, although his verbal conservatism has been consistent since he broke with liberalism and the Democratic party in the 1950s when, as president of the Screen Actors Guild, he felt Hollywood liberals were too tolerant of Communism.

In 1964, Reagan was saying: "Unemployment insurance provides prepaid vacations for a segment of our society which has made it a way of life.". . . "The entire graduated income tax structure was created by Karl Marx. It has no justification in getting the government needed revenues." . . . "We should declare war on North Vietnam. We could pave the whole country and put parking stripes on it, and still be home by Christmas."

By 1974, he sounded like this: "It is time we realized that profit, property, and freedom are inseparable. You cannot have any one of them without the others." . . . "The truth is that government is responsible for inflation. Government deliberately planned an inflation by deficit spending." . . . "Private business is the most over-regulated, over-taxed, and under-appreciated part of America's society . . . Labor sets its own goals, often without regard to the inflationary and even destructive impact those goals may have on other Americans. Businessmen react by raising prices because they must meet the demands of labor."

Reagan, however, has usually been smart enough not to confuse rhetoric, even his own, with reality. He seems to have a gut feel for the current of theoretical conservatism and operational liberalism that has always flowed through American politics—there are a lot of Americans who like to gripe about government spending but would crucify a politician who suggested cutting Social Security. As governor, Reagan contented conservatives with his words while winning a second term rather easily as a moderate and moderately effective chief executive. He ran in California for eight years—stepping down voluntarily in 1974—and it's still there.

The Reagan years in Sacramento began sloppily. The man didn't have the slightest idea how to play his new role, so he declared that he would cut the state budget 10 percent across-the-board. That was laughably impossible—realities like federally mandated programs, union contracts, and scheduled construction and salary increases

rudely intruded. His proudest claim is that the number of state employees increased by only about 10 percent during his tenure—although the budget was climbing from $4.6 billion to $10.2 billion. He
instituted a widely imitated welfare reform program—basically
tougher verification procedures—that reduced California's welfare
rolls by 350,000 people while increasing benefits for the most needy.

Obviously, neither Reagan nor Ford is an intellectual or political
giant. Republicans could choose between a man who likes to talk
about his favorite television program, *Cannon* (Ford), and a man who
likes to talk about his favorite television program, *Mission: Impossible*
(Reagan). Fifteen rounds for the lightweight championship of the
United States! Well, lightweights fight by the same rules as the big
guys, so Reagan–Ford shaped up as a contest of campaigning skill,
issues, character, experience, and controlled and uncontrolled events:

• *Campaigning Skill*—No matter how much each man has to say,
Reagan says it better. The Californian may be the best public speaker
in America; the president is one of the worst. In his autobiography,
Reagan remembered his first important public speech, as a student
demonstration leader 40 years before at Eureka College: "It was
heady wine. Hell, with two more lines I could have had them riding
'through every Middlesex village and farm'—without horses yet." I'll
bet he could have, too. With practiced moves and inflections, he has
choked me up, swelled my proud American chest, made me laugh,
then almost cry, and done magic with the hair on the back of my neck
—and I don't particularly like him or a lot of what he has to say. Ford
has only one resource to throw against that: stamina. Reagan either
lacks it or is lazy; he likes to go to bed by 10 P.M. and usually does.
Early in his political career, Reagan had problems with a combination
of fatigue and a very quick temper (lately hidden). He stormed out
of the middle of a Republican primary debate in 1966 muttering, "I'll
get that son-of-a-bitch!" when he felt he had been called a bigot.
Another time, when reporters questioned him about complicated state
housing legislation, he said: "I know I can sit down and straighten this
out in my mind . . . I'm not sure I know what I'm talking about, I'm
so pooped . . . You're boring in, aren't you? You're boring in because

you know you've caught me so pooped that I don't know what I'm doing."

• *Issues*—Détente with Russia, which Ford appears locked into as part of his foreign policy apprenticeship with Henry Kissinger, seemed the issue most likely to provoke real Republican debate in 1976. Reagan's views have sounded like this: "We must ask ourselves if we are willing to risk all that we call the American way on the naive hope that our potential enemies have mellowed so much that they no longer have aggressive designs." Reagan, of course, will also hit the Washington issue hard, and Ford, or his supporters, will be implying that the Californian is an extremist who cannot win a general election. There was also an early Reagan position with potential for self-embarrassment—a hazy plan to transfer $90 billion worth of federal social welfare programs to state governments. Unless Reagan is willing to admit that what he really wants is for the states to kill or diminish the programs, he will find himself in the unhappy position of advocating increased local taxes.

• *Character*—Ford and Reagan are both pretty solid citizens, for politicians. So, "What is Jerry/Ronnie really like?" could deteriorate into, "How dumb is Jerry/Ronnie?" Reagan is smarter. One way he shows it is by using three little words: "I don't know." Ford, as President, has persistently tried to sound sensible about things of which he is essentially ignorant. That includes many things, large and small. Reagan was criticized in Washington when, during his announcement press conference, he said he did not know enough to intelligently comment on three current topics: the details of the Defense Department budget, the New York City financial crisis, and the Federal Bureau of Investigation's dirty tricks. That was extraordinary in Washington, a place where everyone has a ready comment on everything. But Reagan has been using "I don't know" as an answer since 1966, and in California that seemed to come across as refreshing candor.

• *Experience*—Ford spent a quarter of a century in Congress and then a year in the White House proving pretty well that such experience should disqualify anyone for the Presidency. Congress is a personality-forming world and the personalities are essentially anti-responsibility—they maximize comment and minimize action. He has been conditioned to avoid leadership and when he tried to imitate it, the exercise came off as parody: the WIN program, his cabinet shuffles, and his shifting positions on aid to New York City. Reagan, on the other hand, had to *do* something in eight years as a governor. Whatever else it would show, Ford–Reagan shaped up as an interesting test of what part of the public (Republicans) thought was more relevant to national government: 25 years of posturing and accommodation, putting out press releases, and making speeches on foreign policy and defense; or eight years of governing one-tenth of the American people.

• *Events*—The great strength of incumbency in presidential contests has always been the power to create or control events—to lower taxes or to declare "peace is at hand." Ford has tried to exercise that power, but there has been an uncontrolled feel about his administration and I'd have to bet that he will just keep on screwing up—that he may have to begin planning again for the lobbying office he was going to open before he was appointed vice president in 1973.

Ronald Reagan for president—the Republican candidate for president. It seems very possible to me. Estes Kefauver in 1952 and Eugene McCarthy in 1968 began as slightly laughable candidates, but each forced the withdrawal of a president, first Harry Truman, then Lyndon Johnson. It seems very possible that Reagan will do the same to Ford—that the Californian's anti-Washington rhetoric will sell in the United States in 1976. Still, I'm not convinced that it will be winning rhetoric in November of the country's bicentennial year. No matter how much common sense is made by the Reagans of the world, there is an inescapable feeling that it is all a cover to protect privilege. They may sincerely want to conserve what is best about America, but you get the feeling that, when they are safely and comfortably hidden from the rabble, what they think is best is themselves. That is no joke. But Reagan is no joke either, even if there will be jokes about him in

Washington and comparisons with Barry Goldwater in 1964. They won't be laughing in California, where he got 25 percent of the Democratic vote when he ran in 1966 and 1970. What they may be laughing about out there are Ronald Reagan's jokes about Washington.

2 | Gerald Ford

I have seen the future and it scares the hell out of me.

I have seen Gerald Rudolph Ford in Troy, Michigan, bringing up busing sixteen times in a seventeen-minute press conference when none of the questions were about busing—generally acting like the Republican county chairman of a very small county. I have heard him at Harvard talking about "that great Russian writer" because he can't pronounce Solzhenitsyn—he has trouble pronouncing or defining anything or anybody east of Portland, Maine, or west of Portland, Oregon. I have seen him, from a chartered airplane, playing golf in the Xanadu isolation of the guarded Annenberg fortress in Palm Springs—choosing to spend his time with the rich, the trying-to-get-rich, and a personal staff that can most charitably be described as being in over their collective heads.

Coming out of that Troy press conference, where Jerry Ford had persistently implied that the Democratic party and its sympathizers were essentially dedicated to forcibly dragging blue-eyed children into the blackest wilds, a network correspondent angrily exploded to no one in particular, "Jesus! He's the vice president of the United States. Doesn't he understand that?"

Ford, standing there kind of blankly with history tapping his shoulder, was a lot more than just the vice president of the United States. He was the guy—a decent, kind, and considerate man—we were all counting on to get us out of that mess. And *we,* the 210 million of us, weren't all frightened Republican congressmen or the people who pay $25 for a plastic glass of Scotch at a Republican fund-raiser.

Two weeks after the Troy number, getting a little carried away with myself, I asked Ford how he could do that. Do you want to be that divisive? Aren't busing and abortion issues so deeply felt on both sides that they can't be handled by the normal political process; don't they have to be defused in the courts or someplace?

"It gets tough," he said, talking about the shifting back and forth from national leader to G.O.P. circuit rider. "Those issues are in the political pot already and all I'm doing is giving the electorate the opportunity to understand there are differences between Republicans and Democrats.

"Look," he finally said, "what I was doing there was laying the groundwork for the campaign in my old district in November."

Laying the groundwork, for chrissake, laying the groundwork in one lousy little district so that Republican Robert VanderLaan could beat Democrat Richard Vander Veen in the Fifth Congressional District, in Grand Rapids, Michigan, in November! In November, I thought, you just may be the President of the United States of America! How about laying the groundwork to run the country and deal with the cold, cruel world? [In November VanderLaan had lost and Jerry Ford *was* president.]

Jerry Ford—it is stunning how many people still call him "Jerry" —is a great guy. He does not have the ego cancer that grows in most national politicians. He is not a calculating man. Flying from Monterey, California, to Palm Springs late one night, Vice President Ford decided to wander up to the press section of *Air Force Two,* and then spent an hour shooting the breeze—with three television technicians —about mortgages and hunting and his days as a forest ranger in Yellowstone National Park.

Now most of the big guys don't even know there is such a thing as television cameramen and sound men, and if they do, they don't talk to them. (Spiro Agnew usually wouldn't let the press travel on *Air Force Two.*) When politicians do their airplane visiting they usually shmooze with network correspondents or writers from *The New York Times* or *Time,* somebody with a little clout.

In fact, that night, Patrick Anderson, writing for *The New York*

Times Magazine, was sitting behind Ford and the TV technicians. The plane dropped into a tremendous air pocket, and Anderson's drink, a Scotch and water, arched gracefully onto the top of the bald head of the vice president of the United States, then dribbled over his ears onto the shoulders of his new double-knit. Anderson started to mumble apologies, but Ford cut him off with "Aw, forget it!" and his high, horsy laugh.

Reporters like Ford very much—and, yes, they tended to protect him against himself, partly out of affection and partly because, like other Americans, they desperately wanted Ford to be Lincoln and get the Nixon taste out of our mouths. On the flight from Monterey, the traveling press gave the vice president a couple of gifts they had picked up while he was golfing at Cypress Point: an "Impeach President Ford" bumper sticker and an "Official U.S. Taxpayer" badge.

The badge was given on the condition that he wear it the next time he went into the Oval Office to see President Nixon. "I don't know if I'm going to be invited again," he said.

But, as much as reporters like Ford, his de-Lincolnization was inevitable. Jerry Ford is slow. Contrary to what Lyndon Johnson said about him, he did wear a helmet when he was the University of Michigan's center in the late thirties, and he *can* walk and chew gum at the same time. He also graduated from Yale Law School while working full time and regularly earning another $25 a week as a professional blood donor.

But he is slow, so slow that many, many people think he is stupid. Charles Goodell, the former senator from New York, is not one of them. Goodell is a friend and one of the Republican plotters—along with Robert Griffin, now a senator from Michigan—who planned Ford's successful challenge for the House minority leadership in 1965. Goodell's description of Ford's intelligence goes like this:

> Johnson thought Ford was stupid because he was predictable. He could maneuver around Jerry . . . Ford is a solid, inertial guy. He is not fast on his feet, but he is an intelligent, hard-working guy . . . He is genuinely naive, and he has no instinct for power, for manipulation . . . It took him a year

or two to adjust to being minority leader—he continued to act as if he were still just a congressman from Grand Rapids. It will be a slow transition to national leader—that's the way it is.

It is very possible—probable, I think—that Richard Nixon selected Ford precisely because he knew what other people thought of the Michigan congressman. The President may have thought that Ford was impeachment insurance, that Washington thought Jerry was just too dumb to be President. But it didn't work out that way. Washington and a lot of other places seem more interested in honesty and decency than in I.Q. or pedal dexterity.

Ford, after all, is a *good* man. Small gauge, very partisan, obsessively loyal, reflexively conservative, but essentially good. Unfortunately, the thrill of high goodness is beginning to wear off and the rest of Ford is beginning to rattle.

Ford is not only the same guy who made something of a fool of himself by trying unsuccessfully to begin impeachment proceedings against Supreme Court Justice William O. Douglas, he is the same guy whom Richard Whalen mentioned in passing in *Catch the Falling Flag*, a book on the early Nixon years: "I listened in disbelief one morning as House Minority Leader Gerald Ford earnestly told a breakfast gathering that the answer to Tet was to *Americanize* the war effort."

The Douglas fiasco grew out of Ford's unbending, undying, unthinking loyalty to the Republican party—he was the Nixon administration's tool of vengeance after the Senate refused to confirm G. Harrold Carswell for the Supreme Court. When he became vice president, he told friends that John Anderson of Illinois would be the best choice as his successor as minority leader, except that Anderson had this flaw: "He's the smartest guy in Congress, but he insists on voting his conscience instead of party."

Ford's devotion to party and President has also led him to lie—or at least consciously deceive—on the floor of Congress. He was one of the handful of congressional leaders who had been informed of secret American bombings of neutral Cambodia for two years before the

1970 invasion by South Vietnamese troops. Then, after the invasion, on November 16, 1970, when President Nixon said that the United States had scrupulously avoided previous violations of neutrality, Ford rose in the House to say: "I can say without hesitation or qualification that I know of no Presidents . . . who have been false or deceptive in the information that has come from the White House."

But he did know. Maybe he would have kept his mouth shut if he didn't have this habit of using White House handouts as House speeches without even reading them first.

He's a "team player"—one of his favorite phrases—and he still seems to think his constituency is his friends, the 187 Republican members of the House of Representatives. "There were tears in my eyes when Jerry was named vice president," said Representative Paul (Pete) McCloskey, the Republican maverick from California, when he introduced Ford in San Jose. "He's achieved more than affection from those of us he led—we love him."

And he loves them enough to go pinballing around the country to Republican banquets and receptions that turn your mind to oatmeal —it's frightening to think of what 25 years at head tables has done to Ford's mind. In San Jose, at the closing banquet of the California Republican convention, Ford was asked whether he and Governor Ronald Reagan had talked about 1976 while sitting side by side for an hour. "No," Ford answered, "we spent all our time talking about 1974."

It happened that they were in animated conversation, with great movement of arms. It also happened that I had wandered into a room with a closed-circuit television receiver, and the microphone between them was open, so I heard every word. They were talking about exercise machines and how much weight each would like to lose in a week.

As vice president, Ford spent entirely too much time at those head tables, at least in the view of one of his constituents. His frenetic traveling schedule—about 50,000 miles in the first six months after his swearing-in—was dominated by Republican appearances, usually to campaign for old friends in the House. (When he became president,

he just switched airplanes—*Air Force One* is a lot more comfortable
—and kept up the same kind of schedule.) When I asked him if he
planned to see and hear any non-Republican Americans, he answered
that he already was: "I'm going to have a private meeting tomorrow
night with another nonpartisan group, the directors of the Hearst
Corporation."

Terrific! Ford seems totally unaware that there is a whole other
America depending on him. He's never really met them, and they're
not going to get inside the ten-foot hedges around "Sunnylands," the
estate of Walter Annenberg, the publishing tycoon, ambassador to
Great Britain, and six-figure Nixon contributor who can seclude himself inside his lush green Palm Springs estate half the size of Hoboken,
New Jersey.

That particular brand of unreality has never been Ford's style, but
he was surprised when I made a point of it. "I don't understand why
you say it's impolitic," he said. "The President set it up with Annenberg when he heard Betty and I were going to Palm Springs the way
we do every year. It was very pleasant."

Key Biscayne and San Clemente are pleasant, too, but many
Americans are fed up with politicians secluded behind rose hedges.
One of the most appealing things about Ford was that his income-tax
returns (taxes of 33 percent on annual income of about $75,000)
showed that he wasn't getting rich on the public teat.

Congressman Ford's 25-year House voting record is a testament to
his benign neglect of Americans who were not satirized by Sinclair
Lewis. The best example, of course, is civil rights. Jerry Ford would
probably use his hulking strength to slap down anyone he saw mis-
treating a black lady—if it happened right in front of him. "He is like
most 60-year-old Midwestern Republicans," said a friend and colleague. "He's for equal opportunity, but he has no real sense of
injustice. He's just never bothered to see what's been going on."

He has been an orthodox, moderately conservative Republican on
civil rights and all the great issues of his professional lifetime. The
N.A.A.C.P. rated him "right" on 28 civil-rights votes over the years
and "wrong" on 26, adding that he voted to emasculate every major

piece of civil-rights legislation but eventually voted for final passage.

"On the whole," said Clarence Mitchell, head of the N.A.A.C.P.'s Washington bureau during Ford's confirmation hearings, "I think that his attitude on civil rights is described by my phrase, which is 'restricted.' . . . When you get to the crunch, and when you have to take a stand because it is right, even though it is unpopular, I fear . . . he falls short . . . [But] he would be the kind of person I would be glad to go on a hunting trip with; I know I would not get shot in the back."

Some Ford defenders, particularly more liberal Republicans, like to use phrases like "grow in office" when they talk about civil rights or his narrow partisanship. But anyone looking for a "new" Jerry Ford was going to have a long wait. "He is what he appears to be," said his friend Charlie Goodell.

"All I can say is," said Ford of civil rights, "in the future I will use those same points of view. It is most likely that if you move from being a representative of 455,000 individuals to having a broader constituency, you have to have a broader viewpoint, but my voting . . . was a matter of conviction and judgment."

"I am a middle American," he told one British interviewer. And is he ever—the double-knit suits that would blend into any salesman's convention and the big "M" belt buckle with "Go Blue" for the University of Michigan. He grew up in Grand Rapids amid Dutch Reformed austerity—he is an Episcopalian—and an elite Eastern journalist likes to call him "the last great piece of furniture out of Grand Rapids."

Ford was actually born Leslie King in Omaha, Nebraska, in 1913, but the name change came when his parents were divorced and his mother moved to Michigan to marry Gerald R. Ford, Sr., a paint salesman and Republican county chairman. The president's youth was plain hard work; football heroics unseen in the middle of the line, captain in the worst year (one win, seven losses) the University of Michigan ever had; Yale Law; the Navy in World War II; back home for law and politics, going to Congress in 1948 by defeating an isolationist Republican named Bartel Jonkman.

Never extraordinary but always plugging, conservative but not reactionary—Ford's Americans for Constitutional Action ratings ranged from 50 to 90 and his Americans for Democratic Action score went from 0 to 40—the congressman from the Fifth District had privately decided to retire at the end of 1976—a respectable, rewarding life, carefully planned. Ford knew what his pension was, and in the kitchen he wants to know what it's for before he gives his wife $20. One of the most revealing insights into Ford came from his son Michael, a 25-year-old divinity student who wasn't all that sure that becoming vice president or president was such a good idea. "Dad might be thrown into the lions' pit and have everything he has built up torn apart."

Yes, that might happen. Certainly Jerry Ford was a modest man with no desperate drive to be President. In his confirmation hearings he was asked about his reaction to Nixon's hint to Federal District Judge Matthew Byrne, the trial judge in the Daniel Ellsberg case, that Byrne was in line to become director of the Federal Bureau of Investigation. Ford replied that he couldn't understand all the fuss because the District Court was a better job than F.B.I. director.

Did you really mean that? I asked. "Certainly," Ford said. "You know Byrne had a good chance to be promoted to the Circuit Court." But the power? "Anyone who wants that kind of power should be watched most closely, most closely," he said. Where was he when Haldeman and Ehrlichman needed watching?

He is determined to cast himself in a safe, narrow role. As vice president he said his role was to mediate and negotiate between the Nixon administration and the Congress, "to find areas of agreement, in language and dollars, to narrow differences." That, of course, is not the role millions of Americans wanted him to play—they wanted him to be the man to make us proud again.

Continuing, for a moment, the search for imperfection: Ford seems to be an indiscriminate judge of other men. He has the same comment about almost everybody he meets: "Gee, what a great guy!"

Well, not everybody is so nice. Most of his staff are nice enough, but they fast became legend—for leaving their own and press baggage in Denver when *Air Force Two* headed for Washington, or for letting their man be set up by a California congressional candidate named George Milias who got a lavish Ford endorsement before the staff found out that Milias was only one of five Republicans running for the same seat.

The quality of the men around Ford was demonstrated for me in a doorway incident at a Midwestern Republican Conference in Chicago. Ford was about to begin a press conference there when his staff director and later counsellor at the White House, Robert Hartmann, a former newspaperman who looks like an aging welterweight who forgot to duck once too often, tried to get in without showing his credentials. A young Secret Service agent politely stopped Hartmann, who proceeded to shout and start swinging short punches at the air. When the thing was finally straightened out, Hartmann brushed by the agent and snarled, literally snarled: "You think you'll like it in Alaska, huh?"

That's how Bob Hartmann, the dark side of good old Jerry Ford, reacted to being close to power. How did Ford himself react? How did it feel to be so close, closer really than a heartbeat away? a panel of television newsmen in San Jose asked Ford three months before he became president.

"The truth is I don't think about it."

*   *   *

The truth was, unfortunately, that Ford was telling the truth. He had not thought about it on the most serious level. On August 9, 1974, Gerald Ford became the 38th President of the United States and he didn't know what to do next. He began, sort of, with a shaky meeting with Nixon's old White House staff, telling them: "I don't like long memos, I listen better than I read, really . . . I like to take reading home, but not a great volume . . . I also like yes/no options without a lot of complications."

As ordered, "Action Memos"—the basic policy instruments of the presidency—began shuffling across Ford's Oval Office desk. Sixteen on administration policy ranging from energy to campaign reform were passed to him on one day by Alexander Haig, Nixon's chief of staff and a man who could only have been called the acting president in the final days of Nixon and the early days of Ford. The new president was being used and locked into positions by men he hardly knew, men who just happened to be in place when he arrived—it is probably stating the obvious to point out that control over presidential options (yes/no) is close to control of presidential decisions.

Gerald Ford's presidency developed a depressing, almost desperate pattern: The president would drift along, seemingly serene above the tumultuous planning and plotting of his subordinates, then would try to gain control of his own house and future with bold, solitary strokes that came off as over-reactions, culminating in the "Sunday Morning Massacre," a staff and cabinet shake-up on November 2, 1975.

That Sunday, Senator Howard Baker of Tennessee told reporters, "This is the real beginning of the Ford administration." But other men close to the president had said the same words before—after he pardoned Richard Nixon, after he moved Haig out of the White House, after the disastrous (for Republicans) 1974 congressional elections, after his 1975 State of the Union address and after a United States air-sea armada dramatically recaptured an American merchant ship, the *Mayaguez,* which had been seized off the coast of Southeast Asia by Cambodian patrol boats.

In fact, there may never have been a Ford administration. The record might one day show that it was a series of memos like the one sent to Ford by a friend and adviser early in 1975: "You have to establish forcefully that *you* are the President!"

3 | Edward Kennedy

Talking with Democrats about 1976, you eventually realize you've heard it all before. Samuel Beckett wrote it:

ESTRAGON: Let's go.
VLADIMIR: We can't.
ESTRAGON: Why not?
VLADIMIR: We're waiting for Godot.

Teddy Kennedy, of course, is Godot. And the dialogue goes on: "And what did he reply?" . . . "That he'd see" . . . "That he couldn't promise anything" . . . "That he'd have to think it over" . . . "In the quiet of his home" . . . "Consult his family" . . . "His friends" . . . "His agents."

The man Beckett's tramps could have been talking about was, in the language of politics, keeping his options open. Edward Moore Kennedy was usually in Washington, the very model of a good senator —whatever that means in the real world—casting his broad shadow over the Democratic party.

Aleksandr Solzhenitsyn's most quoted observation is that a great writer is like a second government. In the United States that might be amended to say that a Kennedy is a second government. A Kennedy is always a candidate for President. It does not matter that Ted Kennedy sat in his dining room and told me, as he has told others, that it is "unlikely" he will run in 1976 after consulting his family.

An old-fashioned rational analysis—dozens of interviews, studying polls, and looking out the window a lot—would convince anyone, including me, that Teddy will run. He looks unbeatable for the Democratic nomination, and, conceding that analysis months before an election is not unlike fortune-telling, has a very good chance to win it all in November of 1976—and that is how politicians make decisions. He will be under almost unbearable political pressure to go because the pending new rules of the Democratic party may make him the only candidate who can get the nomination without breaking up the party like peanut brittle.

My head says yes.

My gut says no.

Almost everyone you talk to who has Kennedy credentials says he thinks Teddy will go; some claim they *know* he will and that the decision was made in the fall of 1973 but things never really got rolling because of the personal trauma of discovered cancer in twelve-year-old Teddy, Jr. "Things are in limbo until he knows about the boy," said one "friend." The catch in those neat answers is that the closer you get to Kennedy himself, to the people he would call friends, the more you get answers like: "I'm just not sure, but I'd bet 'no.' " And the reasons then get more and more personal, the name of his wife starts coming up, and, well, Ted Kennedy seems to have more trouble keeping the most private parts of his private life secret than any public figure since Secretariat. He's a wine, women, and song Irishman—actually he doesn't like singing that much—who can't seem to grow out of shouting gross things at parties like: "Hey, it's George McGovern, the man who sleeps with _____."

"A lot of people want Teddy to run because they think politics will be fun again," said Martin Nolan, the *Boston Globe*'s Washington bureau chief who has followed the Massachusetts senator since his precocious election at 30. "It's not going to be fun, it's going to be ugly."

There are a hundred stories, many true, that will make Teddy look like a hyperactive teenager. He is the senator who once had to issue a public statement denying he was having an affair with Amanda Burden, a New York socialite. He is the man of whom Cleveland Mayor Ralph Perk, campaigning for the Republican nomination for senator in Ohio, said: "People ask me how Republicans will explain the eighteen-and-a-half-minute gap in the tapes. I tell them it will take the Democrats a lot longer to explain the twelve-and-a-half-hour gap at Chappaquiddick."

"He's the one man who can override Watergate," said one of the country's leading pollsters. "If he runs, Teddy becomes *the* issue. He polarizes the nation unbelievably."

The people who know Kennedy slightly, senators and other politicians and journalists, often debate his fitness, his character, his personal priorities, among themselves. Many, including those who admire his politics, are uneasy or afraid of a President Edward Kennedy —maybe he's not a full-grown man, or maybe he's just been unlucky (or self-destructive) enough to get caught. If he runs, those late-night Brendan Behan conversations become a national debate. Maybe he'll wait, postpone it until 1980. He'll still be only 48 then.

His grandfather, John (Honey Fitz) Fitzgerald, chose not to run for re-election as mayor of Boston in 1914 when his opponent, James Michael Curley, announced he planned to use the campaign to discuss "great lovemakers from Cleopatra to Toodles." It seems that a cigarette girl named Toodles Ryan was, depending on whom you believed, a casual or not-so-casual friend of the mayor.

Returning now from those thrilling days of yesteryear and beginning with more conventional, and comfortable, political analysis: Kennedy, after fourteen creditable, sometimes distinguished, years in the Senate, is probably the most popular politician in the country, certainly the one with the best chance of putting together a Son of New Deal coalition of academic liberals, working-class Catholics, and the poor—and he turns people on. He also turns a lot off—the pollsters I talked with estimated the fervent anti-Teddy constituency at between 25 and 30 percent of the electorate—but Franklin Roosevelt, too, was many men's devil.

"He can have the nomination by asking for it; nobody can beat him in the Democratic party. But Republicans will eat him up in the general election." That wisdom is so conventional that I heard it almost word for word again and again from state chairmen, gover-

nors, senators, and just plain old "observers," Democratic and
Republican. I had just heard it from a covey of Southerners—they
forecast 2-to-1 and 3-to-2 victories for Gerald Ford over Kennedy in
their states—when I picked up the Texas Poll, 501 voters surveyed by
the Joe Belden organization in March, 1974. The results in trial heats:
Kennedy 41-to-35 percent over Ford; Ford 35-to-29 over Henry Jackson; Kennedy 44-to-24 over Nelson Rockefeller.

Trial heats do not an election make—Peter Hart, the Washington
pollster, is convinced that head-to-head pairings are meaningless until
after the first presidential primary, and he's on to something—but
with someone as well known, loved, and hated as Kennedy, they speak
volumes. So do other numbers: 37 percent of voters surveyed nationally early in 1974 identified Kennedy as the man who "best represents
my views," by far the highest of any public figure (Roper); 44 percent
of Democrats surveyed nationally "would like to see" Kennedy nominated in 1976, compared with 17 percent who preferred George Wallace and 8 percent for Jackson (Gallup).

"Some of the famous anti-Kennedy vote is a myth," said Tully
Plesser of Cambridge Opinion Studies. "The educated liberals who
reject Teddy's saying 'I want to be President' will react quite differently when he is Edward Kennedy, The Democratic Candidate.
. . . He is very, very formidable because he has a unique hold on the
Catholic vote in this country, particularly at the blue-collar level. He
is the Catholic's Catholic . . . All the talk about Chappaquiddick will
only reinforce the feelings of people who are against him anyway.
What could destroy him would be some new event reflecting on his
character. A divorce, oh God . . ."

Plesser and other pollsters agreed that Kennedy could not win big
in a general election—too many voters have already made up their
minds against him—and when asked to bet their own money, all
agreed that a Kennedy–Anybody race would fall within a 53-to-47
percent range either way. Unless. Unless Wallace actively supports
Teddy—then, they said, Kennedy wins big. (In case you were wondering why Teddy went to Alabama one July 4 to say what a great guy
ol' George is.)

That's politics. And Ted Kennedy is a hell of a politician: a great, lusty campaigner; finely tuned Boston Irish instincts; and enough guts to know what he's for—amnesty, for instance—and what he's against —abortion on demand. On the same day he could argue articulately, almost brilliantly, on the Senate floor against reinstituting the death penalty for a bizarre range of federal crimes and twice take time out to call Matty Troy, the Democratic Leader of Queens, to get him to pull the right strings so that a Kennedy friend could get a couple of hotel billboards raised over the highways to La Guardia and J.F.K. airports.

It's all in a day's work. So is snapping at his staff to "Get me an energy program by next week—I'm sick of Scoop Jackson being called 'Mr. Energy'!" And grimly warning a bright young legislative assistant never again to whisper information to him in front of reporters or cameras.

Teddy is not timid with the manners and the freedom of a young lord. He doesn't have to bend as deeply as other politicians—and he often doesn't. He went to a cathedral of orthodox Catholic attitudes, the Iona College Alumni Association, after May Day, 1971, and told the hissing crowd: "The arrested demonstrators were your children, your nieces and nephews or your friends' children or nieces or nephews." In the late sixties and early seventies, after he had effectively lobbied for a fairer draft lottery—students would be drafted along with truckdrivers—he went to college campuses to speak against a volunteer Army. "How many of you favor an all-volunteer Army?" he would ask, and the raised hands would fill the auditoriums. "How many of you would volunteer?" and there would be no hands. "See? You want someone else to do it for you, and I'm against that."

His standard routine is less challenging as performed for 50 delegates to a Textile Workers Union political conference in Washington.

"I remember when my first opponent in 1962 ended a television debate by saying, 'Furthermore, ladies and gentlemen, this man has never worked a day in his life.' Well, I was north of Boston the next morning and some big labor fellow grabbed me at about 5:30 outside a plant gate and he said: 'Kennedy, I heard what they said about you last night, that you never worked a day in your life. Well, let me tell you something—you haven't missed a thing.'

"Your union has had a long relationship with my family . . . Like President Kennedy and Robert Kennedy before me, I serve on the Labor and Education Committee. . . . There's been no increase in the minimum wage since 1967 and inflation has . . . The American Medical Association doesn't agree with my health care plan, the insurance companies don't . . . We want health to be a basic right . . . hospital bills marked 'Paid in Full' . . . Where does the President go when he wants a medical checkup? Walter Reed. But the working men and women of America . . . Tax reform. The tax code is the greatest welfare system of them all . . . when the President pays less tax than the average workingman earning $8,500 a year . . . Private contributions to political campaigns produce private benefits for private interests . . . Okay, I'll take a couple of questions and then we'll pose for pictures."

The questions, as always, begin with his 1976 plans and move to Teddy, Jr.—"We appreciate your thoughts and your prayers"—then a man with "Duke" across a royal blue Local 710 bowling shirt, asks: "Do you think these big companies, these conglomerates, should be broken up?"

"Yes, I do. The energy companies are an example . . ."

"Your brother was a good man," Duke says. "He was working on it when . . ."

In 1976, or whenever, the issue will be: What manner of man is Edward Moore Kennedy? The little brother, the ninth child? The nicest guy? The plugger? The dumb one? The perpetual adolescent? The best one?

There is a family photograph taken in 1944 of John F. Kennedy and the crew of PT-109 standing with their arms around each other on the lawn at Hyannis Port, proud and strong in their young manhood. Kneeling in front of them is a twelve-year-old boy in a little striped polo shirt—Teddy, who was so much younger. It reminded me, sadly, of a movie that was made that year, *The Sullivans,* about five Irish brothers from Waterloo, Iowa, who were killed in World War II. The youngest, Al, who was called "Short Change," had spent most of his short life trying to catch up with the big guys. The movie ended in heaven with the four big brothers striding through the clouds and Short Change running behind, shouting, "Hey, fellas, wait for me!"

The father, Joseph P. Kennedy, once said he was going to "sell the name Kennedy like soap flakes." Well, he did, and Teddy has been running after larger and larger images. Even today, when he has more or less mastered his habit of answering questions that get too close with phrases, grunts, and sentences that don't end, he said this about being a Kennedy: "The extraordinary sense of expectation . . . the comparison . . . is a constant . . . constant . . ."

Being a Kennedy, of course, may have the same end as being a Sullivan. An attempt on his life when he runs seems inevitable— "They have to miss sometime" is one of the grimmer jokes around Kennedy—and what can you say? He lives with it—"Life is unfair," Jack said—and he has been seen to flinch or double up when a car backfires. But occasional fright is not necessarily fear, and he has also been known to elude the Secret Service and bodyguards to seek his own pleasures.

One of those pleasures, interestingly, is drinking with a couple of New York policemen who are his friends, and crawling the East Side of Manhattan. For a guy whose family chauffeur waited nearby when he camped out as a kid, Teddy has a strong pull toward the verities of middle-class America, especially Irish-Catholic middle-class America. "They must have talked good sense around his kitchen table" is Kennedy's highest compliment about another political man, according to his friend and former administrative assistant, David Burke—and the Kennedys talked at dining room tables with servants to the left. Burke, whom Kennedy described to me as the one man he would turn to in a crisis, as he did after Chappaquiddick, is now secretary to New York Governor Hugh Carey, but he is also the son of a Brookline cop, a background not dissimilar to that of many of the men closest to this Kennedy.

Does he wish he had been born Edward Moore? No, he told me.

Would he have made it if his name were Edward Moore? "Yes, I think so! Oh, I think so!"

Maybe. He is very determined, dogged—but that may be because his name *is* Kennedy and not Moore. "I've got to go at a thing four times as hard and four times as long as some other fellow," Kennedy said a couple of years ago. Perhaps because father Kennedy's soap flakes machine so smoothly convinced us that Jack and Bobby were brilliant, perhaps because we remember Teddy was thrown out of Harvard for getting another student to take a freshman Spanish final for him, or perhaps because his justified insecurity as a 30-year-old *dauphin* senator made him sound like one, the impression is abroad that Kennedy is some kind of dope. At any rate, I found friends asking me about Kennedy, as they did about John Lindsay a few years ago: How smart is he? (Or, how dumb is he?) My answer, then and now: smart enough.

Successful modern politicians, for better or worse, have a special kind of intelligence—like an oil slick, broad, restless, and only deep enough to make sure everything is covered. The phrases that you hear about Kennedy are "short attention span" or "a great instinct for getting right to the heart of the matter, for asking the right question" —one is unfriendly, the other friendly, but they both really mean the same thing. He is no scholar, and he is neither reflective nor imaginative—he has people to do all that for him—but on any day he can absorb two twenty-pound briefcases of memos and background papers, take a couple of dozen verbal briefings ranging from 30 seconds to an hour, handle a dozen confrontation situations with senators, reporters, or bureaucrats trying to trap him, juggle the egos of 50 staff members and ex-officio advisers, interrogate the presidents of four drug companies and their counsel about their business, debate Senator John McClellan about the death penalty and Senator Jesse Helms about handgun production in the South, read the newspapers, remember 500 faces and names, and be witty at dinner. You try it.

On that day, as chairman of the Health Subcommittee of the Senate Labor and Public Welfare Committee, Kennedy was taking testimony from the presidents of four of the largest pharmaceutical manufacturers in the country. Subcommittee investigators and Kennedy's staff had investigated industry sales practices to try to prove Teddy's contention that tens of thousands of Americans are dying each year because drugs are being peddled and prescribed without adequate safeguards. The drug executives had been briefed, too, and Henry W. Gadsden, who presumably had something on the ball to become the chairman and president of Merck & Co., was defending the use of salesmen-detailmen and industry sales manuals urging them to "appeal to the pride, ego, and fear" of pharmacists and physicians when this exchange took place:

KENNEDY: You think detailing is a valuable service, then?

GADSDEN: The fact is we wouldn't spend the money on detailing if we didn't think it was worthwhile.

KENNEDY: Exactly. But you only talk about *your* drugs.

GADSDEN: Sir, I believe Xerox salesmen only talk about Xerox machines.

KENNEDY: How long can you stay in the hospital or can you die from overuse of a Xerox machine?

Someone who knows Kennedy very well described him to me as "canny," a good word to describe the kind of Irish-Catholic intelligence that comes from coexisting with the doctrine of the church and the realities of life. There is a great deal that is very Catholic about Edward Kennedy: the almost instinctive respect for institutions (Congress and unions, for example) that makes him more conservative than many people would like to believe, and the separation between public and personal morality that the church's rigid regulation forces on its children very early in life.

"Whatever you think of Teddy's personal morality," a friend said, "he is a publicly moral man. The rules of the church are so rigid that we have to develop a separate personal morality to survive—then the question of how good a Catholic you are becomes a question of how much do you stray and how soon do you return."

Kennedy strays often and clumsily, which really doesn't have much to do with being a good senator or President—unless the straying is part of a pattern, a lack of what might be called character, a bent toward self-destruction, or just an immature sense of priorities.

Do you want Teddy Kennedy to be President? "Everybody hesitates when you ask that, don't they?" answered a congressman who has campaigned with Kennedy and votes the same way. "I'm not sure, but then I'll never be sure, and in a crunch I would say yes."

The word that kept coming up was "maturity," and I finally asked Kennedy for his definition of it.

"I suppose it's an approach to life," he said, "an ability to be able to perceive the important rather than the unimportant, balance the real dimension of existence. I'd say it doesn't include being right all the time, but having reasons, views, actions, and attitudes that are sound."

And are you mature? "Certainly more than I used to be. I'm getting there," he said, breaking into a huge grin, and that was the end of that.

Someday, 80 million American voters are going to judge Kennedy's maturity—it will be the basic question that decides whether he is to be their President. Because of that there is tremendous political focus in Washington on his relationship with his wife, Joan, the neglected and insecure woman called "The Reluctant Kennedy" in the title of one book.

"Gossip is fun, we all love it," said one of the wiser old heads in the Democratic party. "But this isn't fun anymore. It's serious. Kennedy can't take another scandal, a divorce or anything, it'd just be too much. Whatever arrangement they have, his wife has a lot of power over what happens to this party."

The Senate is a comfortable, comical imitation of what the Founding Fathers had in mind. Like a hundred grandees trailed by a hundred attendant entourages, the elders wander from committee rooms to the floor to National Airport for a quick flight back home to dazzle the folks with the glamour that has attached to them since the television networks and major newspapers decided to concentrate their national coverage in the Capitol. Washington, of course, is not the nation, and the great national debate of the elders is a farce, with two or three senators at a time gesturing dramatically at empty desks and glancing into the galleries to see if *The New York Times* or *The Washington Post* is taking notes. When Kennedy was effectively arguing against capital punishment in March, 1974, his distinguished adversaries were yocking it up around the Republican cloakroom about Chappaquiddick, getting up a phony amendment about "swimming away from the scene of a crime."

If Senate sessions were televised, we would be talking about governors and mayors for President. At any rate, we are talking about senators, and Ted Kennedy is in the upper half of the class, working hard and manipulating the public attention that comes with his name to push his favored interests—national health care; draft, tax, and campaign finance reform; world refugee problems; and the eighteen-year-old vote, which became law because his staff figured out a way to do it without a constitutional amendment.

He has had his moments—like trying to make Francis X. Morrissey, his father's old coat-holder, a federal judge—but the third Kennedy has been a more diligent and effective senator than his brothers. He has grown to be the best orator the family has produced —although I haven't figured out why anyone would want to orate in an empty room—and kept his liberal credentials shiny with Americans for Democratic Action ratings above 85 and Americans for Constitutional Action ratings below 5. He is also a nice guy, which counts for a lot in those hallowed halls.

When the Senate went into session in 1969, Kennedy wanted to prove something—probably that he could rise above being a Kennedy, could function away from charisma and media—and got himself elected assistant majority leader (whip) of Senate Democrats over Russell Long of Louisiana in closed caucus.

In 1971, Kennedy belatedly realized that Robert Byrd of West Virginia was trying to take his little job away, and did, because Teddy had been a lousy whip—that is, he hadn't done enough piddling services like making sure certain senators got back from martini time to discharge their sacred trust on some inconsequential roll call. When the secret vote was over and some of his colleagues had betrayed their word that they would vote for him, Kennedy walked out and found, as usual, Marty Nolan of *The Globe* waiting for him.

"This is the first time you've ever lost anything, senator, isn't it? How does it feel?" Nolan asked.

"The Kennedys have known personal tragedy before . . ." the answer began. So have the Nolans. But Kennedy couldn't rise above being a Kennedy.

A Kennedy lives all his life in public; that's the way they've wanted it. Burton Hersh, the author of *The Education of Edward Kennedy,* believes that decision was made in 1946 after an enormously successful reception for congressional candidate Jack Kennedy at the Commodore Hotel, just off Harvard Square in Cambridge. He wrote:

> [It] may have marked that moment when the Kennedys began knowingly to market an apprehension of themselves as something more than people, stimulate somehow that oversweet awareness of the beauty and meaning and predestination of their lives which was to excite the longing and hatred and adoration of millions and millions everywhere, and finally of those insane little moths who flew at them in Dallas and Los Angeles . . . At the time the idea of the reception came up it seemed an absurdity to the regulars in the organization—a kind of costume put-on to which 1,500 local scrub-women and taxidrivers were invited by embossed invitation along with a sprinkling of openly tongue-in-cheek Harvard faculty, all filing together in confusion along a protocol-ordered reception line headed by the Ambassador [Joseph Kennedy] himself in white tie and tails before fanning out to play hell among the teacups and petits fours; the line of communicants stretched across the lobby and out of the door of the little hotel, across the street and into a park nearby. The Kennedys had stumbled onto what was to remain their most successful publicity recourse, their ability to minister to the sharpening pretension among ox-tongued ethnics across America, their ability to involve other people as unaware of the traditional moorings as *they* were in their own exhaustedly derived intuition of pop class.

So, 30 years and 100,000 carefully arranged family pictures later, it comes down to Teddy in 1976. I asked him what he wanted from the President who will take office in 1977 and he answered in part:

> To rebuild the confidence of the United States in the United States . . . Build a series of early warning systems in domestic areas: energy, food, the economy. We can't go on like this from crisis to crisis . . . There are

no *answers,* but you can have approaches. There has been resentment about special programs, and we have to have programs that reach out . . . I'm obviously thinking about things like national health care and social security. They have to help the Cambridge cop and the inner-city poor. If approaches are equitable, the cop is then glad to help the person in harder straits . . . In foreign policy, he should move away from balance of power to interdependence . . . We should not try to reshape and change the world, but have the United States represent something, the things we all believe it is supposed to represent . . . You don't give military aid and credits to military governments like Chile . . . You don't favor Pakistan—even if you're doing it to get into China—when they're using force to oppose an elected government . . . We believe in influencing the world toward humanity and humanism.

There are a couple of interesting things about that recitation. One is that Kennedy is still very much a domestically oriented national politician—I say *still* because that seems to change when a man becomes President and realizes that outside the twelve-mile limit he is the United States of America. The other is that he is of a new generation of liberals who, unlike J.F.K. and his contemporaries, the junior-officers-in-World-War-II generation, don't believe that the great problems can be solved. The next generation that comes to power, and he may be the first of them, has faith only that the problems can be lived with—if they are lived with fairly, if the burden of discomfort is distributed more equitably.

If Edward Kennedy does become President, it is going to be different from what some people think. He is not one of his brothers and he has his own style and his own people.

Teddy consults his brothers' men often and listens to them with great deference, but later he is as likely as not to turn to one of his own men, Dave Burke or Paul Kirk, and say with a smile: "Jeez, what bull . . . !" Ted Sorensen and the rest will be talking about running the country, but they'll be doing more of it on *The Tonight Show* than in the White House.

The new Kennedy men, with Burke as *primus inter pares,* are more his own age, more Irish, and earthier than, if not as academic as, the men around Jack or Bobby. They are also likely to have served on his staff at one time or another. Their names, except perhaps for Stephen Smith, his coldly calculating brother-in-law, are practically unknown: James Flug, former chief counsel to Kennedy's Subcommittee on Administrative Practice and Procedure; Paul Kirk, the political liaison in the Senate office; Burke Marshall, a professor of law at Yale who was the "one man" Bobby said he would turn to for advice. Then there are Tim Hanan, a New York attorney; Richard Drayne, his former press secretary; Edward Martin, his administrative assistant; Carey Parker, legislative assistant; Gerald Doherty, John Nolan . . . the list goes on. His gurus would include former Senator Philip Hart, the gentleman from Michigan, and Archibald Cox, whom Kennedy would almost certainly like to make a Supreme Court justice. And the old friends, or "the jocks," as they are known in Washington, Senator John Tunney and Senator John Culver of Iowa, a Harvard fullback when Teddy was an end.

Out there are the Kennedy Minutemen. The Kennedy Machine has always been something of a myth, a clanky thing at best, but there are hundreds, perhaps thousands, of people willing to drop their own careers and families if the call comes—it can only be described as a phenomenon, a calling.

Kennedy isn't going to say much more, not for a while. He has to play his game and play out his options. The hell with the Democratic party. Let them eat turnips!—that's what Vladimir and Estragon ate while looking down the road for Godot.

Edward Moore may be the best of the Kennedys—even if, as I assume, he spent six days of his life sitting at Hyannis Port talking about payoffs or whatever else it would take to cover up how a 28-year-old girl died. He may be the real Bobby—that is, he may be the guy who can make the magic connection, the bringing together on some levels of working white ethnics and the poor. Certainly his feel for those people near the bottom, all those ethnics working two jobs, is more genuine than Bobby's. He just might put it together.

The country might be ready for Teddy—if he's finally ready. The public and the press has been sensitized by the Nixon charade of '72 and Watergate. We have to believe the '76 gauntlet can test character as well as anything. If Kennedy survives it, he deserves to be President —whatever goes on at that $750,000 house in McLean or whatever the hell really happened at Chappaquiddick.

4 | Henry (Scoop) Jackson

Sen. Henry Jackson (D-Wash.) has suddenly emerged as the most powerful Democrat in the country.

Joseph Kraft, *The Washington Post*

Sen. Henry Jackson of Washington is filling the role Churchill pursued in the prewar days . . .

Editorial, *The Detroit News*

If required to take a wild guess and identify the most likely next President of the United States we would incline right now to pick Senator Jackson.

Joseph C. Harsch, *The Christian Science Monitor*

Scoop Jackson would be just about a sure thing in 1976 if he didn't have to run. He is the Institutional Candidate for President; he could be the candidate of the Congress, big labor, the military-industrial complex, Protestant morality, Jewish money, and Rotary Clubs. He might even end up as the candidate of Allard Lowenstein and other anti-war Democrats who were cursing him only a few years ago.

There have been sunshine days for the most powerful Democrat since his embarrassing run for the Presidency in 1972. Lowenstein, who considered moving to Seattle to run against Jackson in 1970 to protest the senator's enthusiasm for Vietnam, sent a nice note saying he was just another admirer and suggesting they get together to talk about much older times. Leaders of the fashionably liberal Committee for a More Effective Congress warned anti-war intellectuals late in

1973 that they might have to join Jackson before he beats them. Even New York City Council President Paul O'Dwyer, who said several years ago that no "true Democrat" could vote for Jackson, says now that the war is over and he has an open mind. Power, thy magic spell is everywhere.

Even on the other side of the national aisle: a former Republican state chairman in the West says his people will support Jackson if his party nominates "a liberal like Nelson Rockefeller." Across the continent, Republicans close to Rockefeller were saying privately that they'll organize "Republicans for Jackson" if the G.O.P. nominates Ronald Reagan.

Forget the Gallup polls that show Jackson is the choice of only 10 percent of American Democrats. Watch Scoop Jackson, The Consistent Man: enemy of Russia, friend of Boeing, Israel, and the workingman, dull small-town boy, hero of the Northwest, great senator, and . . . and the rest we will find out in 1976.

A foolish consistency is the hobgoblin of little minds,
adored by little statesmen . . .

Ralph Waldo Emerson

The Argus, a weekly newspaper in Seattle, posed the Jackson dilemma in an editorial a couple of years ago: "We don't know whether to applaud Jackson's consistency or condemn his stubbornness." Neither do I, although I will say it's extraordinary that a man could studiously collect information and ideas for 35 years and find that it all confirmed what he originally believed.

"A stubborn people," he says of his Norwegian forebears. "They don't care whether other people think they're right."

He was consistent even in what the Vietnam generation considered his inconsistency. "A flaming liberal on domestic questions," a magazine reported, "Jackson, unlike most Senate liberals, is one of the staunchest advocates of continuing military buildup." That may sound like last week's criticism of Jackson, but that report was actually filed in 1962—before we ever heard of Da Nang.

Political fashion has rarely touched Henry Jackson—neither, incidentally, has fashion itself; he wears black wing-tips, and when he periodically loses weight, he bunches up his oversized pants in the back. When other liberals became environmentalists, he remained what he had always been, a conservationist. He was, in fact, in the 1960s, the country's leading conservationist, toiling hard and effectively to preserve endangered forests, rivers, and species for future generations of production and recreation. He was the author and prime mover in 1967 and 1968 of the National Environmental Protection Act, establishing, for the first time, national conservation goals and requiring "environmental impact" statements for all federal projects. In 1969, after using his clout as chairman of the Senate Interior Committee to push through North Cascades and Redwood national parks on the West Coast, he became the first and only politician to win the Sierra Club's John Muir Award.

But within a year he seemed to be on the other side, attacking "environmental extremists," fighting for a supersonic transport, and struggling in frustration as the new legions of ecology used the N.E.P.A. to file the "environmental impact" suits that blocked the Alaskan oil pipeline for four years. Environment for environment's sake is beyond his functional mind. As he read *The Washington Post* column by column one morning in 1971, he read these words by Nicholas von Hoffman: "Sludge, crud, grinch, gunk, funk, blue algae, black air, oil slicks, and general industrial barf have found an advocate and defender in Senator Jackson."

Make ye no truce with Adam-zad—the Bear that walks like a Man!
                                                    Rudyard Kipling

"I regard the Soviet Union," Jackson has said, "as an opportunistic hotel burglar who walks down the corridors trying all the door handles to see which door is open."

Then Scoop Jackson appointed himself America's house detective.

The senator traces his obsession with the Russians to December, 1945, when he was a 33-year-old congressman visiting Norway for the first time. He got pneumonia—he almost died—and spent ten days recuperating in Oslo. At that time, the Norwegians were trying diplomatically but a little desperately to get rid of a couple of thousand Russian troops that had fought the Germans in northern Norway. "They had a hell of a time getting the Russians out and I started thinking," Jackson remembers now. Like hotel burglars the Russians hung around Norway for almost a year, jiggling doorknobs.

By 1951, he, like everybody else, was a Cold Warrior—others have changed in 22 years and Jackson is now routinely called "The Last Cold Warrior"—and he sounded like this: "When it comes to dealing with Russian leaders, atomic explosions often speak louder than words."

In 1965, when he was calling for bombing of North Vietnam, mining of Haiphong Harbor and "Inchon-type" amphibious invasion of the north, there was no doubt in Jackson's mind about who the enemy really was: "If we don't stop Russia in Southeast Asia, we might as well sign a quitclaim deal to the rest of Asia and grant Soviet entry into the United States."

"I love the Russian people, but . . ." is a standard Jackson beginning —then he retraces Russian imperialism to Potsdam, to Catherine the Great, and back through history. For twenty years he has been the boy who cried Bear!—and he has often been right. In the early fifties, he warned and warned that Russia was no longer a cart-and-sleigh society—then came their H-bomb and Sputnik. In the late fifties it was the missile gap—he blew that one and blames lousy C.I.A. information. In the early sixties he warned John Kennedy that the Russians would violate nuclear testing moratoriums—boom! they did. And in 1970, he warned that the Russians were secretly arming the Arabs and a Middle East war was coming.

"Our government took the Russians at face value in the Mideast in 1970," he told the Jewish Community Relations Council of Greater Philadelphia. "I don't want that to happen again . . . The last SALT agreement was a disaster for us. There is no détente—it's a direct subsidy from us to them so they can bully people around all over the world . . . We need a rascal-proof agreement because we're dealing with rascals."

Jackson voted with the Senate majority in approving the SALT I strategic arms "freeze" treaty, but only after forcing through an amendment mandating an American position of "rough numerical equality" in future (and permanent) treaties with the Soviets—the SALT I treaty allows the Russians about an 8-to-5 advantage in missiles, although Secretary of State Henry Kissinger and others have argued that U.S. multiple warhead systems neutralize any numerical gap. The numbers argument is too much for most laymen—and it may mean that there will never be a SALT II—but what is startlingly clear is that one senator had enough power to exert control over White House diplomatic and military prerogatives. Jackson tried to do it again with the "Jackson amendment," which would deny trade credits and most-favored-nation status to the Soviet Union unless it relaxes its immigration laws, including allowing Jews to migrate freely to Israel. Opponents of the amendment, like Kissinger, argued that we have no right to interfere with the internal affairs of Russia or any other country, but Jackson, the perennial pragmatist, chastised the opposition with moral arguments.

"I'm not a Russian-hater, I'm a realist," Jackson said during a two-hour interview about what has become his Horatioic stand against the Soviet Union. "My plea is that the American people understand that we are dealing with totalitarianism, with tyranny . . . The seventies will be an era of confrontation and negotiation, but on a more sophisticated level than in the past . . . The Russians aren't as crude as they used to be, gobbling up Eastern Europe. They're interested in primacy now . . . The situation has changed, the Soviets are not in an inferior position anymore—and look at the risks they were willing to take in Cuba in 1962, when we still had a 7-to-1 advantage in strategic arms . . . They can take greater risks now—and they will . . . My point isn't that there's going to be a nuclear war . . . but the level of risk-taking will keep going up."

Jackson is not the primitive anti-Communist often caricatured, but he is religiously anti-Russian. He rarely discusses the Chinese—he was an early advocate of diplomatic recognition of Communist China, in 1969—except to speculate that there is a 50-50 chance of a Russian-Chinese war. I am convinced he would welcome that war because it would weaken Russia.

YALE: *Jackson is either a stupid, dangerous man or a clever demagogue.*
HARVARD: *The frightening thing is that he's not a tool of the military-industrial complex. He really believes that stuff.*
Dialogue Between Two International Affairs Instructors

"I can't conceive of any American President using nuclear weapons except in retaliation or self-defense," Jackson told me when I asked whether, as President, he would think or do the unthinkable. But, until he became a serious Presidential possibility himself, he certainly talked about it.

In 1967, he was asked about a war with China over Vietnam and answered: "I think the probability is we will not use nuclear weapons. But one should not rule out the use of nuclear weapons."

In 1968, when the *Pueblo* was seized by the North Koreans, he said: "If they really make an all-out effort in Korea, I'm afraid we will be getting into the use of nuclear weapons."

Jackson on weapons is both impressive and disturbing. He has effectively championed every instrument of destruction from the nuclear submarine to the A.B.M., and part of his power is that other members of Congress are a little afraid to vote against his certainty and sheaves of classified documents. What if he's right?

In a 1970 biography of Jackson, *A Certain Democrat,* William W. Prochnau and Richard W. Larsen point out that Jackson takes his certainty seriously:

> As a young congressman . . . he made countless inspection trips throughout the country to the supersensitive, hidden installations that stored America's first primitive atomic weapons. His curiosity often astounded the military brass . . . Jackson, in his systematic way, actually walked down the rows of weapons and counted the big grim-gray, potbellied bombs.

Scoop Jackson, "The Senator from Boeing," is not interested in bombers simply because they are made in the state of Washington. There is a lot of myth in the Boeing connection; Jackson is a weapons counter whether or not the damn things are made by Boeing, Lockheed, or Republic. That is not to say that Jackson—and his Washington colleague, Senator Warren Magnuson—don't do their best for

Boeing. They do, and for good reason: at one time, as many as 100,000 Washingtonians have been employed by Boeing. When Magnuson, Jackson, and Richard Nixon failed in their 1971 congressional fight for continued financing for the Boeing supersonic transport (S.S.T.), the unemployment rate in the Seattle area reached 13.2 percent. A couple of other numbers: in 1965, 80 percent of Boeing contracts were military; in 1971, the figure was down to 30 percent. In fact, Connecticut, with about the same population, gets three times as much money from Department of Defense contracts as Washington gets.

No, Jackson believes what he said in 1971: "The true test of a man is where he stands on national defense."

Who is this Henry Jackson from 6,000 miles away—more Jewish than the Jews, more Zionist than the Zionists?
    Jamil Baroody, Saudi Arabian Ambassador to the United Nations

Henry Martin Jackson is a Presbyterian who was baptized a Lutheran—the "Martin" is for Martin Luther—and changed churches 50 years ago because his mother thought the local Lutheran minister was too dictatorial, too much like a Catholic priest. Since World War II, he has been one of Israel's firmest and most devoted supporters, taking a secular advocate role that could be filled only by a non-Jew.

The press-release version is that Jackson's concern for international Jewry began with a visit to Buchenwald as a congressman three days after the liberation of the death camp in 1945. Possibly more important is the fact that he simply grew up in the Nordic tradition of social justice; one of his earliest memories of his mother is the uncharacteristic anger she showed when some kids yelled "Kike" at a Jewish junkman.

Now he cherishes and romanticizes—and Jackson is anything but a romantic—his attachment to the Jewish state. When Abba Eban was named Israeli ambassador to the United States, he called on Jackson and was told, "Don't worry, we small countries have to stick together."

"Small, Senator? The United States?"

"No, I meant Norway and Israel."

Whatever its origins, Jackson's Jewish connection is obviously sincere, a political plus, and a personal joy.

Politically, American Jews are an integral part of the financial foundation of the Democratic party—which is why potential Democratic candidates for President begin their pilgrimages to Manhattan and Beverly Hills three years before an election. Jackson went to East 80th Street to help raise some elegant money for the Coalition for a Democratic Majority—a centrist group formed to prevent a reincarnation of George McGovern—at the townhouse of Meshulam Riklis, chairman of Rapid-American. "There's more than enough money in these rooms . . ." Jackson said to the black tie and silk crowd, "to get the coalition off to a real beginning." In fact, there was enough to get a Presidential campaign off to a beginning and a middle, as Riklis, a 1972 Jackson (and, later, Nixon) contributor, welcomed the senator by saying, "You know my home is your home."

Personally, Jackson is turned on by Jews. He acts differently in front of Jewish audiences—a little excited, more animated, his voice rising, arms waving, hands clasped over his head like a fighter, grinning, bouncing. With a yarmulke placed squarely on top of his head like a beanie, and with his oversized head, short arms, and stumpy body, he looks like a hand puppet.

That is not your stock Jackson; he usually is and does drone, an acceptable, slightly out-of-focus speaker, no more. There is also something in his relations with Jews that suggests condescension, as if these people were somehow exotic to a self-described "small-town boy." He uses lines like, "The Israelis have guts and brains . . . we gentiles just don't have a chance." When Paul Delaney of *The New York Times* reported in 1972 that there were no minority group members on Jackson's Senate staff, the senator sent the reporter a staff list with the Jewish names underlined.

The Jewish connection may also be part of the bridge-building between Jackson, the stubborn hawk, and the Vietnam doves. The Harvard instructor quoted above, who is Jewish, put it this way: "A lot of us felt a lot different about war when it was Israel; then a guy like Jackson doesn't look so bad, not bad at all—it's interesting to watch the conflict in so many young Jews."

You're my kind of people! I don't have to be briefed about what plain,
ordinary Americans are thinking about.
Senator Jackson to the Hudson County (N.J.) Regular Democrats

Robert Low, the former New York City councilman, once shared
a small house in Georgetown with Henry Jackson when they were
both bachelors in the 1950s. So, Low was in charge of putting together
Jackson delegate slates in New York before the 1972 Democratic
National Convention . . . and it was tough. He couldn't get a slate
balanced along McGovern Commission minority-women guidelines
in Ulster County, because, as his man in Ulster said, "How can we
get women? What respectable woman's husband is going to let her go
down to Miami alone?"

Those are Jackson people. Scoop, and everybody does call him that,
is plain people—at least for a major politician. The first time I met
him was in a Jacksonville hotel lobby early in the 1972 campaign, and
he suddenly said, "Wait for me, huh, fellas? I want to get a paper."
Wait for me! It may not seem like a big deal, but most of the big-timers
I've covered have people to get their papers, carry their coats, and rub
their backs—full-grown men fought to put Robert Kennedy's shirt on
and slip in his cufflinks. I was almost convinced that Bobby didn't
know how to work a doorknob.

Being ordinary and finding the middle, of course, is not a guaran-
teed strategy to win the White House. Jackson kind of tried that in
1972. His campaign stuck so close to *The Real Majority* by Richard
Scammon and Ben J. Wattenberg that reporters wanted to write that
he was the first book ever to run for President. Wattenberg will be
back in the 1976 Jackson campaign—it's not clear who is using whom
—and it will be a New Deal/Keep America Strong campaign.

The candidate is an Elk, Eagle, Mason, and American Legionnaire.
In 1972, he spoke in Appleton, Wisconsin, telling a joint meeting of
the local Lions and Kiwanis clubs: "Now this is what I call true
integration . . . This is basic America." If it weren't for his pro-labor
bias he could be the *Reader's Digest*'s candidate for President.

"Jackson would complete the New Deal," said Thomas Kahn, one
of his former speechwriters who is now assistant to A.F.L.–C.I.O.

President George Meany. "His agenda would be national health insurance, mandatory full employment with the federal government providing jobs or using the federal budget to create employment, general expansion of the public sector, and national economic planning—stronger federal intervention in the economy."

Kahn was right on target, I confirmed later with Jackson. Then I wanted to know whether or not a President Jackson would try to move the United States toward a corporate/labor state on the Japanese model. "I'm not suggesting we copy the Japanese," Jackson answered, "but we can learn from them. There has to be a better working relationship between American labor and management . . . I would hold regular, scheduled meetings with labor, business, and academia . . . unless we get them working together we're just not going to generate the revenues we need to reach the quality of life we want."

If any American politician has the capability of acting as the Grand Arbiter of business and labor, it is Henry Jackson. He is labor's man and has a visceral appeal to business types who see him as "solid." He sometimes seems to be on both sides, especially on days when he tells businessmen his father was a small contractor, and unions that his father was secretary of Plasterers and Cement Masons Local 190. His father, a Norwegian immigrant whose name was originally Peter Gresseth, was on both sides, at different times. And, Jackson remembers vaguely, his father and the family stayed inside the house on November 5, 1916, the day of "The Everett Massacre."

On that Sunday afternoon, when Scoop Jackson was three years old, a boatload of 250 singing International Workers of the World were landing on the waterfront down the hill when gunfire broke out between the Wobblies and hundreds of merchants, millowners, strikebreakers, and assorted employees. At least a dozen men were killed. "That didn't affect us—or me," Jackson says. "My father was *very* middle-of-the-road."

The men here care for nothing except grim, hard work.
        The Diary of Rev. Louis Tucker, Everett, Washington, 1909

"Everett was a church town, a reform town, and a wage earner's town. It was an American Federation of Labor town, among the most highly unionized in the country," wrote Norman H. Clark in *Mill Town,* a social history of the town 30 miles north of Seattle.

The town—today it has 60,000 people living in American sprawl over the harbor—was going to be "The Pittsburgh of the West," financed and developed by John D. Rockefeller and James Hill of the Great Northern Railroad. It never happened, of course: Rockefeller pulled out because of depressions and phony reports on silver and iron in the mountains; Hill decided to make Seattle the western terminus of his line; there were strikes and violence in the bloody, asthmatic shingle mills. The prettiest home in town, then and now, was the Butler place, a white Colonial house overlooking the Sound. It was owned by William Butler, a cruel Dickensian banker who ran the town and was the brother of Nicholas Murray Butler, the president of Columbia University and a big-time Republican thinker. The Butler home is now owned by Henry M. Jackson.

"Symbolism?" he said to me. "There is no symbolism. My wife picked it by herself—we paid $62,000. She had never been to Everett before. I certainly never had any animosity toward Butler."

So much for triumphant drama in the life of Henry Jackson. He was a Boy Scout, a newsboy who won an award for delivering 74,880 Everett *Daily Heralds* without a customer complaint; and in the third grade at Longfellow School he told the teacher, Mrs. Dootson, that when he grew up he would be President of the United States. His sister nicknamed him "Scoop" because he looked like a newsboy of that name in the comic pages of the *Herald.*

Mainly, he grew up without pain as the son of hard-working Norwegian immigrants—his father was from Oslo and his mother from the village of Bodo, north of the Arctic Circle. He learned, he says, the Nordic code of "rugged individualism and a social conscience." He also learned thrift—he takes two free mini-bottles of Scotch when he flies first class and sticks them in his pocket—and he learned to function without emotion. "We are people who can say 'no' without a big scene," he says, and his evaluation of other men makes it clear that he considers emotion a sign of weakness.

Working his way through college, Jackson finally graduated from the University of Washington Law School in the top third of his class

—a seemingly fair ranking of his intellect. He works hard and is a quick study; he usually knows what he has to know, maybe not too much more. Work, in fact, seems to be his only drive. He didn't marry until he was 49 years old—"I was too busy"—and then he interrupted his Hawaiian honeymoon to attend naval briefings at Pearl Harbor on "the increasing Communist submarine threat in the Pacific."

After law school, he worked for a while in the Everett welfare office, joined a small law firm, and at the age of 26 was elected Snohomish County prosecutor. They still talk fondly out there about "Soda Pop" Jackson, a name he earned by energetically pushing every bottle of liquor and pinball machine out of the dry county. He moved on to Washington, D.C., in 1940, a 28-year-old congressman, and he lived in small apartments cluttered with newspapers and reports for 21 years before he found time to marry Helen Hardin, a pretty 28-year-old secretary. They have two children, Anna Marie and Peter.

Does all work and no play make Scoop a dull boy? A friend of his asked me, "Are you really going to spend three weeks with Scoop?"

Nothing astonishes men so much as common sense and plain dealing.
Ralph Waldo Emerson

Henry Jackson made his first move into Washington State politics in 1936 when he and his friend, John Salter, a clever Irishman and seminary dropout who was Jackson's alter ego and right arm for 28 years, spent their lunch hours at the relief office scheming to make their mark. What they decided to do was issue a press release—they stated that they had been elected leaders of an Everett chapter of the Roosevelt First Voters' League. A small story appeared and the established Everett Young Democratic organization became concerned about the "growing" new group. There were merger talks, and Jackson and Salter—the only members of their "league"—were named president and secretary of the Y.D.s.

That was the beginning. Now the debate about Scoop Jackson in his home state sometimes seems to center on whether he can walk across the Snohomish River—it is assumed he can walk across Puget Sound because that's salt water and it's more buoyant. In 1970, Jackson won a vicious Democratic primary with 87 percent of the vote, then won the general election with a phenomenal 84 percent. "The well runs dry for us when Scoop runs," says Mort Frayn, a former Republican state chairman and speaker of the Washington House of Representatives. "No one wants to run against him and he gets most of the Republican money. The fact is that he's the personification of a straight guy."

The 1970 primary seemed tough because anti-war people were out to get Jackson—Eugene McCarthy came into Seattle to campaign against him—and Washington does have a radical political history. His primary opponent, Carl Maxey, whose young supporters carried PENTAGON PIMP signs at Jackson rallies, went this far: "Every time I see Jackson in that television commercial, walking in the woods with his child, I see the trees and I'm reminded of the coffins they are sending our children home in from Vietnam."

Jackson grimly told friends, "I'm not going to beat Maxey, I'm going to bury him." Scoop can be a very tough or a very nasty politician, depending on your perspective. A pretty cheap shot helped him get to the Senate in 1952 when he was in a tough race against a conservative Republican incumbent, Harry Cain, and exploited a defense vote where Cain had voted the same as Senator Glenn Taylor, the Idaho Democrat who was Henry Wallace's running mate on the 1948 Progressive party national ticket. "Cain can talk from now until doomsday," Jackson said, "but he cannot escape the fact that he and the left-wing senator from Idaho were the only two senators who voted against a 70-group Air Force."

Grace under pressure is not Jackson's strong point. Despite his stoicism, he can flash a wicked knife when he's pushed, as he did again and again in his 1972 Presidential campaign. That dark streak, hidden deep behind the easy grin, may yet be his undoing.

But he's not under pressure anymore at home. The folks see him as a straight talker, an honest man, and a guy who delivers for them —Hanford nuclear power complex, North Cascades National Park, Fort Lawton Park, irrigation projects, and now, the proposed home base for Trident submarines in Bangor.

One Washingtonian, District Court Judge Philip Sheridan, told me he had a good three-word description of Jackson that I might want to use.

What's that?

"The Ideal Man!"

Phil Sheridan is an old friend of Scoop's—they were in the Snohomish County prosecutor's office together—but you'd be surprised how many other less-committed people at home said roughly the same thing. Some of them, without knowing it, are in Jackson's file, a compilation of everyone he meets, with thousands of entries like this:

> KUBOTA, Takeshi (Dear Tak) . . . 1817 55th So. Seattle (PA 2–6868) . . . Kubota Gardening Co., 9727 Renton Ave., So. . . . Wife: Kiyo . . . On Christmas Card list . . . 1963 (fund-raising) dinner—1 ticket purchased . . . helped: 1–11–64—luncheon for Helen; 4–15–65—Arranged dinner meeting of Jackson Street Community Council and gave gift to Anna Marie.

> *Henry M. (Scoop) Jackson was rated as the "most effective" senator . . . in a survey of Senate legislative assistants released yesterday. The telephone survey was taken by the Ralph Nader-backed Capitol Hill News Service . . .*
>
> *The Washington Post,* October 27, 1973

Twenty-one years before the Senate staffers named him the most effective senator, *Liberty* magazine had rated him one of the ten outstanding members of the House of Representatives on the basis of his "independence and leadership." It has been a very distinguished 35-year career for Jackson; whatever happens from now on, he will be remembered as one of the great men in the history of the U. S. Congress:

• *Independence*—He was one of the first congressmen to vote against funding the House Un-American Activities Committee and once refused appointment as its chairman; he played a small but significant role in the destruction of Senator Joseph McCarthy, deftly cross-examining the senator and his aides almost into incoherence and becoming something like a television star of the early fifties; he practi-

cally invented Admiral Hyman Rickover, forcing the Navy to promote him three times, and played a key role in the development of the
nuclear submarine fleet which is now the heart of America's national
defense.

• *Leadership*—He became Congress's leading authority—the man
other senators looked to before they voted—on national defense,
atomic energy, and the energy crisis in general; he is a voice always
taken seriously on foreign policy; he wrote the nation's first comprehensive environmental protection laws; he has been probably the most
effective advocate of the American Indian in Congress, writing the
Indian Education Act and the Alaska Native Claims Act.

These days the waves part when Jackson walks through the Capitol. He is chairman of the Interior Committee, dealing daily with the
energy crisis; chairman of the Permanent Investigations Subcommittee, which he has used to look into the causes of the energy crisis, the
Soviet wheat deal, Mafia infiltration of the financial world, wiretap-
ping and bugging; and a ranking member of the Armed Services
Committee and the Joint Committee on Atomic Energy.

With his committee prerogatives, Jackson commands one of the
largest staffs on Capitol Hill—81 men and women he can juggle to his
interests of the moment. His chief defense staffer, for instance, Dorothy Fosdick, a stereotyped hardliner and daughter of theologian
Harry Emerson Fosdick, is officially listed as a member of the Investigations Subcommittee. That unit, not incidentally, is a political gold-
mine that can get Jackson, as it got Joe McCarthy, national headlines
any day he chooses—and as his ambitions have flowered, Jackson has
used it more and more recklessly. It was that subcommittee that
allowed a professional criminal to publicly accuse Elliott Roosevelt of
plotting the assassination of the Prime Minister of the Bahamas—if
there's proof of that charge, no one outside the committee knows
about it.

Jackson was into brainpicking before the Kennedys and pretty
regularly calls on outside experts like economist Walter Heller and a
small army of Soviet scholars, particularly British students of Russia,
men like Robert Conquest, author of *The Great Terror.* He thinks "we

just don't have the same kind of American expertise anymore, since people like Chip Bohlen have moved on." And, as always, he flashes his secrecy classification, talking about "Top Secret" documents, sources high in the Nixon administration, and people with "covers" in Europe. Just about the only people he turns to for advice on any subject, for judgment, are Rickover and John Salter, a public affairs consultant whose most impressive client is—who else? Boeing.

"I am the *liberal;* other people have lost their way," is a favorite Jackson line. Obviously the words "liberal" and "conservative" mean all things to all men these days—the fairest way to judge where a senator actually stands these days is *Congressional Quarterly*'s compilation of how he voted on issues of concern to the "Conservative Coalition" of Republicans and Southern Democrats.

On 152 Conservative Coalition roll calls during the 93rd Congress, Jackson voted with the coalition 38 percent of the time and against 37 percent. Teddy Kennedy voted with them 4 percent of the time; Hubert Humphrey, 5 percent; Jacob Javits, 20 percent; and James Buckley, 82 percent.

> *"They say Scubadoo could go all the way in '76."*
> *"Boy, if they knew what we know!"*
> Dialogue Between Two Reporters Who Covered Jackson in 1972

A few years ago, *Christian Science Monitor* columnist Roscoe Drummond privately polled the 100 members of the U.S. Senate about who of their number was most qualified to be President. The overwhelming choice: Henry M. Jackson.

There is no doubt that Jackson is that qualified. There is little doubt that he would be a strong, effective President, partly because he is a man who knows what he believes in and is willing to fight for it. That's a rare quality among members of Congress who concentrate their energies, minds, and souls trying to divine what the folks back home want them to do.

If all that's true, then what could reporters *know* about Scoop Jackson? They know they don't like him—what's more, they know that most of the Secret Service men assigned to protect his body in

1972 also came to dislike him. Jackson, they found, was petty, testy, and a little mean; he couldn't take the pressure.

"Whenever Scoop has been under pressure, the threatening kind, when he's on unfamiliar ground, he's gone for the cheap shot," said a man who has known him for twenty years in both Washingtons. "Go back to that stuff about Harry Cain being a left-winger."

In 1972, running for President, Jackson was on very unfamiliar ground and that campaign was a necklace of cheap shots:

• *The Amendment*—It was the year of busing and Jackson outdid them all in the smelly Florida primary by introducing an amendment to the U.S. Constitution that said: "No person shall be denied . . . the right to have his or her children attend their neighborhood public school." We haven't heard about that statesmanlike gem since the primaries.

• *His children*—Whenever it was suggested that The Amendment had racial undertones and overtones—or even when it wasn't suggested—Jackson repeated and repeated that he was the only Democratic candidate with his children in a public school with black teachers and a black principal. True, but it wasn't exactly a ghetto school —it's a 70 percent white school in an all-white Washington, D.C., neighborhood and is considered just about the District's best school.

• *Other men's children*—Scammon and Wattenberg's *The Real Majority* pointed out that the American electorate is un-black, un-poor, and un-young. Jackson was at least un-young. Perhaps he won older votes by going to colleges and gratuitously saying things like "I'm not going to tell you that I think you're the best student generation we have ever produced, because I don't think you are." His feelings seemed to go deeper than that; he liked to slap kids down. In Florida, a young man asked him a serious and pertinent question about the proposed Cross-Florida Barge Canal, but, in asking it, the youth identified Jackson as "chairman of the Interior Commission." Jackson answered by ripping into anyone dumb enough not to know it's the "Interior Committee."

• *His religion*—In Florida, a very Protestant state, Jackson would find a half-dozen ways to mention his Presbyterianism or Masonry in most speeches, including the fact that John Kennedy picked him as Democratic National Committee chairman because a Catholic candidate needed a Protestant chairman. "That's ridiculous," said Brian Corcoran, his press secretary. "He doesn't say that because his audiences are Protestant. It's really the only funny story he knows."

• *The three A's*—It was a Republican senator, Hugh Scott, who first said George McGovern was for "amnesty, acid, and abortion." But it was Jackson, campaigning in the Midwest, who propagated and popularized that remark, and did his part in destroying the Democratic candidate. Now he says he was only trying to warn the party that the Republicans would raise the cry if McGovern was nominated.

Jackson was also the only Democratic candidate who flatly refused to release a listing of the campaign contributions he received before new federal disclosure laws took effect on April 7, 1972. Most of his money—which almost certainly totaled between $1 million and $2 million—was raised through committees in the two Washingtons, neither of which had local disclosure laws at that time.

The two facts that have come out are negative: Gulf Oil Corporation has pleaded guilty to illegally contributing $10,000 to Jackson, a contribution the senator says he did not know about; a minor Boeing executive was caught writing $299.63 in company checks to pay for Jackson advertising in Wisconsin, and the senator put that down to "youthful over-enthusiasm."

There has never been a hint of scandal in Jackson's 38 years in public life; quite the opposite: in Washington State even Republican opponents have called him Mr. Clean. He says that he won't release the '72 list because it would be embarrassing to others, contributors who are Nixon appointees and who publicly supported other candidates.

In fact, since 1952, he has donated his speaking and writing honorariums ($18,000 in 1971) to a scholarship fund for needy Everett students—and those donations were secret until the 1972 laws forced Jackson to make his charity public. Any questioning of his personal integrity is one of the few things that bring temper to Jackson's Nordic surface. When McGovern attacked him for the Boeing

$299.63, Jackson, who rarely says "damn" or "hell," began shouting, "That prick!"

Obscenity is not his thing, but Jackson is a plain, tough talker. Listening to speech after speech, I was struck with the repetition of blunt phrasing. He sounded like a twangy Jimmy Cagney as he pinballed around the country in 1973, urging the Israelis on: "We'll wait until they beat the hell out of the Arabs." "Push the Arabs into the canal." "We're not going to get down on our knees."

"I just don't want to be mush," Jackson told me. "I don't like mushy people." In an interview with his biographers, Prochnau and Larsen, which was not used in their book, the senator said he was physically sickened when he saw a matador killing a bull in Juarez, Mexico. Then the subject switched to Vietnam and the writers pushed Jackson into talking about his trips to battle zones, about death he had seen and parts of arms and legs scattered around artillery hits.

"Did you become sickened at the sight of that?"

"No."

"Why did the bull's death sicken you and not the soldiers'?"

"Because killing the bull was not necessary," Jackson said after a pause.

He has never killed anyone. His press-release biographies state that he enlisted as an Army buck private in World War II but was ordered back to Congress 90 days later by President Roosevelt. True enough, but he enlisted in September, 1943, almost two years after Pearl Harbor—and after the fact that a healthy, 31-year-old bachelor was still a civilian had become a political issue in Washington State.

If the men who run America sat down to pick the next President, they might very well settle on Scoop Jackson. He appeals to other men of power—Richard Nixon, remember, offered him two cabinet positions in 1969: first, secretary of defense; then, secretary of state.

But that's not how it works, thank God or James Madison. Scoop —he was the first Democrat to announce his 1976 candidacy—has to run, and the certain Democrat may be uncertain again.

Jackson was close once before. In 1960, he had good reason— including a public endorsement by Robert Kennedy—to believe that he would be John F. Kennedy's vice president. But, in the closing hours of the 1960 Democratic convention, he was rejected. Then he was coldly ignored during the thousand Kennedy days by the brothers he had considered among his closest friends.

"That was a terrible hurt for Scoop," a friend said. "The Kennedys just cut him off. He was different after that. The bitterness and inflexibility in 1972 may go back to that—I think it does."

So much of Jackson does seem to go back to 1960, as if the last sixteen years never happened. In the spring of 1973, another friend, Chicago's Mayor Richard Daley, introduced him by saying: "With God's help, Scoop Jackson will lead this nation in 1960!"

Just a slip—I think.

5 | Edmund G. Brown, Jr.

"I am going to starve the schools financially until I get some educational reforms," said the Governor of California, Edmund G. Brown, Jr.

"What reforms? What do you want?" said Jack Rees, the executive director of the California Teachers Association.

"I don't know yet."

Jerry Brown is different. He is the most interesting politician in the United States. And, at the moment, he is one of the most popular, phenomenally popular in his own state where polls show that only 7 percent of voters disapprove of his performance in office. Although he is not a particularly likable young man, he has piqued the imagination of Californians by choosing to sleep on a mattress on the floor of a bare, $250-a-month apartment in Sacramento rather than in a $1.3-million mansion, by trading in a bulletproof Cadillac limousine for a Plymouth Satellite and by roaming around state government asking hostile and irreverent questions like this one of the University of California's Board of Regents: "Why is it better to have a smaller number of students in each class?"

The people of California thought they were just electing the son of a former Governor, Edmund G. Brown, Pat Brown's kid, another liberal Democrat like his old man. Instead, they have inherited this loner who sometimes sounds like an erudite George Wallace, attacking big-government spending, "government gibberish," "the bureaucratic maze" and saying that it's about time some people on welfare picked up shovels and went to work. And they love it. Jerry Brown

is popular not so much because he is telling them what they want to
hear, but because he is saying what they are saying these days. He has
a perfect ear for the grumbling anti-politics of America, and he is in
tune with the strain of rhetorical conservatism and operational liberalism that has always run through American politics. (A lot of Americans are against big spending and against cutting Medicare.)

But Brown is not at all like Wallace or anyone else in American
politics. He is almost impossible to classify as liberal or conservative
—it is hard to classify a governor with a special assistant like Jacques
Barzhagi, a former French sailor with a shaved head who has opened
meetings of California cabinet members with a touch of Zen: "How
is the Governor different from a shoemaker?" Intellectually, Governor Brown may be farther left than anyone holding high executive
office in the United States: He calls on his staff to work "in the spirit
of Ho Chi Minh" and he has proposed equal pay raises for all California state employees because he is willing to consider seriously the
proposition that janitors should earn as much as judges. Emotionally,
he is extremely conservative: At twice-a-week cabinet meetings that
sometimes last until 2 A.M., in the style of college bull sessions, he has
said, "Hot lunches for school children? No one ever gave me a hot
lunch!" and "I don't believe in disability benefits for pregnant women.
Giving life is not a disability."

"Jerry has no ideology," said his executive assistant, Gray Davis,
quite accurately. Rather, Brown, a very serious man who tends to
think each man is an island, has an individual philosophy, an evolving
cerebral mix of the teachings of St. Ignatius and Thomas Aquinas,
Buddhism, Existentialism, and Machiavelli.

On his first day as Governor in January, 1975, Brown was asked
by Davis whether he wanted to issue a statement of objectives, to
which he answered, "What do you mean?" Well, said Davis, what are
we trying to do? "It'll emerge," said the Governor of California.

When I asked Brown the same question after he had been in power
six months and produced a couple of pretty solid achievements, including farm-labor laws that might just end decades of wrath in
California fields, he answered: "Reduce the sum of human misery a

bit, I guess. Help people expand their lives a little bit, give them an awareness of their own potential." Then he stopped for a moment and said, "Do you think that what you do or what I do will really make a difference in the long run?"

What he does in the next few years might make a difference. In his own mind, I think, he has set himself an incredibly ambitious objective: Jerry Brown would like to lead people into changing their values, American values. He wants Americans to question materialism. Ho, Mao Tse Tung and Gandhi are political idols of his not because of their ideology but because of the ascetic and spiritual quality of their leadership: They were able to motivate large numbers of people with visions of a better life not linked to material reward.

What does that mean? One thing it means is that other California politicians should read a book called *Small Is Beautiful—Economics as If People Mattered,* a minor underground classic by an English socialist, E. F. Schumacher, the former chief economist of the British Coal Board. Brown is a student of the book. He is in fact a student of many books, *prima facie* evidence that he is a politician aberrant. When I mentioned Schumacher, he seemed annoyed at the possible suggestion that his thinking was not original, and he ended that part of our conversation with, "I had those ideas before I read the book."

He probably did. Obviously, he has a complex and searching mind, an extraordinary mind for a politician. But, in a month around Brown, Schumacher's work—particularly a 1966 essay titled "Buddhist Economics"—was the most trustworthy guide I could find to the current that runs through the individualistic political philosophy, rhetoric and action of Governor Brown. Some excerpts from *Small Is Beautiful* could have come from a long conversation with Jerry Brown:

> The substance of man cannot be measured by Gross National Product. For the modern economist, this is very difficult to understand. He is used to measuring the "standard of living" by the amount of annual consumption, assuming all the time that a man who consumes more is "better off" than a man who consumes less. A Buddhist economist would consider this

approach excessively irrational: Since consumption is merely a means of human well-being, the aim should be to obtain the maximum of well-being with the minimum of consumption. Thus, if the purpose of clothing is a certain amount of temperature comfort and attractive appearance, the task is to attain this purpose with the smallest possible effort—that is, with the smallest annual destruction of cloth and with the help of designs that involve the smallest possible input of toil. The ownership and consumption of goods is a means to an end, and Buddhist economics is the systematic study of how to attain given ends with the minimum means. . . .

There is the immediate question of whether "modernization," as currently practiced without regard to religious and spiritual values, is actually producing agreeable results. As far as the masses are concerned, the results appear to be disastrous—a collapse of the rural economy, a rising tide of unemployment in town and country, and the growth of a city proletariat without nourishment for either body or soul.

It is remarkable that a politician who reads stuff like that, much less thinks it, could be elected to govern 22 million Americans. The secret, of course, is to be Pat Brown's kid. Nobody ever gave Jerry Brown a free hot lunch at school, but he practically inherited the governorship without political trial or conditioning. This Governor has none of the mellow heartiness of professional politicians, but he also did not begin with their conditioned caution or share their assumptions of what is possible in American politics. Officially challenging materialism is a young man's vision, and Brown is a very young man. By very young, I mean that Brown is even younger than his 39 calendar years. He has had limited life experience—Governor's son, Jesuit seminarian from 1956 to 1960, student and law clerk until he was 28 years old in 1965, and a high state official after practicing law for five years. He is sometimes portrayed as a veteran of the movements of the 1960s, a veteran who was at Berkeley during the Free Speech Movement, went to Mississippi in 1962, marched with Cesar Chavez and the United Farm Workers, but that list is stretching things a bit. His involvements were brief and limited, and he emphasizes that he was "an observer—never a participant."

Brown's political training began in his father's office: He wandered around the State Capitol asking, "What are you doing that for?" Now he's asking the same question again. But his political career began when he walked into the Ambassador Hotel in Los Angeles one day late in 1968 and told Joe Cerrell, his father's old campaign adviser, that he wanted to run for the city's Community College Board. Cerrell laughed and said, "With your name on the ballot, you could sit in that chair from now until April and still win. What do you really want?"

"I want to make a name for myself," Jerry said, "so I want to run for something where I'll win and win big."

Running for the Community College Board, he won big over a field of 133 candidates. Eighteen months later, he was the only Democrat to win statewide office in 1970, with his election as Secretary of State by 300,000 votes. Pat Brown was Trumanized in California after losing to Ronald Reagan for Governor in 1966 after serving eight years as Governor. The electoral power of the Brown name was proved again this May when 29-year-old Kathleen Brown Rice won big as a candidate for the Los Angeles Board of Education. But, by then, there was no way to tell whether Kathy's name recognition and popularity came from being Pat's daughter or Jerry's sister.*

Any analysis of Jerry Brown has to begin with his father and go on to his training as a Jesuit seminarian—and any emphasis on either subject tends to annoy the hell out of the son. Five months after he was elected, the new Governor Brown was introduced to the California League of Cities annual meeting with ten minutes of anecdotes about what a wonderful man his father was and the speaker turned to the Governor at one point to say, "I don't know if your father ever told you this . . ." The son cut her off with, "My father never told me anything!"

During his campaign, Jerry Brown would sometimes mock his father, who loses his mellow heartiness when his son is near: "This

*Brown, Jr., was called Jerry at home because no one in the family really liked the name Edmund and the middle name of father and son is Gerald. (Pat Brown says his nickname goes back to the time he won a citywide Liberty Bond oratorical contest when he was a schoolboy in San Francisco during World War I. His winning speech ended, "Give me liberty or give me death!" and his friends began calling him Patrick Henry Brown.)

old man wants to make a speech. You want to make a speech, old man?" On election night, when the younger Brown barely won after losing a huge lead in early polls, he turned on his father and said, "I almost lost because of you. People remember you as such a big spender."

Pat Brown was, in fact, an enormous help to his son during the campaign, raising hundreds of thousands of dollars and lining up such traditional Democratic support as the leadership of organized labor which found the son, in the words of one union leader, "a little weird." But that does not mean the first Edmund Brown was really prepared to see the second take over the microphones and spotlights—that made Pat Brown an old man, and he does not see himself that way. In 1970, the father, then 64, wanted to run for Governor again, but his son was already preparing to run for Secretary of State. Bernice Brown, wife and mother, finally stepped in, telling her husband: "You can't do that. It's Jerry's career now."

When it was Pat's career, he was a politician first and a father second, out every night winning friends and influencing people, then coming home to line up the happy family for a few photographs. "When we were young, my father paraded us before the public," Kathleen remembered. "He was so proud of us, but I didn't like it. I'm sure Jerry didn't, either." One of Brown's other sisters (he has three), Cynthia Brown Kelly, remembered that her brother, even at 12 and 13, had trouble admitting his father was sometimes right. "If he thought Dad was wrong, he'd say so," Cynthia said. "But if he thought he was right, he just didn't pursue the argument anymore." And, when he was 22, Jerry convinced his father of something: In a long telephone call from Sacred Heart Novitiate, the young seminarian persuaded his father to stay the execution of Caryl Chessman, a convicted rapist who became a symbol in national debates over capital punishment. That was 17 years ago, but Pat Brown still talks about that single decision retarding his political career, costing him the chance, perhaps, to have been a Senator or a Vice President.

These days, if Pat Brown wants to see his son, he usually has to corner him at public events or wait outside his office like a supplicant.

Occasionally, there are phone calls when the Governor wants some information or a bit of advice, but invariably the former Governor asks acquaintances and reporters: "How's Jerry? What did he say? Tell him I . . ."

"I was attracted and repelled by what I saw of politics in my father's house," Jerry Brown told me. What attracted you? "The adventure. The opportunity." What repelled you? "The grasping, the artificiality, the obvious manipulation and role-playing, the repetition of emotion without feeling; particularly that: the repetition of emotion."

In 1956, when Pat Brown was State Attorney General after serving as district attorney of San Francisco, Jerry Brown left his father's house to enter Sacred Heart in Los Gatos to prepare for the Jesuit priesthood. "Don't make too much of the Jesuit thing," he told me. But it is impossible not to. The *Compania de Jesus,* the soldiers of Christ, oversaw much of young Brown's life at St. Ignatius High School, at Santa Clara University, and in the seminary until he left to major in Latin and Greek at the University of California at Berkeley and then went on to Yale Law School.

There is a little question-and-answer joke among Catholic priests that goes: "Are you a Jesuit?" "No, but I'm glad they're on our side." The Jesuits are something special—at least, other people perceive them as seeing themselves as special: an elite and zealous corps, the Pope's defenders, the missionary shock troops of Roman Catholicism. "Wherefore, if you would perfect others, be first perfect yourself," the 16th-century command of St. Ignatius of Loyola to the first Jesuits, is a standard attractive only to certain men.

Jesuit perfection requires 15 years of rigorous, total training; it is spiritual, intellectual, emotional and physical indoctrination. Brown stayed at Sacred Heart for three and a half years, including a year of almost total silence, long days picking grapes in the order's vineyards, intensive philosophic study and Socratic dialogue peculiar to the Jesuits. "Is an egg an unborn chicken or a ripe egg?" he once said lightly while campaigning; and when no one laughed, he added, "It's an old Jesuit question."

The training has been developed over centuries, designed to suppress the ego into service to God through service to mankind. All things material are to be rejected, and the Jesuit definition of material things is encompassing—wealth, pride, will, the ways of man. "I learned what there was to learn for me, so I left," Brown says. "I wanted a more independent existence, control of my own life, a chance to follow the precepts of the Church within a more practical context."

The more practical context he knew was his father's—politics. The irony of the tortured father-son relationship is that Pat Brown was the ultimate winner. At visiting time at Los Gatos—two hours a month —the first Governor Brown would try, as subtly as he could, to persuade his son to leave and go on to law school and politics. Well, Pat Brown's only son is indeed following in his footsteps.

Secretary of State of California had always been more title than job; secretaries had confined themselves to duties like regulating laundry marks and cattle brands. Brown, in the words of his staff, "seized the imagination of the media"—filing suits against oil companies for campaign contributions, calling press conferences to attack other politicians for incorrect finance reports, and generally raising sanctimonious hell whenever cameras or reporters were around. His most effective seizure was identification as the principal sponsor of Proposition 9, a tough campaign reform initiative that regulated political contributions and did things like setting $10 as the maximum amount lobbyists could spend on lunches for state officials.

With Watergate dominating national headlines, Brown had the name and the issue to become governor. He should have beaten any Republican by 2-to-1. As it was, he easily won the Democratic primary against five opponents, but got less than 50 percent of the vote in the general election, winning by only 187,000 votes over State Controller Houston Flournoy, a pleasant but not particularly formidable opponent.

Brown likes to call campaigns "a fair test of the essential character and personality of the candidates." Within that definition, he was failing the test, at least in the judgment of California politicians and journalists, who almost unanimously agree that he would have lost if the campaign lasted a week longer. (A secret-ballot survey by the *California Journal* of 15 reporters who covered both candidates showed that eight voted for Flournoy, although not one of the 15 identified himself as a Republican.)

His essential personality, as described by a *Sacramento Bee* reporter, came across as, "the new kid in the fifth grade looking for a fight to show how tough he is." Two women who know him were less kind: One said he was "without compassion," the other said "without grace."

Certainly, he has no social graces, although that is tempered by an equal lack of social artifice. "Did you ever notice that Jerry never says 'Thank you'?" said Gray Davis, his executive assistant. "Perhaps you can't hear him," replied the mysterious Mr. Barzhagi, the special assistant who lives in and takes care of Brown's California casual and glass home in the Hollywood Hills.

"This is no place to be if you need positive feedback to keep going," said Rose Elizabeth Bird, Brown's Secretary of Agriculture and one of the two women in his seven-person cabinet, the first two women cabinet members in state history. "Jerry doesn't need approval, and he doesn't think other people do."

That void could lead to great problems for Governor Brown: Politics, after all, is the institutionalization of other people's approval. Brown has a great gift for unintentionally and unknowingly hurting or humiliating people. Brown's basic platform style is based on humiliation. He almost never gives speeches (his inaugural address lasted just seven minutes), but takes questions and then tends to pick sarcastically at a questioner for the edification and amusement of the crowd. When a Woodside councilman tried to ask him questions about local problems at the League of Cities conference, Brown kept cutting him off with such lines as "That just means you're not doing your job, you're not trying hard enough." Or: "Hold it, every time I hear the word 'comprehensive' I know what follows will be gibberish." Or, when a reporter complained at a press conference that there was no advance notice of an important appointment, Brown came

back with, "What do you want? Bells? Bugles? . . . You know where
he lives, go find him!"

"He is contentious, an intellectual provocateur," said J. Anthony
Kline, Brown's legal services secretary (counsel) and former room-
mate at Yale. "He has contempt for the ability of people, particularly
politicians, to question fundamental assumptions. Should government
be involved in this? Can government do anything about the problem?
Should anything be done? That can appear to be contempt for the
process itself or for people."

Whatever it is in Brown, it can be unattractive, particularly when
he is contending and, like a kid in the fifth grade, he's always ready.
He is a small man, almost frail, with fine features often called hand-
some and a voice strangely nasal and gravelly at the same time; the
contentious Brown has edges of scorn in his voice and cruelty in his
face. The candidate came across as quite the opposite of, say, good old
Pat Brown or good old Jerry Ford—and it almost cost him the
election.

There was also more than an edge of contempt in the strategy and
tactics of his campaign. It was cynical and dirty, although the voters
of California had no way of knowing that at the time. Brown played
politics as if he had learned contempt for the process itself in his
father's house. Or, as if he literally applied the Jesuit maxim *Tantum
. . . Quantum,* Ignatian shorthand for "inasmuch as material things
help you to achieve your goal, use them," which can be further
translated into "the end justifies the means." The means of Jerry
Brown's campaign included strategy designed to discourage people
from voting and tactics that verged on blackmail.

"We were ahead so we wanted a dull, dull, dull campaign," said
Thomas Quinn, Brown's 30-year-old campaign manager and now
Secretary of the California Air Resources Board which Brown plans
to elevate into a cabinet-level Environmental Protection Agency. "We
wanted to avoid any discussion of substance. We found obscure,
boring issues and talked about them. Jerry's real ideas were dangerous, but we were generally successful in avoiding them. It was sometimes hard to restrain him because he is essentially an activist. We

wanted people to think he was a 'don't rock the boat' guy. Obviously, we were successful: We won."

In the primary, Quinn said, Brown used investigators to compile dossiers on the two opponents he feared most, Assembly Speaker Robert Moretti and San Francisco Mayor Joseph Alioto. "Some very interesting property transactions, sex, things like that" were in the files, according to Quinn. Then, the campaign manager said, "I informed Moretti and Alioto that if they tried anything we'd let this stuff go." (Moretti's campaign manager, John Fitzrandolph, confirmed that he had received several calls from Quinn warning him to be careful because he had "stuff that could destroy Bob's life." Moretti, incidentally, was later appointed to the State Energy Commission by Governor Brown.)*

The campaign manager said Flournoy was also investigated, but the Republican was "too damn clean."

Why was all this going on when Brown began both the primary and general campaigns with state polls showing him 20 points ahead? The Brown people were afraid their opponents were going to call him a homosexual. There was already a whispering campaign—a common tactic against bachelor politicians—and Alioto was helping it along by calling Brown "effeminate" and demanding that he "come out of the closet and debate." (Brown and his advisers are so sensitive to such whispers and the national press that a young woman sometimes hovers in the background during his interviews with important reporters —the girl used is Jacques Barzhagi's girlfriend.) During the campaign, Brown aides joked that they were putting together a television commercial with a gorgeous Scandinavian blonde turning to the camera saying, "I don't know anything about Jerry Brown's politics. All I know is, he's a great lay."

That commercial would not have surprised Californians any more

*Quinn discussed his role in the campaign at a closed conference of the Candidate–Media Interaction Study of the California Center for Research and Education in Government at which I was present as an adviser. Some details of the meeting on March 20, 1975, were later published by the *Los Angeles Times* and *Sacramento Bee*. Both newspapers requested release of the tapes of the meeting when Quinn denied their accounts, but Quinn has refused to agree to the release.

than their new governor did when he took over. Under a meaningless slogan, "A New Spirit," Brown's campaign themes were hazy enough to give politicians, press and public the vague impression that they were getting Son of Pat Brown and Son of New Deal, Fair Deal, New Frontier, and Great Society: just another liberal.

The Sufi Choir, a Buddhist group "in the world but not of it," sang, *"Om sri ram/Jai sri ram,"* at the Governor's swearing in, and then he gave his 950-word inaugural address. He began ungraciously by saying, "My father never thought I was going to make it. But here I am." Then he reminded his audience that fewer than half of California's voters went to the polls, calling that statistic "a vote of no-confidence in government," although the low turnout could have been a tribute to his campaign strategy.

The new Governor then repeated his campaign pledge to avoid any general tax increase and made only six promises, five of which he has already kept with the cooperation of a heavily Democratic legislature. Four of them were easy—legislation fulfilling long-time Democratic commitments to move toward eliminating the state oil depletion allowance and three other business-oriented tax breaks. The unkept (for now) promise could take much longer (Brown is committed to full collective-bargaining rights for public employees), but the Governor had made his point: "Lowered expectations"; government should promise only what it can reasonably expect to deliver.

The final promise led to triumph for Brown. "It is time," he said, "to extend the rule of law to the agriculture sector and establish the right of secret-ballot elections for farm workers." After years of strikes and boycotts between California growers, the Teamsters Union, and Chavez's United Farm Workers, those secret-ballot representation elections began in November, 1975. Under Brown's farm labor law, which was modeled after the National Labor Relations Act, farm workers, for the first time in the United States, had the same collective-bargaining rights as other American workers. Others, on both the federal and state level, had tried to get such a law for almost 40 years. Brown and his Secretary of Agriculture, Rose Bird, drafted the law and won the approval of the contending parties and the Legislature in just two months. "The timing was right, everyone was tired," Brown said, but there was more to it than that. Brown is a friend and something of a student of Cesar Chavez, the ascetic Catholic U.F.W. leader—there was trust there and also an informed knowledge of the U.F.W.'s real strength and weakness and of Chavez's bottom-line position. At the same time, the Teamsters and growers were persuaded, and surprised, that Brown did not act as a U.F.W. advocate. So, in a twelve-hour, closed-door negotiating session, Brown hammered out revisions that produced a law all three sides endorsed.

But it was not the farm-labor law that set the tone of the first six months of the Brown administration, it was the Sufi. The tone for most of those directly concerned, politicians and press, was confusion: What the hell's going on here?

Some of what went on, like saving $153,000 a year by refusing to give state officials free briefcases, was clever gimmickry—"working the press," in the envious phrasing of State Treasurer Jesse Unruh; "symbols of doing with people, not for people," in Brown's phrasing. Some of it, like delaying minor decisions for months, was personal style—"He wants to do everything himself, he can't delegate authority," in the words of a friendly critic, State Senator Anthony Beilenson. "I reject get-it-done, make-it-happen thinking . . . I want to slow things down so I understand them better," in Brown's words.

Some of it, however, like the Governor's constant public questioning of other public officials and governmental assumptions, is more profound and widely misunderstood—Brown's Socratic dialogues are not the prologue to a detailed Brown program; the dialogue is the program. This Governor does not see his function as crisis-resolution and consensus-seeking, but as perpetual crisis-generation or, at least, perpetual critical examination—in the sense of Plato's: "The life which is unexamined is not worth living." Brown is offering process, not programs; synthesis, not solutions.

The gimmickry, of course, is great public relations and Brown is very aware of that. He is the kind of new politician who insists that television cameras stay on his "good side," his left profile. Brown probably prefers a crash pad across the lush park from his office to an empty mansion twelve miles outside Sacramento, but he also knows there is no harm in projecting a lifestyle that has already scored once with the American public—the role model is Ralph Nader.

Brown's work-style is a kind of Puritan existential. He has no official schedule and makes almost no ceremonial or formal appearances, going and doing wherever and whatever strikes him at the moment—and doing it with focused intensity for sixteen or eighteen hours at a stretch. That is why his cabinet and staff meetings sometimes go from 7 P.M. to 2 A.M. "Free-form time," his counsel, Tony Kline, calls it. "Disorganization," his critics call it.

It is free. "Agenda" is one of the words Brown has practically banned in his presence, along with "systems analysis," "data," "expertise," "redevelopment," and "comprehensive planning." The entire cabinet has spent two hours debating and free-associating on topics as trivial as a one-week extension of the Silver Salmon season. At one session, someone reminded Brown that he had to do something about scheduled salary increases for state employees in his 1975–76 budget. "I don't think they deserve anything. They don't do anything," Brown began.

"That's garbage, Jerry," said Rose Bird, the most impressive of the appointments the new Governor made after personal interviews that sometimes lasted five hours. She pointed out that the Federal Government estimated that it took about $20,000 for a family of four to live moderately in California last year. The Governor countered that most Californians made less than that. "There's no crisis," he said. "If there was, there'd be a revolution"—and the government of California was off on a rambling discussion of why there was no revolution in the United States.

That may sound a bit sophomoric, but, in fact, out of that dialogue came Brown's proposal to give each of 175,000 state employees the same raise of $90 a month. The Chief Justice of the State Supreme Court, making $54,000 a year, would have gotten the same increase as a $5,000 a year janitor. The Legislature was horrified and quickly squelched the plan—state employees will receive percentage increases of about 8 percent.

"You'll hear more about this," he told me. "I'll be back. I don't believe that janitors should be paid more than judges, but I think the gap between them is too great now. If work is interesting and challenging—and a judge's is—people should be paid less. Those are the people who get great psychic rewards: Their lives are better because they have the privilege of interesting work . . . I'm trying to put things like this in the public domain. I want these ideas discussed. Let people react. See what happens."

Brown opposed an $11,000 increase in his own salary of $49,100 and ordered a 7 percent cut in his staff's salaries, the only pay scales he has direct control over. That frugality, budget increases lower than those tolerated by Ronald Reagan and a tough line on crime—Brown thinks penitentiaries are for penance, not rehabilitation—has delighted California conservatives. But he is not one of them by any means. His concept of social justice is consistent with most liberal thinking, but he does not equate social justice and material equality.

The appointments Brown has made are the best indicator of his directions on immediate social problems. His staff and cabinet are young—the oldest person who spends much time with him is the 44-year-old Secretary of Resources, Claire Dedrick—and have been drawn almost exclusively from three movements: public-interest law, anti-poverty work, and environmentalism. Tony Kline founded Public Advocates, Inc., a law firm that specialized in suing the state; Claire Dedrick was a Sierra Club vice president; Rose Bird was a public defender in Santa Clara County; Mario Obledo, Secretary of Health and Welfare and the first Chicano in a California cabinet, was the director of the Mexican-American Legal Defense and Educational Fund.

The appointments that Brown has *not* made are also revealing. After almost a year in office, he had not filled the position of Education Adviser to the Governor, one of the most important in California, because he had not gotten around to it yet; he had not filled 68 new and vacant judgeships because he wanted to, in his words, "heat up a crisis in the criminal justice system."

I'll do it when I get to it, in my own time," he said when I asked him about the education position. "My own time"—the phrase indicates just how much California decision-making has become a one-man operation. The most persistent friendly complaint about Brown concerns delegation of authority or the unwillingness of his appointees to move without a personal blessing from him. "It's impossible to get an answer on anything without talking to Brown himself," said Jerry Smith, a state senator who was at the University of Santa Clara with the Governor.

Brown, who reacts to almost any criticism by saying, "That's not true" or "That's wrong," insisted that one of his major goals was to drive decision-making and responsibility deeper into the pyramid of state power. No doubt he does—he wants to begin the dialogue and let college presidents, councilmen, and cops on the beat exercise the authority of the state.

Good theory, but in practice California seems to be governed by one man doing one thing at a time. He personally reviews extradition orders before signing them—that's ten or twelve each day from deputy sheriffs who want to go to, say, Texas, to pick up a prisoner there who is wanted on California charges. He had Tony Kline prepare a ten-page veto message (never used) for a special bill allowing a Sacramento stadium to be used for the annual Camellia Festival even though the stadium is classified as seismically unsound. He was considering vetoing the bill to make the point that government was deluding people by certifying anything safe against earthquakes.

While Brown and his top assistants focus on such things, there is apparently nothing else happening in his administration. Brown's involvement in education has not touched on court-ordered deadlines to restructure the state's system of school district financing. Instead, he asked his questions ("Why are administrators paid more than teachers if the business of schools is teaching?"), most of them quite consistent with E. F. Schumacher's thinking in *Small Is Beautiful:*

> The problems of education are merely reflections of the deepest problems of our age. They cannot be solved by organization, administration or the expenditure of money, even though the importance of all these is not

denied. We are suffering from a metaphysical disease, and the cure must therefore be metaphysical. Education which fails to clarify our central convictions is mere training or indulgence. For it is our central convictions which are in disorder.

The appointment or nonappointment of judges is a case study in the operations of the Brown administration. He has indeed triggered a public dialogue on the role and working habits of judges and, also, a crisis in court backlogs, according to the State Judicial Conference. "The answer in government always seems to be to add more people. I think that's wrong," Brown said. "Compare the number of judges per capita they have in England—fewer—and they have speedier justice. Why is that? You tell me."

The view from the Governor's office of that controversy and others —school financing and the cost of medical malpractice insurance among them—where Brown says he is deliberately letting crises heat up, is one of the things that makes Brown very different from other American leaders.

"Crises are gifts to political leaders who are willing to address fundamental problems," says Tony Kline. "What an opportunity Abe Beame has in New York."

"Maybe we can change the patterns of government," says Gray Davis. "As it is, interest groups make demands and government accedes to all or part of what they want."

"You don't have to *do* things," says Brown. "Maybe by avoiding doing things you accomplish quite a lot. Maybe if Kennedy had avoided the Bay of Pigs or Vietnam, that may have been quite an accomplishment."

"Does that make sense?" Brown said to me during one long conversation. "I guess I'm just stringing words together." Well, some of the time the new Governor of California and his people are winging it, just stringing words and actions together. Brown likes to talk and, to a certain extent, govern existentially: "Life just is. You have to flow with it. Give yourself to the moment. Let it happen."

Since running for governor is not exactly letting it happen, Brown's existential credentials may be doubted, but very little else about him is being questioned these days in California—he's just too popular. "If he ran again today, he'd get 65 percent of the vote, more," said Ed Salzman, editor of the *California Journal*. A state Republican leader put it this way: "He's been good. People are after me to attack, but what am I supposed to attack him on? He's doing a real good job of getting to that silent majority vote, and if I attack him, I just make them mad."

Brown calls it all "oneness with the people." "To be a leader you have to be at one with the people you lead. You have to feel it." This time he reaches back to Lao-tze, the founder of Taoism, offering Chinese that translates into: "You can't go across the grain." Can he, a loner, a man without attachment except to ideas, really be at one with the people out there, people worrying about children and lousy jobs, mortgages and money? "It is my impression that I can," he said, pausing, then adding, "And I'm perfectly willing to test it."

It was a very good answer. He will probably test it again: Value-changing politics cannot stop at the border of California. A couple of years ago, just after Brown moved to Hollywood Hills, he stopped his car on one of the winding little roads there when he saw a new neighbor and old friend, Paul Schrade, a liberal activist and former Western regional director of the United Auto Workers.

"Hey, Paul," Brown said, "we have to get together and talk about taking over the state of California."

"Just California?" Schrade asked. "What about the country?"

"Yeah, but I have to wait until 1976," Brown said and drove off.

It seems that 1976 will be much too soon to tell whether Jerry Brown's difference will make a difference in California. Kline calls the exercise "The Great Attempt," but then concedes it could end as "The Spectacular Failure." If Brown does fail, it will probably be for the wrong reasons, just as he succeeded for the wrong reasons. He got where he is not because of his ideas but because he was Pat Brown's son and if he fails it could be because of flaws in his own personality and because he became a prisoner of his own popularity and ambition. The ideas, the real commitment to nonmaterialist reform, may never be fairly tested.

There is a sense of tragedy about Jerry Brown. He is *too* popular and his deep, cold ambition may drive him too far in trying to hold the acclaim of both left and right. And his feel for "the people" is for people in the abstract, not for individual human beings. Stepping outside Brown's small circle of friends and assistants, it is very difficult to find anyone who knows him and says they *like* him—the people out there who like him have never met him.

Brown, in fact, is beginning to show signs of trying to remain all things to all sides. When the conservative *Oakland Tribune* discovered state memoranda proposing discussion of a community jobs program for welfare recipients, a state-owned bank like New York's, and cooperative food markets, the newspaper headlined in red: "Governor's Secret Worker-State Plan." Co-ops, according to the *Tribune*, were "communes" and the paper demanded and got the dismissal of the proposals' author, Employment Development Director James Lorenz, the founder of California Rural Legal Assistance. Then, to placate conservatives, Brown announced he would form an informal council of economic advisers including the *Tribune*'s publisher, the presidents of the Bank of America and Standard Oil of California, and David Packard, the first finance chairman of President Ford's 1976 campaign committee.

Brown does not think in terms of individuals and their problems. When he took over as Governor, he made a series of late-night phone calls—he is a classic "night person," often working or talking until dawn—to friends and acquaintances asking them to come to Sacramento for a few weeks and help him get started. Everyone turned him down. "What's *wrong* with these people?" he blurted out one night. What was wrong was that they had families and jobs that they could not just up and leave. Later, when he heard that Lieutenant Governor Mervyn Dymally was complaining that he never saw the Governor, Brown said, "That's nonsense. I saw him yesterday"—they had walked past each other at Los Angeles International Airport. He refuses to answer the calls of his largest contributors—"He thinks we're unclean because we gave a politician, him, some money," one said. Because he despises the ceremonial, he refused to step outside his office one day last month to say a few words and shake a few hands of 400 officers from senior citizen organizations around the state.

There are a lot of people, some of them quite powerful, waiting in line to be the second to kick Jerry Brown on his way down. Of course, none of them has the guts to be first—not when he's on top. But if he slips, he has no network and few friends, no personal or political power base to stop the fall.

Politicians, like any other establishment, have the patience and procedures to punish aberrant behavior. Congressman Philip Burton, the chairman of the House Democratic Caucus, is not likely to forget that Brown did not even bother to answer his letter recommending the appointment of his brother, Robert Burton, to a state commission. State legislators, too, will still be there if Brown stumbles—a fading Governor could find his desk piled with popular bills, giving him the unhappy choice of vetoing or raising taxes.

"We're protecting him now," said Assembly Speaker Leo McCarthy, a political friend at the moment. "I'm killing bills like tax exemptions and deductions for veterans and senior citizens that could embarrass him. But he'd better be much more sensitive to us a year from now or there will be problems. He could talk to us more. At least he could let us know when someone from our counties is being appointed to a judgeship or state job."

If things don't work out, Jerry Brown will be alone, on his own— which is the way he always wanted it.

6

Hubert Humphrey
George Wallace
Birch Bayh
Lloyd Bentsen
Jimmy Carter
Frank Church
Fred Harris
Henry (Scoop) Jackson
Milton Shapp
R. Sargent Shriver
Morris (Mo) Udall

I am one of those Americans who can measure his entire adult life by one continuous event: Hubert H. Humphrey running. My agony of watching the long distance runner began with my first vote in 1960 when the senator from Minnesota was running against John Kennedy in the Democratic primaries; then came the run for vice president with Lyndon Johnson in 1964, the race against Richard Nixon in 1968, and the challenge to George McGovern in the 1972 primaries. My whole life flashes before my eyes when I think of Humphrey— the thing that hits me first is that as my hair started turning grey, Hubert's was getting darker.

With dyed hair and special double-knit pants with a girdling waistband, the happy warrior—"The Politics of Joy" was his 1968 rallying cry—seemed ready to try it again in 1976. An awful lot of people—maybe it was just my tired generation—reacted by saying

"Ohhhhhh!" as if that were his middle name, Hubert Groan Humphrey! But you had to take him, The Great Seal of American Politics, seriously. And you had to like him—after all, he's the same religion we are.

No matter what your religion is, it's Hubert's. A. M. Keith, a Minnesota politician, used to tell a story about traveling the state with Humphrey, who was, a long time ago, mayor of Minneapolis. Each time he met someone, Humphrey would ask about their family, then about their religion. The first person said, "I'm a Lutheran," and Humphrey happily replied, "I'm a Lutheran, too." If someone said, "I'm a Baptist," so was Humphrey. Or a Methodist, or an Episcopalian. Humphrey would always say, "Great! So am I. Glad to meet another."

Finally, Keith pulled aside Humphrey, who happens to be a Congregationalist, and said, "You can't do that. You can't tell everybody you belong to their church." Humphrey was bewildered: "Why not? I'm a good Christian."

That story is the essential Humphrey anecdote. The "essential anecdote" is a time-honored journalistic device for telling as much as you can about a public figure in as short a time as possible. In 1976, with a dozen Democrats running for President, a reporter was pretty much reduced to dealing in essential anecdotes. How much did people really want to know about Lloyd Bentsen or Milton Shapp or Frank Church? The only one of the dozen that most people had ever heard of was Hubert Humphrey.

Name recognition brought groans but it was also a most visible political asset in a field crowded with guys determined to prove their last names were not *Who?* With Edward Kennedy's name removed from the Gallup and Harris lists after he declared he would not run for president under any circumstances in 1976, Humphrey consistently led national Democratic polls in 1975, scoring as the candidate who was the first choice of the largest number of party members— he was usually the choice of about 30 percent of polled Democrats.

Except for George Wallace, who was recorded in the same polls as the choice of about 20 percent of Democrats, the rest plodded along in statistical obscurity. Henry Jackson stood at about a 10 percent Gallup/Harris rating and the rest stretched out toward zero—reminding themselves all the while that George McGovern won the 1972 nomination after standing at 6 percent or lower in similar 1971 polling.

The essential Wallace anecdote of his fourth try for the presidency was the story of the 1975 Democratic Governors' Conference in Washington that December. Ten announced candidates for President were scheduled to address the assembled chief executives at the Mayflower Hotel. Nine did. The tenth, old George, never came down from his room upstairs. Why? "I didn't mean to be rude. I tried to be gracious in the sense of curtailing their time since no one in there was going to support me . . . I think I was reading a newspaper, maybe the funnies, and watching television for the news."

There's no news on television at three o'clock in the afternoon, but the governor had proved that he can pretty much do anything he pleases without destroying the faith of millions of Wallaceites in his capability to run the country.

The other nine, plus Senator Frank Church, who was then considering a candidacy announcement, had to peddle their wares wherever they were asked. Even then most Americans ignored them, not even picking up their names. "Oh, yeah," a New Yorker said of Senator Lloyd Bentsen, "Ezra Taft Benson, the Secretary of Agriculture." But if you wanted to know just a little, essential anecdotes might suffice, and these were told, for want of a better reason, in alphabetical order:

Senator Birch Bayh of Indiana

When you speak of Birch Bayh you have to remember you're talking about a guy who conceded that a major factor in his election to the U.S. Senate in 1962 was a campaign song that went, "Hey, look him over/ He's your kind of guy/ His first name is Birch/ His last name is Bayh." A credit to Jaycees everywhere, Bayh became known in Washington as a first-string back-slapper and flesh-grabber who had his own speciality, the affectionate punch in the arm. "If he does that to me once more," Robert Kennedy once snapped, "I'm going to punch him in the nose."

Senator Lloyd Bentsen of Texas

Lloyd Bentsen had a 7 A.M. tennis date one day in 1974 with another senator and two reporters. When the others arrived, Bentsen was already sitting alongside the court at the Washington Hilton Hotel, apparently deep in thought. He didn't hear the others come up until one said, "Hi, Lloyd." He looked up, startled, and said: "Boy, I sure would like to be President!"

Former Governor Jimmy Carter of Georgia

In 1972, Jimmy Carter, prohibited by the state constitution from seeking re-election as governor, was just another stop on the endless road for presidential candidates seeking local endorsements. Hubert Humphrey, Edmund Muskie, Henry Jackson, and George McGovern all stopped by in Atlanta, posing for photographers and staying awhile for ritual discussions of the state of the nation and the world. "You know," Carter told a friend after hearing them all, "I know as much as they do, maybe more."

Senator Frank Church of Idaho

In 1959, when he came to the Senate at the age of 32, Frank Church was asked whether he wanted to be president. "No," he said, looking over at Senator Theodore Green of Rhode Island, who was 92 years old. "My ambition is to serve as long as Senator Green."

Former Senator Fred Harris of Oklahoma

When Fred Harris was a sophomore at the University of Oklahoma, he and a friend drove to Oklahoma City to spend a day watching the state legislature in action. He loved it. On the way back to school he said to his friend, "Goddammit, Charlie, there ought to be some way we can figure out how to stay around that place some."

Senator Henry Jackson of Washington

Did you hear about the night Scoop Jackson gave a fireside chat? Halfway through, the fire fell asleep.

Governor Milton Shapp of Pennsylvania

In 1960, Milton Shapp was a rich businessman who wanted to talk to the Kennedys about this idea he had for sending young Americans overseas to help poor countries. He tried to get to Bobby Kennedy after a meeting with local politicians in Philadelphia, but the pols just muscled him out of the way. Shapp went to the airport, found out Kennedy was flying to Pittsburgh, bought a ticket on the same flight, and elbowed his way into the seat next to the Democratic candidate's brother. Since then, Shapp has claimed credit for conceiving the Peace Corps.

Sargent Shriver

Peter Jenkins, chief Washington correspondent of *The Guardian,* filed this report back to England after a long conversation with Sargent Shriver when the Kennedy brother-in-law was the 1972 Democratic nominee for vice president: "It had seemed a stimulating talk. The Shriver charm is powerful and the enthusiasm infectious. No doubt he is a good man, earnest to do good. But when I looked in my notebook later there wasn't much there."

Representative Morris (Mo) Udall of Arizona

When people asked Mo Udall why he thought he had any chance of being president, which they often did, he would answer: "Just imagine that in 1940, on pain of death, you had been forced to predict the next three presidents of the United States. You would have had to pick an obscure Missouri senator who was so identified with a corrupt machine that his re-election was in doubt, an even more obscure Army lieutenant colonel in the Philippines, and a kid in his second year at Harvard."

Many of those anecdotes, and others I could have used, are variations on a theme: super-ambition. I suppose it goes without saying that a man or woman who wants to be President of the United States is "ambitious," but that word alone does not do semantic justice to presidential aspirations. That kind of drive is awesome, more than a little frightening to people who themselves are used to being called ambitious or driven—to men like Walter Mondale, ambitious enough to become a senator from Minnesota, but who withdrew as a potential candidate for president in 1975 because he just did not have super-ambition.

Frank Church, who could talk, even casually, about spending 60 years as one of the 100 most honored representatives of a society of 200 million, probably did not have it either—at least, people who knew him did not believe he did, which was the reason for the anecdote they told about him. More than one of the dozen candidates in 1975 would be eliminated because they had overestimated their own ability to give of themselves to ambition, to crowds, to strangers, to the nation. They could not pass the Humphrey Test: persistently, shamelessly, happily pushing themselves, like a bologna, into a delicatessen slicer. Humphrey, a man of extraordinarily quick intellect, charm, and energy had given so much of himself away in 30 years of public life that there was always a question of whether anything was left.

In 1975, there also was a question of whether Humphrey himself was still able to pass the test. He asked the question himself, wondering with old friends whether he could stand—emotionally, not physically—another effort and perhaps another rejection. So he waited—"hesitated" would be a better word—leaving the field, at least for early practice, to the Bayhs, the Bentsens, and the rest.

All the candidates got on the lists the same way: each just said, "I want it. Hey, look at me!" That's really all there is to the first stage of a presidential campaign. There is some speculation and learned discourse on the role of the press in projecting potential candidates —Russell Baker, *The New York Times* resident humorist, has had fun creating The Great Mentioner who mystically begins promoting people for the presidency in columns and on the nightly news. But if there were such a creature, different names might be mentioned. Perhaps Senator Philip Hart of Michigan and Senator Charles Mathias of Maryland. Or Representative Donald Fraser of Michigan and Representative John Anderson of Illinois. Or Governor Reubin Askew of Florida. In 1975, you would find a consensus of politicians and political reporters that those five were among the most impressive men in American public life, if not *the* most impressive. But the only one mentioned for the presidency was Mathias, a Republican who mentioned himself rather halfheartedly in his disappointment over the performance of President Gerald Ford and the prospect of Ronald Reagan's candidacy.

All the men who publicly mentioned themselves—and had, along with their staffs, been mentioning themselves privately to the press for months or years—had records of public service which were rarely explored in the early months of their candidacies. It is in the nature of the campaigning process and the press's emphasis on politics rather than government that those records would not be closely scrutinized unless their bearers reached the presidential semi-finals—the two or three candidates in each party who survived earlier elimination rounds and had some kind of reasonable chance to move into the White House. (The press preoccupation with politics is so ingrained that in 1972, when President Nixon essentially refused to campaign, newspapers and television expended their energy in attacking him for not traveling, rather than using their resources to examine how the Nixon administration had actually governed for four years.)

The records of the candidates, in barest outline, looked like this as their campaigns began:

• *Humphrey,* who was 64 in 1975, was a pharmacist and University of Minnesota instructor before being elected mayor of Minneapolis in 1944 and senator in 1948. He retired from the Senate to become Lyndon Johnson's vice president in January, 1965. Returning to Minnesota to teach again after his 1968 presidential defeat, he was once more elected to the Senate in 1970. More than any other individual, he was the voice of American liberalism in the 1950s and early 1960s, speaking early, often, and persuasively for civil rights, welfare and anti-poverty programs, Medicare, tax reform, and co-existence. Then, as Johnson's sycophantic vice president, he burned his credentials and credibility with a new generation of liberals by defending the war in Vietnam: "This is our adventure, and what a great adventure it is!"

• *Wallace,* 56, became an assistant attorney general and state representative in Alabama after service in the Army Air Corps during World War II. He was a state circuit judge before first being elected governor in 1963 and embarking on four runs for the presidency; the fourth, in 1972, was cut short when he became paralyzed from the waist down as the result of being shot while campaigning. The state he has dominated for more than a decade is one of the poorest in the nation and most significant "quality of life" indicators have declined relatively during his stewardship— Alabama now ranks 50th among the states in per-pupil education expenditures, 48th in percentage of residents passing armed forces mental tests, 49th in per capita income, 48th in percentage of residents living above the poverty line, 48th in infant mortality.

• *Bayh,* 47, studied agriculture at college and worked at it until he was elected to the state House of Representatives; he earned a law degree in 1960, when he was the youngest speaker in Indiana's history. In 1962, he was elected to the U.S. Senate and has won a reputation as a consistent, cagy liberal who, at the urging of A.F.L.-C.I.O. leadership, led the fight to reject two Nixon Supreme Court nominees and was the principal sponsor of the 25th Amendment (on presidential succession). More than anything he is seen as a younger and more calculating Humphrey, a cornbelt professional whose staff has instructions to brief him on what reporters are wearing before press conferences so that he will know exactly who and where questions are coming from.

- *Bentsen,* 54, was an attorney at 21, a major in the Air Force at 24, a congressman at 27, and was 30 when he suggested in a House speech that President Truman use the atomic bomb in Korea. At 34, he quit Congress to "make money" and did, a lot in insurance and land dealings, before he was elected to the Senate in 1970. He is a product of the Sam Rayburn-Lyndon Johnson-John Connally school of Texas politics, and his Senate ratings from the liberal Americans for Democratic Action have ranged from 33 to 55 out of a possible 100. As a senator, he is considered about the most efficient—the only one who retains a management consultant for his office—and a reliable tool of the Democratic congressional leadership.*

- *Carter,* 51, graduated from the U.S. Naval Academy and once served as a nuclear engineering aide to Admiral Hyman Rickover. Returning to Georgia after seven years in the Navy, he went into peanut farming and wholesaling and was elected a state senator in 1962, then won his one term as governor in 1971. After saying he was "proud" to run with segregationist lieutenant-governor candidate Lester Maddox, and repeatedly praising George Wallace, Carter won acclaim nationally as a spokesman for the "New South" by beginning his administration saying, "the time for racial discrimination is over." He reformed state budgeting techniques and reorganized 300 state governmental units into 22 agencies, which he claimed saved Georgians $50 million a year in taxes—an unprovable claim because it was based on projected future budgets.

- *Church,* 51, practiced law in Boise for just six years before becoming "the boy Senator" in 1956, often being mistaken in the Capitol for a new page. Now a very senior member at a relatively young age, he is in line to become chairman of the Foreign Relations Committee and is second in seniority on the Interior and Insular Affairs Committee (where he zealousy protects Idaho's water interests, vital concerns in a state largely dependent on irrigation). A dependable liberal (80 ADA ratings) on most issues, he uses issues like gun control, which he energetically opposes, to keep conservatives happy at home. An old-fashioned plains orator, Church really does concentrate most of

*On February 11, 1976, Bentsen withdrew as a national candidate, running for President only on the Texas primary ballot.

his energy on foreign policy and, consequently, is considered poorly informed, or lazy, on domestic problems that fester far from Idaho.

• *Harris,* 45, a lawyer, practiced three years before being elected to the state senate in 1957 and then the U.S. Senate, where he served from 1964 to 1973. He did not seek re-election—many Oklahomans believed he could not have won again after voting more and more with Eastern liberals. Until the 1970s he was "one of the boys" in Washington, a moderate liberal who served a year as Democratic National Chairman, but by 1972 he was restless and disillusioned enough to begin his first "New Populism" campaign for the presidency. If nothing else, he is considered, along with Mo Udall, one of the wittiest public men in America.

• *Jackson,* 63, was elected a county prosecutor soon after graduating from the University of Washington Law School, then elected to the House of Representatives in 1940 and the Senate in 1952. As dull as most people thought he was, Jackson stood among the most powerful men, if he was not the most powerful man, in the Senate. He has used that power to promote himself—he is a master of the press release and television comment—and his major concerns, including national defense, Israel, and a planned economy. He considers himself a Roosevelt liberal, but most of his peers consider him a moderate and his ADA ratings generally hover in the 40s and 50s. They also consider him eminently qualified for the presidency. Not that they necessarily want him to be—he has few friends.

• *Shapp,* 63, worked as an engineer before forming Jerrold Electronics, the company which developed much of the technology for cable television. Selling the company in the early sixties, he spent millions of his own dollars seeking public office, losing races for senator in 1964 and governor in 1966 before being elected Pennsylvania's chief executive in 1970. He turned out to be an effective, if not spectacular, moderate liberal governor with a dead-end problem: because of a state constitutional limit, he cannot run for a third term in 1978. He has to find something to do. He is also the first Jew to campaign for the presidency.

• *Shriver,* 60, has never held elective office, although at various times he considered running in Illinois, Maryland, and New York. His life, in fact, has been dominated by a single event, marrying John F. Kennedy's sister, Eunice. For years, he represented Kennedy family interests as director of the Merchandise Mart in Chicago, serving also as chairman of the Chicago Board of Education. He was appointed the first director of the Peace Corps by his brother-in-law in 1961, then was named the first director of the Office of Economic Opportunity and ambassador to France by President Johnson. He became the Democratic nominee for vice president in 1972 after several men had declined to run with George McGovern and Senator Thomas Eagleton had stepped down as McGovern's running mate when it was revealed that he had a history of emotional problems.

• *Udall,* 54, who spent a year as a professional basketball player, was elected a county prosecutor in 1952 and a congressman in 1961. A thoughtful, witty liberal, he played the House game—respect for the elders—until 1968 when he ran against Speaker John McCormack in the House Democratic caucus. He was clobbered, but the contest set the pattern for his career as a professional outsider who criticized both the rules and the members themselves.

No matter what they had gone through before, these men had volunteered for an adventure and an ordeal that few others would ever know. There were 29 Democratic primary elections scheduled for 1976, compared with the seven John F. Kennedy had run in during his 1960 campaign. Elizabeth Drew, writing in *The New Yorker,* put it this way:

> In selecting those who might occupy the most important office in this country—the Presidency—we put our potential leaders through a process that is both strange and brutal. The people who might make crucial decisions about war and peace, about our taxes, who will have enormous effect on the quality of our lives, our social order, the civility of our public discourse, undergo an experience from which few human beings could emerge whole. Some do not. The evidence of the damaging nature of political campaigns—the scarred veterans, the burnt-out cases, the bitterness—is all about. "They never come out of it the same," one senator said

of colleagues of his who had run for the Presidential nomination or the Presidency.

One who knows about it, George McGovern, said: "In a Presidential campaign it's as if you were always in the seventh game of the World Series—one error and it could be all over. The sense of excitement and tension is always there—day and night . . . You literally live for months on the flow of adrenalin. I was tired, but I went at a pace that couldn't be sustained at any other time. It couldn't be sustained by the staff, by the press—they had to be rotated."

How could they do it—these men or Edmund Muskie in 1972? "It's a very heady business, really," Muskie said, "to suddenly find yourself near the top, and to breathe constantly the atmosphere of those who take it for granted that you're going to be the next President of the United States—not just the staff but also the press and your foes. It does things to you. You begin subconsciously to believe it yourself . . . It was a rather wonderful feeling."

7 | Nelson Rockefeller
Ronald Reagan
John Connally

The people are right. Politicians *are* a bunch of no-good, lying hypocrites.

I don't always believe that, but then I haven't always just spent a weekend in Atlanta watching Nelson Rockefeller, Ronald Reagan, and John Connally campaign for President at the Southern Republican Conference. The three "superstars," as the conference program called them, stopped by to assure Strom Thurmond and 1,200 other practicing politicians that there was nothing wrong with the country or Richard Nixon—and especially that there was nothing wrong with them.

The problem, it seems, is us. Some of us have gotten confused by malicious publicity about Watergate and other things and have gotten the impression that the country is being run by knaves, fools, and liars. That's ridiculous, said the superstars. Then Rockefeller told the troops that New York's dope pushers are in jail, Reagan blamed us for the energy crisis, and Connally graciously volunteered to save the Republic.

The bastards.

Rockefeller crawled. These people—state and county chairmen, their troops and ladies from thirteen sunshine states—have always hated him, but they invited him, smiled at him, told him he had a chance with them—just to prove that they could make a Rockefeller from New York come down and pay court to the people who ground his face in the mud of 1964 and 1968.

"I don't think the ideological differences were as important as they seemed then, or as some of us made them out to be," said the man who had been brutally shouted down by the legions of Barry Goldwater at the 1964 Republican National Convention. "I'm so tired of the tapes. Americans are tired of the tapes. They wish you would change the subject, and so do I."

When reporters, at least, wouldn't change the subject, Rockefeller winkingly retreated into this Watergate rhetoric: "I don't know much about it. I don't know the facts, how can I know the answers? . . . I'm just a local politician." It was a slight variation of the rhetoric he used to dodge Vietnam questions for five years. And Clarke Reed, the shrewd ultra-conservative conference chairman from Mississippi, approved, saying that things had changed since 1964, adding with his own wink: "Y'all think Goldwater has changed?"

Reagan may have sunk lower than Rocky. They cheered and cheered him on his night in Atlanta, but it may very well have been the end of his Presidential hopes—even if his political death may not be apparent for a long time. The fact is that he needs a solid Republican South to make a run for the party's nomination, and they also cheered Connally—the big Texas demagogue is going to hold big enclaves in Reaganland.

I've always thought Reagan was something of a fraud, and nothing happened in Atlanta in December, 1973, to change my mind. He is either a better actor than most people thought he was when he openly did it for a living, or he is without shame. The American people, he told a press conference, were warned about the energy crisis. How? He remembered a Conoco Oil advertisement about a year ago in *U.S. News and World Report* or *Newsweek*, he couldn't remember which. The "average American," he said, could deal with it "by turning off the lights as he goes through different rooms to go into the den and watch television." How many average Americans do you think have dens, governor? "The Republican party has traditionally been the victim of shenanigans worse than Watergate. There is documentary proof." What's that? Well, he said, the *New York Herald Tribune* almost published stories documenting that 200,000 votes were stolen from Nixon in Chicago in 1960. Reagan, it turns out, doesn't believe what newspapers do publish but is convinced by the things they almost publish.

Connally just ran away. There are two visions of him in Atlanta with his new party: a series of statues as he magnificently gestures through classic oratory, his silver hair gleaming under the lights; and the hasty exit with a *New York Times* reporter pursuing—"I'm sorry, Chris, I'm so busy, I'm sorry!"—to get in a question about that $10,000 from the milk producers' attorneys. I also have a fantasy vision of Connally throwing his arms around himself, hugging the magnificence, and murmuring, "I love you so much!"

No press conferences for Governor Connally. What he has to say he says from behind the high podium in Condor Hall—it's named for the world's largest vulture. And what did he say? Charlie Coy again: "He's a great Fundamentalist orator. My wife's going to get home and say, 'Wasn't that a great speech?' When I ask her what he said, she'll say, 'Well, I don't know, but it sounded wonderful.' "

"We are the only hope for the future of this nation" was one of the Connally lines. Then there was: "In this Golden Age of Opportunity, I pledge my total commitment to the preservation of this republic and to the preservation of capitalism." My favorite, however, was about Nixon: "Remember, this man has done some incredible things on the domestic front."

The reporters covering the conference snidely referred to Rockefeller, Reagan, and Connally as "the dirty old men," but the three superstars were real giants compared with Louis (Skip) Bafalis, a freshman congressman from Florida. Bafalis, one of the new Southern Republicans who does pride to his dentist, barber, and tailor, raised the level of American political humor by regaling the crowd with gems like this:

"There's a story going around Washington about changing the name of the Watergate to the Chappaquiddick Inn, and they've hired a couple of managers named Bobby Baker and Billie Sol Estes. Ted Kennedy's going to be the swimming coach. And the locker room boy is Walter Jenkins."

The Hyatt Regency in Atlanta is an adult Disneyland, a spectacular structure with 23 floors of interior balconies facing an indoor court dominated by a huge column supporting five Plexiglas bubble elevators which shoot up into the indoor sky.

The people are very attractive, very careful about how they look. There is something to be said for women who from the age of about fourteen seem to spend two hours getting ready to be seen any place a man might be. My depression on leaving the Peachtree lobby wasn't related to Republicans, ideology, or the South—it was about American politicians, about what our system really seems to be producing as leaders. Hell, it's not just Republicans. I kept expecting to run into Hubert Humphrey.

The hotel for 48 hours was a nest of hypocrisy, self-delusion, and lies. I was going to slug the next man who used charming moral arguments to defend immorality. A young vice president of a national corporation, the treasurer of the Georgia Republican Party, and I had this conversation:

"There is something wrong with the country. We've got to get people working together again, living by the rules of decency. Even in small things, like not cheating on income taxes, not fixing tickets or violating the speed limit when no one is watching . . ."

"Not erasing tapes?"

"I support the President because he is *The President,*" he said and turned away.

This was the hardest core of Nixon support eight months before he resigned. Nixon was, in the eyes of the people who convened in Atlanta, the Southern President and the underdog President. And they, after years as both Southerners and Southern Republicans, saw themselves as the ultimate underdogs—an irony to an outsider because they aren't underdogs anymore; this was a meeting of the small-town country club set. Loyalty to Nixon, who they feel has been loyal to them, was an article of absolute faith. Rockefeller was acceptable as a contrite guest, even honored in a perverse way, because he had been blindly loyal.

Southern Republicans, right now, are one of the most vital and committed political forces in the nation. The men and women who gathered around the bars of the Regency—they drink Scotch four-to-one over bourbon, according to bartenders—are putting time, money, and incredible energy into politics. And it shows: starting with virtually nothing in the one-party South ten years ago, they now have three governors, nine U.S. senators, and 32 representatives; in June, 1973, in Mississippi they elected fourteen mayors.

Men like Thurmond and Reed, who is the chairman of the Association of Southern Republican Chairmen, do not believe that they can pick the G.O.P. nominee for President in 1976—but they do believe they have veto power over that nominee as they did over the vice presidential nominee in 1968. In many ways these Southerners are to the national Republican party what Manhattan reformers are to New York City Democratic politics—they work like hell and they're an uneasy conglomeration of true believers and believing pragmatists. All of them would veto Percy; only the true believers would veto Rockefeller. A couple of hours and several drinks past midnight, a professional from Macon, Georgia, drawled: "We *caint* go for a fella who says *cawn't* instead of *can't*. Rockefella's a librul."

The Southerners were kidding Rocky a bit by inviting him down and treating him as one of the boys and repeating over and over again that "he's acceptable." "They're very polite," said one Republican. "They won't go for Nelson, but they'll drink a lot of his liquor before they tell him." [They didn't go for Nelson even after President Ford appointed him vice president. After Rockefeller announced in November, 1975, that he would not seek the job in 1976, he traveled to another Southern Conference and told a closed meeting of chairmen: "You got me out, you sons of bitches! Now get off your asses and work for the party!"]

Rockefeller has finally understood, or accepted, what the Republican party really is: the political institutionalization of America's small towns and corporate ethic. The Rockefeller political operation in Atlanta was smooth, with New York Republican Chairman Richard Rosenbaum and Rocky's personable advance man, Joe Canzeri, laying the groundwork.

Gone are the days of Freddy Young, fondly as they are remembered. Young was in a glorious tradition of New York politicians who offended other Americans, an upstater Rockefeller adopted and successively made state chairman and chief judge of the Court of Claims. In 1964, Young was traveling the country for Rocky and cornered a Colorado Republican brahmin at a country club cocktail party. Grabbing the man by the pinstripes, Young asked: "How can you be for that goddamned bum Goldwater?"

"I *beg* your pardon!" said the Westerner.

Young thought the man was hard of hearing, so he shouted it: "I said, how can you be for that goddamned bum Goldwater?"

Rockefeller arrived in Atlanta first, on Friday evening, December 7. At the afternoon session before he arrived, Republican National Committee Chairman George Bush had set the tone for the conference by saying everything is almost fine, there is no grass-roots pressure for a Nixon resignation or impeachment, all that talk comes from George Meany and Ralph Nader, and, anyway, the Republican party had nothing to do with Watergate. Art Fletcher, the director of the Black Political Division of the R.N.C., welcomed the eight blacks in the audience to the party of opportunity.

Nelson from New York bounced into his half hour with 40 reporters saying, "There sure are a lot of you. Is this the convention or the press conference?"

"This is how many votes you're going to get in the South," mumbled Hubert F. Lee, the octogenarian editor of *Dixie Business.*

Age was very much on some minds over the weekend. Rockefeller was 65 and Reagan was 63, and parts of them look it. The happiest billionaire's years show only in the throat and around the jawline— in fact, that strong line is beginning to crumble. Reagan is two-faced: the face above his mouth looks about 45 with dark bronzy hair untouched with white or gray but obviously touched with something else; the mouth, chin, throat, and neck look in their seventies, when he occasionally stops grinning his boyish grin to breathe. Reporters, a nasty bunch, amused themselves during idle hours by speculating about Rockefeller's twice-a-week physicals and multicolored pills and speculating whether he or Reagan had had facelifts, and how many.

After evading most questions with a wink, Rockefeller circulated among the clear-eyed women, Instamatics, and American flag pins until the band struck up "Dixie" and Robert Shaw, the state chairman of Georgia, sang "The Star-Spangled Banner" and called out, "Y'all hush—come on up here and listen to me." They and Rockefeller listened to him and to a parade of elected Southern Republicans, who agreed that there was no Watergate and everybody knows it.

The one note of reality that crept in was a joke by Representative LaMar Baker of Tennessee, a very funny man, who said we ought to laugh at ourselves, and repeated an old new joke: "Let's get crime out of the White House and back on the streets where it belongs."

Finally, they brought on Rocky to what I would call a pro forma standing ovation. He cut his prepared remarks in half, leaving out a page about "the party of Abraham Lincoln." Except for excising Lincoln, his message was not altered for a Southern crowd. He has become a genuine tough-talker, and Reagan's advance man said, half-jokingly: "The bastard stole our speech."

Among other things, Rockefeller said:

"Let us not forget what Richard Nixon did for this country . . . The Congress this year voted about $20 billion to $30 billion more in expenditures than we had in revenues—only Richard Nixon had the courage to stand up and cut back on these so we could live within our means . . . In New York, we got the cheats off welfare and off the taxpayers' backs. We got the hard-drug pushers into jail and let the people back on the streets. We gave them life sentences, but we got them off the streets . . . We've got to revitalize the old American morality and apply it to the problems of today. We have to regain a sense of integrity."

What do you mean, we?

Connally followed Representative Wilmer Mizell, who used to be Vinegar Bend Mizell, the Cardinal and Pirate pitcher. Ol' Vinegar Bend fired it right down the middle: "Motivation? Let me share with you a list of the people who are demanding the impeachment of the President . . . the A.C.L.U. . . . the U.A.W. . . . the A.D.A. . . . Common Cause . . . Brother, if that's not enough motivation for us to win, I don't know what is!"

Connally hustled off after promising to save the Republic. Ironically, Connally's great political flaw in the rest of the country—the turncoat factor: he's been a Republican only seven months—is a benefit in the South. Almost every man and woman in Condor Hall was a turncoat Democrat from the sixties when the new Republican South emerged from the ashes of civil-rights battles and entrenched Democratic indifference to the rising white-collar middle class of the suburbs and small towns. Almost every speaker began by saying, "I converted in . . . ," precisely the way evangelists say "I found Christ when . . ." Clarke Reed, for example, converted in 1960 when he believed John F. Kennedy planned to unilaterally disarm the United States.

Reagan was terrific. Whether or not the South is solid for him, they'll still love him. He spoke at the conference's closing banquet on Saturday night, while outside the hotel a couple of hundred young people milled around with signs like DIG UP THE BODIES IN THE WHITE HOUSE LAWN.

Reagan played the audience . . . well, like an audience. He seems to make up some of it—five out of eight Wall Street lawyers are Democrats; the Democrats spent more on television advertising than the Republicans in 1972; this inflation is "a deliberately planned policy of the Democrats." Then he begins talking about prisoners of war visiting his home, his voice becomes throaty, then cracks, he has to stop for a moment . . . "Holding out was the only thing we could do, they told me, the only thing we could still do for our country . . . Where did we find men like these, just ordinary guys . . . American guys from the farms, from the small towns, from the cities . . ."

You've got to see it. I don't want to make fun of those words, but the reporters who travel with him say they're always the same words, and the voice always starts to crack, then stops at the same points in the speech.

I've never heard so many reporters—and they were the only outsiders in this particular fantasy world—saying the same thing: "I've got to get out of this place. I'm going to hit somebody or they're going to hit me."

Big John Connally got the loudest cheers of the conference by saying: "I predict and I assure you that if the election were held again today between George McGovern and Richard M. Nixon the results would not be measurably different."

Maybe he's right about the winner. But there would be a measurable difference. Most Americans would stay home; they wouldn't vote for any of the bastards. At the moment, I can't think of any reason they should.

Two

The Way It Was: 1972

8 | Edmund Muskie

MANCHESTER, N.H.—There is a small plaque near the scuffed old front desk of the Sheraton-Carpenter Hotel that reads: "In this lobby, John F. Kennedy, the 35th President of the United States of America, personally opened his first campaign headquarters in the nation—Jan. 4, 1960." Twelve years and three days later, Senator Edmund Muskie was doing the same thing, and more than a thousand people pushed into the little ballroom. The candidate's advance team had made the night an event; even with the temperature outside at 15 degrees below zero, large families came, and so did young men with their dates, plain girls with fancy lacquered hair. They weren't disappointed. Ed Muskie from Maine gave what his oldest friends called the most emotional speech of his life—no text, no jacket, confetti in his hair and sweat on his huge face. The next day The New York Times *reported on its front page that Muskie had called for an almost unconditional withdrawal from Vietnam. But that's not what the people there would remember after he euphorically plunged into the crowd with the Alpine Drum & Bugle Corps right behind him blaring "God Bless America." The moment that stuck in their minds, that had frozen the crowd with a vision of what America used to be, was when he shouted: "This is a country we love and believe in and want to fight for and die for."*

"He is such a decent man, with an inner security that makes him so much more attractive than Richard Nixon," said a sometime adviser to Muskie. "But I have this picture of him sitting on the porch in Kennebunkport and this kid comes up to him, dodging the draft and everything else, broke and strung out on drugs, with his pregnant girlfriend. They all talk for an hour and the kid knows he's into something real; then Muskie leans forward, pats him on the knee and tells him to go back home, get a job, marry the girl, and everything will be all right."

The President, of course, wouldn't have been able to think of anything to say to the kid once the football season was over—but Nixon would have wanted to give him the same advice. That may have been the good news-bad news joke of 1972. First, the bad news: Ed Muskie is a kind of likable Richard Nixon. Now, the good news: You *will* like Ed Muskie—there is something real there.

Nixon and Muskie are men of that generation that produced Navy lieutenants in World War II. (Both were lieutenants in the Pacific, as were John Kennedy, Gerald Ford, and John Lindsay.) Whatever their differences on issues and approaches, and there are significant differences, they are both men with a firm grip on America's past and no clear vision of a different kind of future—Muskie wanted to bring us together again; when he said, "We can do better," he meant he was a better man than Nixon to do the same thing.

Muskie brought almost everyone together in Marathon, Wisconsin (population: 1,214), three days after Manchester and told them he would preserve the family farms, reminiscing a bit about his father and the land of Maine. The Marathon High band played "America the Beautiful" and Muskie chatted with the band director—he is a small-town politician who understands the stature of bandmasters— and the kids behind him were talking to me about getting the hell out of Marathon as soon as they graduated.

Edmund Sixtus Muskie, the poor boy, the Polish tailor's son from Rumford, Maine, was well to the left of the poor boy from Whittier, California—3,000 miles and 70 Americans for Democratic Action points, according to their Congressional voting records. But, though they looked at it from different sides, they both saw the great middle of the country and felt its past. The President—Muskie always called him, uncharitably, "Nixon"—talked about train whistles in the night. The challenger, at the moment of his emergence as a potential President, the day he invited that anti-war student, Rick Brody in Washington, Pennsylvania, to debate him in 1968, answered the young man by describing how his father, Stephen Marciszewski, "tore himself out of his home life, away from a family he would never see again, to go to a foreign land with only five years' formal education, with a newly learned trade as a tailor, to find opportunity for himself and for children who were yet unborn. And the year before he died, his son become the first Polish-American ever elected Governor of an American state. Now that may not justify the American system to you, but it sure did to him."

It was impossible not to be moved when Muskie spoke that way—which he rarely did, by the way. One reason Muskie was liked is that he didn't take the cheap shots—when Nixon talked about those days by the railroad tracks he always seemed to be asking you to feel sorry for him.

Muskie's essential likability, the undeniable fact that he looked and sounded *good,* was elevated into his platform. The Politics of Trust, or Truth, Candor, Honesty, Character, Believability—all the words in Muskie literature—also happens to be the politics of bankruptcy. He hadn't had much to say beyond the inspirational—Muskie said it so much better, but he said only a little more than Nixon did in 1968. In February, 1972, it was early yet and the candidate said he was "establishing credibility," but reporters traveling with him had already composed a song saying Muskie looks like Lincoln and then rhyming into the line: "Being ugly sure beats thinkin'." (Muskie and his wife, Jane, roared with laughter when they heard the ditty at a party.)

Muskie was saying that the "credibility" phase is coming to an end, that he would soon swing into specifics. He talked with enthusiasm about the 27 task forces he had packaging ideas for his own campaign. But, in a conversation one night for an hour and a half on a flight from Columbus, Ohio, to Des Moines, Iowa, he seemed to have no clear direction in mind yet—he was saying what he had said in public: trust me.

What was clear that night was his view of himself as Senator or President. "Compromise and accommodation" was a phrase he leaned on—he talked of drawing in a wide range of ideas and molding them and pushing them into legislation and programs as close as possible to the line of his own liberal conviction, but still acceptable to anyone else, Republican congressmen or a divided nation. He talked consensus, referring proudly more than once to the months of persuading and educating he did to win 86–0 Senate approval of his Omnibus Water Pollution Control Act of 1971.

"No President," he said slowly, "has the experience, background and knowledge to make decisions in all these areas. He's got to have *instincts,* he's got to put ideas together, he's got to put people together and draw them out. He has to apply the insights he gets, the perspective that he gets to fit the directions he has in mind. In the process, you grow yourself . . . That's what I really enjoy. You can never guess in advance whose idea I'll pick.

"It's obvious that this country is going to be different. We know change is coming . . . If you're asking whether I think it's possible to re-create the America of 1910 or some date in the past, of course it isn't. I think, nevertheless, we must find an answer to it, this search for identity, a way for an individual to make an impact . . .

"You go back to [Franklin] Roosevelt. He had a relatively simpler job because everybody was in the same boat. Everybody was broke. It was easier to bring the poor and the rich, the black and the white together. Today it's different. A lot of people, with all the difficulties, are satisfied with the way things are for them.

"I've said I'm not completely sure that I'm the one man out of 200 million who should be President . . . I'd like to contribute to the reunification of this country—a reunification that makes it impossible to learn from those who are different rather than fear them. If I should become President, that would be my highest priority."

When we finished talking, someone asked me what he had said and I answered: "He said something really had to be done but he wasn't sure what or how to do it."

SPRINGFIELD, ILL.—"I am deeply grateful to you, Adlai, for your support and kind words. I am delighted to be in Illinois. Delighted and, at the same time, humble. For only in humility can a man run for President in the state that gave the nation Stephen A. Douglas, Abraham Lincoln,

John Peter Altgeld, Paul Douglas and Adlai E. Stevenson." The endorse-
ments by the big names of the Democratic Party have become so routine—
this is January 10, it must be Illinois and Adlai Jr. the Senator—that the
traveling reporters amused themselves during the news conference with as-
sorted Illinois politicians by composing mock statements: "I am deeply
grateful to you, Lyndon, for your support and kind words. I am delighted
to be in Texas. Delighted and, at the same time, humble. For only in
humility can a man run for President in a state that gave the nation Bobby
Baker, Billie Sol Estes . . ."

Edmund Muskie was winning endorsements for the Democratic
nomination for President because his people, particularly Jack English, the ex-county chairman from Hempstead, Long Island, recognized first that 1972 was a whole new ball game in the Democratic
party. Specifically, they saw that the party reforms of the McGovern,
etc., commissions meant that there were going to be no more big
favorite-son and uncommitted delegations at conventions.

"The Teddy White thing—entering a couple of psychologically
important primaries like Jack Kennedy did—was dead," said English,
whose title is political co-ordinator and whose job includes body-
guarding the candidate through excited Manchester crowds with the
still face of a professional killer. "There was only one tactic: go across
the board into every state and tell them, 'Either you're with us or
against. Just tell us now. Because if you're against us, we have to run
a primary against you.' "

Beginning in the spring of 1971, Muskie operators, spread so thin
they didn't know where their next paycheck was coming from, started
the tedious business of pushing around or flattering local politicos and
citizen politicians, collecting petitions, learning about new state filing
procedures, and taking care of a thousand other details necessary to
get the name Muskie on the ballot of every primary state and getting
a maximum voice in states where delegates would be picked by
McGovernized—that is, democratized—conventions down to the
precinct level.

There was the smell of victory about the Muskie campaign—jokes
instead of the quietly desperate predictions by the staffs of the other

candidates as their planes passed in the night. Muskie steps off his plane—a ten-year-old, 52-seat Electra named the *Josephine* after his mother—and hears his communications (read television) director, Robert Squier, gasping to a small crowd, "My God, it's Raymond Massey!" And there is the candidate, playing poker with reporters on the plane back to Washington after telling the people of Iowa and Wisconsin how much they should trust him, reaching for a couple of bucks to cover a shy pot and grumbling: "It's depressing that no one ever trusts me."

(Not that Muskie is a great humorist, good poker player, or friend of the press. Maine hilarity has always lost something in translation —dry, they say—and he mixes desiccated wit with truncated puns: "We can't take the Granite State for granted." His poker runs to baseball, high-low, and wilder games with Polish names—it doesn't square with a man who counts the money in his wallet before taking out a dollar and measures his words the same way, and I can't figure out the significance of that lonely excess. And he doesn't like the press; he tolerates reporters as people doing honest work that sometimes complicates his own. When I asked him for his personal evaluation of George Wallace and John Lindsay, he answered: "You're not likely to get much from me on that. At this point I don't see that it serves my purposes to comment on other candidates.")

As happy as Muskie staffers were in their work, the Muskie political operation was thin and stumbling—although it was probably the most expensive ($10 to $15 million before the convention) ever built around a non-incumbent national candidate. They left notes to the candidate lying around in hotel rooms, like this one in Miami:

"I happened to notice when we arrived at the hotel that former Boston Mayor John Collins and his wife were in the lobby. A courtesy telephone call might be in order if his image is still good at home."

TALLAHASSEE, FLA.—Even a two-hour visit to Tallahassee gives you an insight into what G. Harrold Carswell, a local boy who didn't make good, was all about. The members of the Tiger Bay Capitol Club listened with fixed, ball-bearing eyes as Muskie talked about America. This was Wallace country, and the local newspaper, The Tallahassee Democrat, *offered its*

*readers their choice of four right-wing national columnists on January 7, the
day Muskie was in town: David Lawrence, Kevin Phillips, Victor Lasky and
John Chamberlain. But the candidate's eyes were just as hard when the
questions started. Carswell? "The man was not qualified to sit on the Supreme Court of the United States." Busing? "It's the least desirable way to
deal with the problems of school integration . . . But it is a tool and I don't
exclude it in answering this question." The $5 billion space shuttle with all
those jobs for Florida? "It's a question of priorities . . . I've seen the way
people live in Newark. What are we going to do for them, build them a space
shuttle?" In Tampa that night: "I didn't announce for President to win an
election, but to lead a country. If I demonstrate to you that at heart I'm
nothing but a Southerner, then I don't want your vote. If you want me to
be concerned only with your problems and no one else's, then find another
candidate."*

The Politics of Trust and Truth probably had an accidental birth
in Watts. Once the flap started after Muskie told some black leaders
in Los Angeles that there wasn't going to be a black man on his ticket
for Vice President because he didn't feel like losing, he really had only
one defense: Look, I told the truth and everybody knows it. Then the
explanation became a crusade. And people seemed to like it—they
knocked themselves out clapping in Tampa—even if the candidate
sometimes had trouble practicing what he had preached.

He was, after all, a politician—in fact, the father of the Maine
Democratic party was probably among the most experienced and
sophisticated professionals ever to seek the Presidency—and he regularly rewrote history, sometimes on two subcontinents. "Nixon dedicated himself to peace," he said in Columbus and a couple of other
places where he uncharacteristically stuck to his prepared text. "And
what did we get? A war in Vietnam. A war in Cambodia. A war in
Laos. A war between India and Pakistan." In Kenosha, Wisconsin,
they remembered that there was some kind of trouble in Vietnam and
Pakistan before Julie and Tricia got to the White House, and a man
at a United Auto Workers rally there walked out shaking his head and
saying, "You know you can't blame Nixon for everything, people'll
never believe that."

And even as he did his *mea culpa*s for enthusiastically supporting the war in Vietnam himself for years, Muskie called it "Nixon's war," just as it was "Nixon's inflation"—not Johnson's, Humphrey's, or Muskie's.

(Muskie's political talents aren't restricted to understanding exactly how organizations work, from precincts in Maine to the U.S. Senate. He had an instinctive sense of crowds and media. When he mesmerized the folk of Manchester by telling them that fighting and dying were obligations of citizenship, he quickly added that if we had the kind of country he wanted, no one would have to fight or die anymore. I thought I heard a click when he realized what fighting-and-dying rhetoric would look like in *The New Republic.*)

The candidate of candor, though, did sock it to 'em with some regularity. But he knew how to duck—and he had to, because the press was beginning to jab with questions that open with phrases like, "Sir, as an advocate of truth in politics, could you tell us . . ."

Witness this exchange with David Broder of *The Washington Post* on *Meet the Press:*

BRODER: Senator, going into the matter of trust in government and yourself . . . One of the greatest sources of distrust in government and politicians is the way in which they finance their campaigns. You've said that you raised about $1 million or $1.2 million for your campaign last year. Will you disclose now the sources of that money?

MUSKIE: I'm willing to do what the law requires.

BRODER: The law does not require that, as you know perfectly well . . .

MUSKIE: Let me say I've done what the law requires. The law is inadequate. I've supported reform of the law . . . Now you're asking me whether it's possible for a candidate unilaterally to write a new standard of conduct. I haven't found that possible.

I asked Muskie later about the questions and the dangers of trumpeting his commitment to truth. He said, "The answer to Broder's question is that if I did that, I'd be out of the race. That's the simple fact."

Now there's an answer you could trust. Muskie the front runner, who spent less than $10,000 in his first campaign for Governor of Maine, was a big-money candidate, an investment candidate—if his books were opened, the country would get a free master's degree in political science.

What the books would show are five-figure contributions from Democrats, many from New York City, who wanted to hide their ideological commitment from business contacts and other candidates and who wanted to hide the amounts involved from the Justice Department. One of the stories about this campaign that will come out sooner or later is how terrified Democratic contributors were that Attorney General John Mitchell, the F.B.I., and the Internal Revenue Service would start nosing around to dry up anti-Nixon money. And the Muskie books also listed Republicans—including Nixon fundraisers, according to his staff—who were covering their bets on the chance that the Senator was going to be the next man in charge of the Justice Department and every other federal agency.

> *MILWAUKEE, WIS.—There is, indeed, something Lincolnesque about Ed Muskie—although a kind of prissy mouth spoils the Mount Rushmore features—but it's not usually his language. For a man with obvious intelligence and a Phi Beta Kappa key he has a public vocabulary seemingly limited to words that have appeared in* The New York Daily News. *This night, January 10, at the Performing Arts Center, rhetoric and generalities came together to produce some superb examples of why it takes advance men to get 1,000 people to a political rally in Milwaukee. The subject was the economy and jobs, and Muskie's applause lines were: "The surest way to make jobs is to make jobs . . . I would challenge the President to explain to us why we cannot fight unemployment simply by employing the unemployed."*

There is always a lack of substance in political campaigns, and probably for good reason—Muskie argued rather convincingly that what voters are really interested in and all that they can be expected to absorb is a reading of a man's character and public priorities.

What Muskie said in Milwaukee was that the federal government could put five million people to work in hospitals, schools, parks, and police stations. The folks cheered and I asked him later how he would do that.

"I don't have the resources to program all of these programmatic answers," he answered. "These are areas we're developing. We've done work in particular fields that indicate the approach we would take. But you can't, in the midst of this kind of effort, put together a total programmatic approach to all these objectives . . . It's all just a job beyond the resources."

Trust me. The answers were the same on the problems of the cities, a problem that Muskie had shown a rather articulate commitment to over the years. But as for specifics, he would only endorse revenue sharing, "education" of the suburbs to the urban dilemma, and a "quantum jump" from the Model Cities legislation he managed through the Senate in 1966.

The Stephens High School *Broadcast,* writing about the new Student Council president in 1931, seemed to get a little carried away: "When you see a head and shoulders towering above those of the common herd in the halls of Stephens, you should know that your eyes are feasting on a future President of the United States."

Well, Ed Muskie was 6-foot-4 even in high school, and he hasn't shrunk. He has come a long way. With all the writing about the man's caution and indecisiveness—("Sometimes," he said, "I see seven sides to a question because there *are* seven sides")—it takes pride and toughness, both of which he has in inordinate amounts, to travel from an $8,000 Cape Cod house in Waterville, Maine, Republican Maine, to the Democratic National Convention in seventeen years.

There is a pride, possibly an arrogance, in Muskie that comes out in his famous temper and when he calls his staff "those faceless bastards." There was a toughness, very similar to John Kennedy's, in the way he stripped away the old Maine advisers as he moved up and they got in over their heads. He started to try doing this campaign with the old crowd. It didn't work, and when he learned that Donald Nicoll, his friend and administrative assistant and one-time executive secretary of the Maine Democratic party, was keeping younger men away from him, he found a new assistant and gave him one order:

"Liberate the talent on this staff."

Muskie of Maine speaks at a rate almost twice as slow as that of any other candidate for President. But there is real turmoil just beyond the edges of the television screen when he's drawling through his favorite story about the Maine farmer and the Texas rancher. His right hand shakes spastically and he almost always works a paper clip in it; his left constantly goes through the motions of buttoning his jacket and placing his glasses in his breast pocket for a half hour.

There has also been a real run of luck for the only Roman Catholic ever elected to high office by the Protestant farmers of his state: he was elected Governor in 1954 against an inept Republican who kept insisting that there were no poor people in Maine; he got to the Senate, where many knowledgeable men consider him *the* best of the 100 members, with the help of the Sherman Adams-Bernard Goldfine scandals of 1958; he looked good as a Vice-Presidential candidate in 1968 because the competition looked so bad; and Chappaquiddick threw Teddy Kennedy and left Muskie with divided and politically flawed opponents.

But more than anything else, Ed Muskie has been successful in establishing some kind of communion with the country. People do trust him and sense that he understands their problems even if he may not know what to do about them. He sometimes rolls on extemporaneously, mentioning "America" in every sentence. The appeal of that chauvinism is often lost in a New York City, or rather Manhattan, context, although Muskie is not alone in that depth of feeling, not alone by 150 million people or so. I remember Senator George McGovern coming to New York late in 1971 to appear at a dinner of liberal Democrats and Liberal party members opposed to Alex Rose, the Liberals' authoritarian leader, and beginning a speech by saying, "It's always good to be with real Americans, people who love their country." The audience just stared at him—they spend their waking hours debating how racist and imperialist the country is; they may not know it, but they hate America.

Ed Muskie loves America. He is the real people, or at least he remembers very well being one of them—he still puts red wine in the refrigerator to chill before dinner; his wife likes to inspect other people's kitchens and bathrooms; he's a tailor's son and he made the drapes in their Washington home.

He also understands what is good, what is best, about America—and he doesn't hesitate about reminding people. In my travels with him for a two-week period, the most graceful and moving thing I saw happened in a union hall, Local 77 of the United Auto Workers in Kenosha, Wisconsin. Someone ended an introduction with, "And now the wife of the slain civil rights leader, Mrs. Medgar Evers."

Somewhere in the back of the white room, a dozen men began an almost imperceptible hissing and Muskie immediately stood and began applauding, beginning a long standing ovation.

PORTLAND, ME.—Mrs. Stephen Muskie, the candidate's 81-year-old mother, who they say still sometimes takes in neighbors' laundry, met him at the Portland Airport to officially christen the campaign plane with her name, Josephine. Muskie made a joke about her safely carrying him for nine months and hoping the plane would do the same. Then someone asked her whether she thought her son would be a good President. "He'd better be," she answered. "If he's going to be President, he has to be a good one to show everybody what a good man he is."

9

George Wallace
Hubert Humphrey
Henry Jackson
Edmund Muskie
George McGovern
John Lindsay
Shirley Chisholm

"I want to talk about all those candidates down here for the Democratic Presidential primary," says the rich Southern voice coming across the piny countryside of north Florida at 1330 kilocycles on *Call and Comment,* a telephone talk show that radio station WMEN bills as Tallahassee's most listened-to show. "About this fellow Edmund Muskie. I heard his name is really Muskovich and he came from Russia."

"Well," says the show's moderator, "if his name's Muskovich, that doesn't necessarily mean he's a Russian. He could be Slovak or something. What if he is a Russian? Would that affect your vote?"

"Possibly," the voice on the telephone says slowly. "Possibly."

"There you have it, listeners," the moderator says. "The question is whether Muskie's real name is Muskovich and did he come from Russia. Our lines are open and we're waiting for an answer."

No one called to answer in the next hour.

Talk shows are big in the Florida Panhandle and a couple of hundred miles down the road in Fort Walton Beach, the callers to WFTW's *What's on Your Mind?* were debating whether President John Lindsay would name Huey Newton as Secretary of Defense and Fidel Castro as Ambassador to the United Nations.

Of course, that's north Florida, the place they call "south Alabama." That's where they love George Wallace, and Billy Grammer of the Grand Ole Opry begins each Wallace rally by saying, "There *are* a lot of us hillbillies here tonight!"

South Florida looks different. That's Miami, the place they call "New York south." They like to talk about how different Miami and the Panhandle are, and say that Florida is a "microcosm" of the United States. In Miami, charity banquets take the place of talk shows and they love Hubert Humphrey and Artur Rubinstein.

Humphrey was at the Oholei Torah Day School Fifth Annual Scholarship Banquet at the Sheraton-Four Ambassador Hotel—"Our International Promenade," the brochure says, "stretches twice the length of the Hall of Mirrors at the Palace of Versailles and is completely air-conditioned"—and he said that if Rubinstein isn't too old to play the piano at 83, he isn't too old to be President at 61. The former Vice President had to wait almost three hours to speak, nervously tapping his brown corduroy yarmulke with the gold brocade "HHH" while $111,000 was pledged to the school. But finally he gave one of the infinite variations of his set speech, quoting the Declaration of Independence and the Gettysburg Address, reciting the entire Pledge of Allegiance, and adding this final flourish: "I'm thinking of three elections tonight—the March 14th primary here in Florida, the general election against Richard Nixon on November 7th and, like all mortals, that final election when we meet our heavenly destiny."

The big election in the sky. That's what the Florida primary was supposed to be, an earthly version of the big 1972 primary election in the brilliant $40-a-day-plus-meals blue sky. It did turn out to be the most fantastic local show since Disney World opened in Orlando: Never before in American politics had so many candidates said so little to so many. And said it so often and so expensively.

What did it all prove? Reporters probably shouldn't quote each other as much as they do, but reporters are usually the most honest people you meet on political campaigns and the one quoted here is David Norton, a Georgia boy born and bred who writes for the *Atlanta Journal* and told a friend after one Florida trip: "It proves either that Florida isn't a microcosm of the country or that the country is in more trouble than we know. Southerners don't deserve a primary—they're too primitive. They should be left alone with George Wallace so they can play 'Dixie' and clap hands."

That's the hyperbole of a weary, disillusioned native son. But the exaggeration is not so great, and disillusionment with the Florida primary increased in proportion to the number of candidates who were placed on the ballot by a seven-member commission of state officials who faithfully discharged their responsibility to list all Presidential candidates "generally advocated or recognized in the news media."

Finally, there were eleven names—George Wallace and the Ten Dwarfs—and Jerry Thomas, President of the State Senate, was grumbling about a "jungle ballot," while Secretary of State Richard Stone dismissed the whole thing as "ludicrous . . . we're right in the middle of the Okefenokee Swamp and hip-deep in alligators."

The eleven alligators, in approximate order of importance, were:

Governor George Wallace of Alabama, who got 29 percent of the vote in the 1968 Florida general election and came on down hoping to do as well this time against the field. "That sawed-off little rat," as he was described to me in the office of Governor Reubin Askew, scheduled 29 days in the state, saying the same thing every day to guitar-pickin' revival meetings of 1,000 to 10,000 people. He shouted some and lied some, but he told those people they were being screwed by pointy-heads in Washington and New York—and they clapped hands. Two pipefitters, Myron Miller and Tom Johnson, argued one rainy afternoon in the Jacksonville shipyard about how much impact Wallace was having. "He's got 90 percent of the vote in this yard," Miller said. "That's crap," Johnson answered, "he ain't got more than 75 percent."

Senator Edmund Muskie of Maine, whose father's name was Marciszewski until an immigration officer changed it the day he arrived on Ellis Island from Poland. Muskie gave Florida twenty days. Most were uninspiring—he got something of a reputation for "crawfishing," a Florida term for scuttling sideways on the big issues, like busing—but he was there, standing tall as the anti-Wallace front runner, even if he was not exactly leonine about attacking ol' George.

A lot of voters had only one positive thing to say about Muskie, and Matthew Kendrick, a 36-year-old black Air Force officer said it in Tampa, as he watched Hubert Humphrey shake hands at the state fair: "I'm going to vote for Muskie because he's got the best chance to beat Wallace and that's what I'm interested in."

Senator Hubert Humphrey of Minnesota, who got 31 percent of the 1968 general election vote in Florida. Humphrey spent 40 days here in colorful ties and double-knit suits, giving out Muriel Humphrey's Beef Soup Recipe "for vim, vigor, and vitality," trying to prove he wasn't a burnt-out case. He proved he was as vigorous as ever and enormously popular among black people (15 percent of the Democratic vote) and among Miamians who can be generically described as 55-year-old blondes. But about the most vital thing he said as he crawfished energetically around the state was: "And we must say to all polluters: 'You cannot take from the land, the water, and the air unless you return that land, that water, and that air to its original source, unpolluted, uncontaminated, and unscarred.' " With those words ringing over 100 people at the Seafood Festival in a place called Grant, the Humphrey motorcade moved around a corner and Lee Strahle, his Brevard County coordinator, threw her seafood platter out the window of the second car. The paper plate, napkins, plastic fork and spoon, and ketchup at the foot of a palm tree could have been the official symbol of the 1972 Florida primary.

Senator Henry (Scoop) Jackson, who spent more time (50 days) and more money (somewhere between $500,000 and $1 million) on Florida than any other candidate. Some of the cash went for polls and Jackson sounded suspiciously like a poll-programed candidate, giving Floridians everything Oliver Quayle said they wanted. He was for defense, reminding each county how many jobs it would lose if Pentagon budgets were cut back; he was against busing and would spend five minutes of most speeches talking about his daughter, Anna Marie, the only candidate's daughter going to a public school with Negroes. There were 517 "Scoop" billboards, his television commercials began first, on January 11, and he was supported by the important newspapers and congressmen in north and middle Florida. But only 150

people came out to hear him in Frostproof, 30 in Fort Meade, 20 in
Auburndale and 200 in Haines City, including 40 members of the high
school band.

Mayor John Lindsay of New York, who spent 25 days and
$500,000 running like a man with nothing to lose—the most exciting
candidate left of Wallace. After his interview with the editors of the
state's largest newspaper, *The Miami Herald,* the paper reported: "He
is telling Florida voters things that no serious candidate for public
office has told them in a hundred years. He endorses 'the progressive
income tax' so easily that it almost seems he is unaware of the hysteria
Florida politicians engage in whenever the subject comes up. He sees
the busing of schoolchildren as a necessary expedient, even as the
Florida Legislature votes overwhelmingly, in effect, against it . . .
Through all of this he manages to remain elegant."

Senator George McGovern of South Dakota, who disappeared after
spending nine days in the state early in the year. The most newspaper
play he received during the closing weeks of the campaign was a story
denying rumors that he was "writing off" Florida to concentrate on
the March 7 New Hampshire primary and the April 4 Wisconsin
contest. In the end the only thing McGovern had going for him was
enthusiastic supporters around the state's colleges and universities,
men like Thomas Gilliam, a political science professor at the University of West Florida who was Escambia County coordinator of a
campaign that didn't seem to exist.

Representative Shirley Chisholm of New York, who spent just 18
days in the state but still left a unique mark. Politically, she was
another "new-priorities" Democrat who sounded like Lindsay or
McGovern, but, of course, she was also a black female running in the
old Confederacy, concentrating on campuses and black neighbor-
hoods. White students who came to see her cheered "Right on!" and
black students applauded, but other blacks, especially men, tended to
watch silently. Voters asked what her husband thinks, what kind of
education she had, whether she would favor blacks over whites; she
answered that her husband approves, she has an M.A. from Columbia, and "My dear, I'm a humanist."

The candidates who never did show up in Florida: Eugene McCarthy, Senator Vance Hartke of Indiana, Representative Wilbur Mills of Arkansas, and Mayor Sam Yorty of Los Angeles. Yorty was campaigning in New Hampshire, but he filed a suit in state court to get his name off the Florida ballot because it would "humiliate" him to run badly. Mills's presence was felt when friendly Panhandle legislators tried to keep his name off the ballot, no doubt for reasons similar to Yorty's.

On the morning after March 14, some of those alligators would come out of the swamp and some would not. An accident of the 1972 political calendar had given several hundred thousand Floridians the power to decide large questions for the rest of us. (No one was sure how many Democrats would turn out and professional estimates varied wildly between 25 and 55 percent.) Who was to be the American opposition candidate in 1972? Hubert Humphrey? Henry Jackson? John Lindsay? Floridians could make or break each or all of them. More important, where was the Wallace movement going? Floridians could decide that, too, and that's what this primary was all about.

It's kind of frightening to travel through Florida, watching the Disney campaigns and talking to bored, confused and, worse, bitter voters in this state and realize that it all does mean a great deal to the rest of the nation.

The place is a swamp, a state with primeval Southern political traditions in transition as hundreds of thousands of small-town and suburban Northerners following the sun become tangled, like the roots of the mangrove trees in the Okefenokee, with the county courthouse heritage of old Florida. The 6.7 million Floridians (2.8 million enrolled voters, 2 million of them Democrats) can much more easily be divided into their 67 counties than viewed as a single state; it's about 850 miles from Pensacola to Key West and that happens to be as far as from New York to Chicago or Atlanta. One political almanac describes the state as well as another.

The sharp growth has created many Floridas, politically and sociologically. The northern Panhandle of the state remains a part of the Old South, much like the adjacent hill country of Alabama and Georgia. But southern sections of Florida reflect the various Northern origins of their residents. The Miami area, for example, with its large Jewish population tends to vote like New York City.* Fort Lauderdale and Broward County just to the north vote like the very conservative suburbs of Chicago, as do the coast cities of Sarasota and Fort Myers. St. Petersburg normally goes Republican, its numerous senior citizens voting here as they did when they lived in New Jersey, or Minnesota, or Ohio. Tampa, with its large Spanish-speaking community, has a significant liberal-labor vote, although George Wallace ran well in its white working-class precincts. Cape Kennedy, nearby Orlando and Orange County, unlike other Republican centers in Florida, are less retirement colonies than Sun Belt boom towns. The politics here are like those in suburban Houston, Texas or Orange County, Calif.—very conservative. Jacksonville, however, is very much like a present-day city in the Old South, with nearly equal numbers of liberal Democratic Negroes, white, middle-class Nixon Republicans, and Wallace supporters.

Wallace is the big alligator and the big story in Florida. If he won by one vote over his nearest rival in the statewide total, he would be projected again as a national force and move credibly on to the Pennsylvania, Wisconsin, and Indiana primaries with his populist slogan: "Send Them A Message." He'd have the power to do anything he wanted to the Democratic Convention; he'd have the base for another American Independent party. But if he lost by one vote in a Southern state, he was going to have a tough time going North as the voice of the little people. I could write the headlines in *Time* and *Newsweek*—"Florida: The End for Wallace?"

Not many people thought the little spellbinder would lose. "With ten liberals running against him in Florida, it is absolutely impossible for Wallace to lose," said David Hurwitz, who is Humphrey's Florida

*This description, from *The Almanac of American Politics—1972* (Gambit Press), tends, as do those in most other publications of its kind, to exaggerate the Jewishness of Miami and of Florida as a whole. In fact, even in the Democratic primary Jews are expected to account for only about 5 percent of the vote, Protestants for 65 percent, and Roman Catholics for 25 percent. The newest group of Floridians, the more than 300,000 Cubans who have fled their island since 1959, are politically insignificant, with only 30,000 registered in Dade County (Miami) and half of those in the Republican party.

campaign manager. Private polls by candidates had shown Wallace moving steadily up from 20 to 35 percent of the vote—but primary polls are the blind dates of politics; it's difficult to predict what will happen because it's tough to determine which voters will come out on Election Day and which will stay home.

Men who know him better than I say ol' George wasn't convinced by published numbers showing him running away from the Yankee pack. They say he started a little edgy this time. What did he think when he got to Pensacola Airport early in February and 50 people cheered (2,000 waited there in 1968)? There were 3,500 people cheering when he stalked on to "Dixie" at the civic auditorium, but he got 11,000 at the high school there in 1968—that's 10 miles from the Alabama border.

Whatever he thought, he put on a good show as his press secretary, Billy Joe Camp, and the boys in red Wallace blazers sold bumper stickers for 50 cents and styrofoam straw hats for $1.50, and plump Wallace Girls passed around buckets for collection. It is pure "good Christian boy" stuff and there is one message. Wallace says the same thing, almost word for word, at every rally. Here it is, edited, and without the usual 36 interruptions for applause and a Rebel yell or two:

> This is the beginning of the average citizen of Florida and of the United States taking back the Democratic party to where it ought to be, with the people . . . You have a unique opportunity here in Florida to take this party back from the intellectual snobs of the East. I want to tell you I have been with all the greats, and the people from our region know as much about the problems of the country as do any of those from the Congress who are now down here in Florida, who created the problems in the first place.
>
> We have been relegated to a second-rate power as far as our national defense structure is concerned. We're going to be No. 1 in military strength.
>
> I'm going to talk about taxes. There is $200 billion of propertied income in this country that is tax exempt. We have $30 billion of the multibillion foundations, such as the Rockefellers', the Fords' and the Mellons' and the Carnegies', who have been given special treatment by the American Con-

gress at the expense of every workingman, businessman and farmer in Florida . . . You know we gave $155 billion of your hard-earned tax money to every Hottentot 10,000 miles away from us, and it goes down a rathole . . . The Government of our country, the bureaucrats, spending $30 billion to $40 billion deficit each year, brought on inflation and when they say freeze wages and prices, we're going to tell the Government they ought to freeze themselves and stop throwing our money away.

You cannot walk safely on the streets of any big city in Florida . . . In Chicago, they got a law that a policeman can't draw his gun until he's been stabbed, until he's cut bad and bleeding. Then he can draw his gun.

We have spent billions and billions and billions of our money on a welfare program that has paid people, in many instances, not to work. The other day a grand jury in New York City said a billion dollars in one welfare program had gone down the drain in one year . . . We want those welfare loafers to be put to work.

A victory for George Wallace is going to result in the taking of the batteries out of the buses that transport the little children throughout the state of Florida . . . They get on the bus dark in the morning, get off dark in the afternoon, and all because some social schemer in Washington says, 'That's good.' I'm the only candidate in this race who has consistently opposed what you oppose . . . I believe the people of Florida should control their own schools.

Those 500 words are the basic Wallace campaign. He traveled the state with his new wife, Cornelia, and a few friends and aides like a man running for county commissioner, rearranging the sentences to answer questions at news conferences, making one 40-minute speech a night, taping the words for $100,000 worth of television commercials.

There is a marvelously mystical and Biblically touching tone to the Wallace pitch. The words, Wallace told a persistent reporter in Pensacola, "mean whatever you think they mean."

They meant different things one afternoon to several hundred men and women, shivering in a chill wind off Cinco Bayou, who were waiting for Wallace in the Brooks Plaza Shopping Center in Fort Walton Beach. As he climbed onto a flatbed truck, hunched down in his black raincoat under a banner heralding "Wallace for God and

Country," three eighteen-year-old students from the local community college timidly held up two scrawled cardboard signs. "Power to the People," one said; the other said, "The Only Dope We Should Shoot Is Wallace." Steve Murphy, a burly man wearing the overseas cap of Okaloose Chapter, Veterans of Foreign Wars, walked over, looked at each poster in turn and said, "That's a good one . . . I want that 'Dope' thing taken down." Before the young men could decide what to do —"Do we have to?" one of them asked me—a middle-aged woman, who could have been their mother, leaped at them, ripped the sign away and began jumping up and down on it like the bad guy in a Popeye cartoon. She was quivering, her glasses almost jiggling off as she looked back for her own children, and I asked her name. "Mrs. George Wallace, you son-of-a-bitch," she screamed, "Mrs. George C. Wallace."

It is easier to judge that kind of Wallace impact than to be positive about what he will do at the polls. "Wallace looks stronger than he is because the 'anti' people make more noise in any election and because none of the other candidates has gotten through yet," said Parker Thompson, a successful young Miami attorney working for Lindsay, before dinner in his Coral Gables home. "People feel strongly about busing around here, too. But I certainly don't know anyone who would vote for Wallace. He can be beaten."

After dinner, two neighbors, a surgeon and his wife, stopped by for a drink on their way home from church. "Wallace voters?" the wife said, nodding outside toward the street of shaded $100,000 homes. "Well, there's the . . ." She proceeded to name a half dozen couples in the neighborhood.

No one, certainly no Florida politician I talked to in early 1972, knew what mix of votes Wallace would get from his true believers and from people casting protest votes. It is hard to conceive that many people in Coral Gables wanted George Wallace in the White House, but they could still get a message across by voting for him. The ironic beauty of primary elections is that the winners don't actually take office, they just get to keep running and talking.

The conversation that night at the Thompsons', three weeks before the election, focused on busing. It is easy for a Northerner to misjudge Southern feeling about busing because Southern school systems have always been funded and administered on a county basis, not on a municipal basis, as in New York or New Jersey. What this means is that you can't buy your way out of integrated schools in Florida. In the North, you can move to Greenwich, Connecticut, and talk about the terrible bigots in Queens while your own children go to alabaster schools. But when Federal courts put pressure on the Miami area, moving to Coral Gables was no escape. The Dade County Board of Education clustered schools, and the Coral Gables Elementary School was paired with George Washington Carver Elementary in a South Miami ghetto. (Before the buses of white Coral Gables kids arrived, Dade County put sidewalks in front of Carver for the first time and began hiring different kinds of teachers for ghetto schools.)

Part of Wallace's strength was rooted in the caution of his most formidable opponents—Muskie, Humphrey, and, to a lesser extent, Jackson, just didn't have the political guts to take him on. Muskie crawfished, and Humphrey and Jackson practically let Wallace manage their Florida campaigns; the Senators from Minnesota and Washington began to sound more and more like the man from Alabama with each new day and new poll.

There was both exuberance and desperation about the $500,000 Humphrey campaign in Florida. "It's the work I enjoy," he told a Tampa radio interviewer who asked why he is running nationally for the fourth time in twelve years. And he ran as hard and joyously as ever, leaping into the saddle of a wooden palomino on a merry-go-round at the state fair and trotting across an airport V.I.P. lounge to make ten minutes of phone calls to old supporters—"Hi, would you tell your daddy that an old friend of his is calling, Hubert Humphrey." He is so quick of feet, hands, and mind that it is easy to believe the apocryphal story that he once saw a tomato flying out of an audience and before it landed he was saying, "Speaking of agriculture, let me say this . . ."

But, away from the handshaking, he stopped for a moment on his chartered Boeing 737 and said, "Florida is the whole ball game for us. This is our national campaign." When the plane landed and there was another in the endless series of staff foul-ups—this time somebody forgot to tape-record a statement on President Nixon—he turned away mumbling, "Oh, for Christ's sake, let's go!"

Most of Humphrey's rhetoric, however, is not only pre-recorded, it's historic. At Spring Lakes Baptist Church in Jacksonville, he didn't talk to the small black audience about Wallace; instead, he recited the Pledge of Allegiance, then explained each line. In fact, "The People's Democrat," as Humphrey is billing himself this time, almost never mentioned Wallace—and often he just echoed his rhetoric.

In St. Petersburg, the subject was education: "Busing is not the answer to quality education . . . Now there are times when you can take a child in a poor neighborhood and in a very poor school with poor teachers and take him to a better school. We've been doing this for years . . . But to use busing as the sole way to get racial balance in your society is both a burden on the child and a burden on the educational system . . . I think it's time to quit using children, and for politicians to quit demagoguing about this issue."

In the Jacksonville shipyard, it was taxes: "The Federal tax system is rigged against you, the workingman. It is rigged against the average family . . . Our tax system penalizes the little man who works, and rewards wealthy investors who get checks from stocks, bonds, and large dividends . . . The time has come for a tax system that says to the wealthy, to the superrich, to big business, to the banker, 'You pay your fair share.' "

On foreign aid: "We loan money to Rio de Janeiro at lower rates of interest and longer term than we'll loan it to St. Petersburg or Tampa. As a matter of fact, we're much more generous with the rest of the world than with our own people . . . We've helped the rest of the world for 25 years and I hope nobody will think I'm selfish when I say that for the next 10 years we might want to help ourselves."

If Florida was to be Hubert Humphrey's last hurrah nationally, there were moments worth remembering. At Edwin Walters College, a small black school in Jacksonville, he lectured 200 students for 40 rambling minutes before finding the right words: "You and I could

do a lot together. I know this country. I've lived here a long time. I
know this Government. I know what makes it work and why it
doesn't. You give me your idealism, your energy. I'll give you my
experience. I'll give you everything I have."

Scoop Jackson also had it all on the line in Florida and his campaign there had been the longest, most expensive, dullest, and, in some
ways, the roughest. He raised close to $10,000 of the money he needed
in one night at a $30-a-plate dinner at the Jacksonville Hilton. The
toastmaster that night was Robert J. Smith, Jr., a local attorney who
is executive director of Jackson's finance committee in the state and
who sported the beginnings of a beard. "I hoped to come here looking
like Robert E. Lee," Smith began, "but I ended up looking like Gabby
Hayes."

Smith's little joke may be the story of the Jackson campaign. The
Senator from Washington came South trying to look like a new Dixie-
crat, the thinking-man's Wallace. But there was a difference: Wallace
is an exciting and instinctive politician, a great campaigner who tells
police escorts not to blow their sirens because it upsets people; Jackson turned out to be boring and clumsy. Seeing no black faces at one
of his dinners, he led reporters into the kitchen where he rushed up
to two black men loading garbage and said, "Boys, how'd you like
some chicken, boys!" The Senator could end up with one of those
campaigns in which morning-after arithmetic will show he spent $10
for every vote he got.

In telling Floridians everything they seemed to want to hear, Jackson was probably guided by his polls, secret surveys by Oliver Quayle.
It's hard not to suspect a politician who begins speeches by mentioning that John F. Kennedy picked him as Democratic National Chairman in 1960 because he was a Protestant—and who then proceeds to
mention his religion a half dozen times.

The tough and essentially negative quality of Jackson's campaign
was displayed in three-foot-wide enlargements of a *Washington Star*
story that were posted at his rallies. The huge headline read, "Busing
Works, Muskie Says." His speeches, delivered in a sleepily nasal
voice, often struck the same note. After emphasizing that he had

introduced a Constitutional amendment in the Senate to prohibit busing to achieve racial balance, he droned on:

"I'm sick of people who say law and order is a code word for racism ... I served as a prosecuting attorney ... The other Senators wanted to cut the defense budget. If Muskie had his way, there would have been a 45 percent cutback in military and civilian personnel and in payrolls in Florida ... I don't buy the nonsense some of the candidates are saying over and over again: 'This is a sick country.' "

But Jackson could not be written off too easily. He had interesting things going for him, including pillars of the state's political establishment and the United Jewish Appeal, which had contacted many prominent Florida Jews to tell them that if they're really interested in Israel they should work for Jackson, a fervent friend of the Jewish nation.

(In one county, Escambia, the line-up of local political leaders told something about the campaign: Jackson had what is known in Pensacola as "the older group," led by U.S. Representative Robert Sikes, whose district got an astonishing $642 million in Federal funds last year, including $460 million from the Department of Defense. Muskie had "the up-and-coming young lawyers," led by Louis Ray, Jr., president of the local Young Democrats. Humphrey had H. K. Matthews, former leader of the local chapter of the National Association for the Advancement of Colored People. Lindsay had Charles Fairchild, a 31-year-old accountant who volunteered after the Mayor's people asked the Young Democrats to please find someone. McGovern had Professor Gilliam, the political scientist. Mrs. Chisholm had Mrs. Augustus Black, a black dentist's wife. Wallace had no organization, but a guy named Eddie at the local Shell station asked: "Is anybody else running?")

Edmund Muskie, running in primaries all across the map, never really got into Florida with both feet. And when he was there, he always seemed undecided about which way to step when it came to Wallace and busing.

The national front runner was determined to ignore the Alabama Governor—"It's not to my advantage to talk about him" he told me earlier in 1972—and the line from Muskie's political chief, Jack English, was: "We'll treat Wallace as if he were Sam Yorty; he's not serious enough for us." Wallace, however, is not Yorty, and Muskie finally began to warn his small crowds about "wasting your vote." Then he moved on to calling the Governor "a divisive candidate who appeals to the worst in men."

On busing, Muskie came in like a lion and went out a little sheepish. In early January, he was bluntly telling the hard-faced men of Tallahassee not to expect him to act like a Southerner and that busing, unpleasant as it was, was a "necessary" tool to integrate schools. Without changing the substance of his answers to busing questions, the Senator soon stopped using words like "necessary" and began emphasizing the unpleasantness.

The hallmark in all of Muskie's Florida campaign was caution. He refused to risk anything, except on one issue: Nixon's proposal for a $5-billion space shuttle, a Florida job bonus that Muskie opposed from the day it was announced, saying that the nation needed those billions for problems in our own part of this universe. "Well, what state are we going to blow next?" he asked as he got back on his campaign plane after defending the anti-shuttle position at a hostile Orlando news conference. "One a day like this and we can all go home."

Lindsay was neither cautious nor cheap. He gambled $500,000 that he could find enough of a constituency in Florida to set himself up as a credible national Democratic candidate. Win or lose that gamble —he would loudly interpret anything better than sixth place as victory—the turncoat Republican ran the most exciting and professional campaign in the state. His staff spotted local issues that others missed and he was at Escambia Bay talking about "fishkills"—that's three or four acres of pollution-poisoned fish piled fifteen feet high, and the kills happen 300 times a year—and attacking American Cyanamid and Monsanto for dumping chemicals. His research was New York-style, and when confronted at one appearance by wives of American prisoners-of-war in Vietnam, Lindsay rattled off statistics and Vietnamese place names on the issue, while a few of his rivals, in the same situation, began by saying, "Huh?" His scheduling and stamina took him to twice as many places in a day, and his looks, well, there isn't much you can say about Lindsay's looks and celebrity except that he's asked a lot of questions about Johnny Carson. He exaggerated his accomplishments as Mayor—"I've reorganized the city government from top to bottom and now we've got some efficiency"—but he did have something to say and people came out to hear it:

"Governor Wallace represents everything that's wrong with this country . . . He represents division, hate, and fear. He would shut people out of our system and he has to be confronted . . . If he's brave enough to stand in the way of little children going into a schoolhouse, he ought to be brave enough to face me man-to-man in a debate . . . When we debate busing now, we are debating what this country stands for . . . We are debating whether we mean to provide justice to our black brothers and sisters . . . I'm for busing because it can bring black and white kids to school together, even though their parents still live apart."

The excitement and easy laughter on the red-white-and-blue "Lindsay '72" buses—"I'm going to get that blonde's vote first," the Mayor of New York said, looking out the window at the one face that stood out in a shopping-center crowd—sometimes seemed to be more entertainment than politics. Even though the blonde, Patricia Shockley of Panama City, after a handshake and a wink from Lindsay, said enthusiastically that she would vote for him, there are only so many Floridians who will go as far left as a John Lindsay—and the Mayor has to divide them with McGovern and Mrs. Chisholm. At the same shopping center, the Mayor of Panama City, M. B. Miller, pushed his way through a crowd of 500 to grab Lindsay's hand and wish him luck. But, the night before, Mayor Miller had introduced Wallace to a crowd of 3,000 as "this greatest of living men." And in a mock election in a political science class at Panama City High, Wallace got every vote but one—the teacher voted for Humphrey.

The timing of the Florida primary makes it the first big elimination contest for the Democrats and, fairly or unfairly, the men judged losers here may be on their way to oblivion no matter how beloved they are in Seattle or Cedar Rapids. There is real irony in Florida having that power because, among other things, Richard Nixon was going to sweep the state on November 7, 1972. The Republican Southern strategy was working. Consider the results of an informal poll taken the day after the *Pensacola News-Journal* endorsed Henry Jackson in the primary as "the only viable Democrat who can be trusted with the national security." Of the paper's twelve pressmen, ten said they would vote for Wallace in the primary—and all ten said they would vote for Nixon in November.

But then irony wasn't the only funny thing in Florida in 1972. Even Disney would have had to hustle to match the way Americans select their leader.

In Maclenny, they asked Henry Jackson whether he believed in God and he answered: "Sir, I am a Mason and a Presbyterian."

In Miami, they paraded the candidates, one at a time, through the Grand Ballroom of the Sheraton-Four Ambassador. Ed Muskie was there on January 8, reading a four-page statement pledging and re-pledging his undying opposition to Soviet anti-Semitism until Jack Germond, national political correspondent of the Gannett Newspapers, slapped shut his notebook and moaned, "My God, what Mickey Mouse!" Hubert Humphrey was in the same room on February 7, attacking Soviet anti-Semitism and calling on President Nixon to issue an executive order including kosher foods in federally-funded school lunch programs. And Humphrey was back on February 20, speaking to the South Florida Bank Administration Institute for 40 minutes about "the American Dream," and, so help me, at Table No. 8, after 30 minutes, one banker tugged at his vest, then leaned over to his wife and said, "You know, this is horseshit."

[Wallace won easily in the 1972 Florida primary, polling 42 percent of the vote against his ten Democratic opponents. Humphrey, whose candidacy essentially destroyed Muskie's, finished second with 18.6 percent, followed by Jackson with 13 percent, Muskie with 8.9 percent, Lindsay with 7 percent, and McGovern with 6.2 percent. In 1976, the Florida primary again shaped up as Wallace against the field with former Georgia Governor Jimmy Carter viewing himself as the principal challenger to Wallace's Southern domination.]

10 | George McGovern

Shirley MacLaine, like thousands of other Americans working to make George McGovern the 38th President of the United States, was ecstatic on the day after he won the Wisconsin Democratic primary election. "One of the remarkable things about him is that he never gets tired; he can campaign from six in the morning until midnight every day and he never gets tired," she said in a taxi coming back from La Guardia Airport. "I asked him how he did it and he told me that the secret is telling the truth. If you always tell the truth you don't have to use up energy trying to remember what you said in other places."

George McGovern was tired as hell a few days later when he flew from the same airport to New Bedford, Massachusetts, in the middle of another eighteen-hour day—and he didn't think he was in the sainthood business even if there is an apostolic bent among his followers. "I'm a politician, that's my business, and I don't regard it as a discrediting label at all," he said. "Running for President forces you to be somewhat more balanced than you would be simply as a Senator. Until you've actually sought the support of people of conflicting and varying backgrounds, you don't realize that you seldom have the luxury of taking a black-and-white position on issues. Politics is a compromising business . . . They talk about my ideologically fanatic supporters, but I have faith that the kids will understand when I have to make a political accommodation and will stick with me. This idealistic constituency of mine is a lot more pragmatic than they get credit for."

Politicians are different from you and me. The business of reaching for power does something to a man—it closes him off from other men until, day by day, he reaches the point where he instinctively calculates each new situation and each other man with the simplest question: what can this do for me? The process is as inevitable, and as frightening, as hardening of the arteries, and it shows in many ways —to a reporter it shows almost comically in interview after interview, year after year, when friends of the candidate invariably say, "You know, no one ever really gets close to John." Or Nelson, or Lyndon, or Jack, or Bobby, or George.

Take George, George McGovern, junior Senator from South Dakota and candidate for President. He was doing a twenty-minute tour of the Massachusetts Correctional Institution at Concord and he began with a walk through the yard with the warden, James L. O'Shea. Their conversation was questions and answers: How many men do you have in here? Six hundred seventy-eight; the capacity, though, is 550. What would be the ideal size for a prison like this? One hundred men, 150 tops.

The tour over, McGovern called a news conference and as the television lights went on he began speaking crisply: "There are more than 600 men here in an institution designed for only 550. Now, I believe that the ideal maximum capacity for an institution like this is 150—100 would be even better. I think the superintendent here would readily agree." James O'Shea blinked dumbly as the camera swung away from him and the candidate offered more instant penology.

At Boston State College, a young crowd of 2,000 or so cheered McGovern's every word on Vietnam, but Leslie Nathan, a Simmons College senior, wasn't sure what to do after McGovern answered her question about abortion by saying: "I really believe that on a matter as sensitive and difficult as this one is, the only recourse for those of you who favor legalized abortion legislation is to work at the state level . . . I personally think this is an extremely sensitive and personal issue and the final judgment will be made by the prospective mother and a good doctor."

It happens that if a prospective mother and a good doctor decide on an abortion in Massachusetts, they could go to jail. It also happened that McGovern did favor liberal abortion laws, but a lot of Roman Catholics in the Commonwealth didn't, and he said privately that he doesn't intend to lose an election over the issue. "It was a beautiful answer," Miss Nathan said, "but he really didn't say anything, did he?" Her friend, Carol Fink, said, "He's a politician!"

Exactly. James O'Shea, Leslie Nathan, and the rest of us were beginning to realize that, at least for that moment, George McGovern was the best in his very rough business. I asked Representative James Abourezk of South Dakota what kind of President he thought McGovern might be and he answered: "You never thought you'd be asking that question, did you? People underestimate George. He works at it, he's a great politician."

With limited physical and fiscal assets, unlimited ambition, and some help from Edmund Muskie's amazing disappearing act, McGovern had handcrafted a necklace of little miracles. I don't mean primary victories, real or moral—I mean that he had gotten this far without shedding too much of his minor-key radicalism; he had advanced "people politics" from slogan to strategy; he had refracted political images to the point that he was viewed as the anti-politician; he had discovered and was exploring a Democratic campaign that might just send Richard Nixon back to wherever he comes from.

Those four points—ideology, organization, imagery, and strategy —deserve a closer look.

• *Ideology*—McGovern, who is 49, came back from World War II service as a bomber pilot (he won the Distinguished Flying Cross during 35 missions over Europe) determined to be a Methodist minister like his father, but soon gave up the pulpit for Northwestern University's graduate school. He was something of a young radical, and on his way to a Ph.D. in American History he took time out to campaign for Henry Wallace in 1948. His views have moderated remarkably little since then—even though he has routinely fudged his ideas in public during times of political crisis.

In the campaign of 1972, in the words of William F. Buckley's *National Review*, he offered "a dazzling array of propositions calculated to comfort the afflicted and afflict the comfortable."

Among many other things, the candidate was really talking about income redistribution—he had proposed taking about $43 billion a year from people making more than $8,000 and giving it to those making less. That would be done by giving federal grants of $1,000 to every man, woman, and child in the country—a family of four would get $4,000 and there would be no welfare. Families earning $4,001 or more would have to start paying the federal money back through sharply escalating income taxes. Families earning more than $12,000 would have to pay all their $1,000 grants back, and anybody earning more than $50,000 would have to pay more than half their income (the rate keeps rising) back to the government—and that's all gross income, no more capital gains, municipal bonds, and all that. In addition, inheritances would be limited to about $500,000 in money and property—the government would confiscate everything else.

Besides that, McGovern proposed cutting the defense budget by about 40 percent by reducing military personnel from 2.5 million to 1.7 million, bringing half our troops home from Europe and all troops home from Southeast Asia and Korea, and scrapping parts of the Air Force and Navy. He would have had the federal government take over one third of local school costs and establish a national health care program not unlike Sweden's and provide a job for every American, hopefully by contracting with private companies for billions in public service work such as mass transportation, and if that failed, giving the unemployed government jobs.

That was only the beginning—the guy wasn't kidding. Or was he? I asked what he would do if the nation started to polarize, with strong feelings for and against his ideas, and he answered: "I wouldn't press anything to that point. I wouldn't press an issue that was tearing the country apart . . . I don't try to advance causes that are impossible . . . I just think the country's ready for major change."

McGovern can back off with the best of them; politics is his business. He may have been "right from the start," as his slogan says about Vietnam, having spoken strongly against the war in 1963. But he did get a little off-track in the middle, saying a couple of years later, "I am against a United States withdrawal from Vietnam . . . I think

President Johnson has conducted the military effort with great re-
straint . . . I support the strafing [of North Vietnamese targets]."

Still, George McGovern, the ideologue, is a whole man. The in-
triguing question was what George McGovern, the politician, would
do as he tried to keep expanding his constituency beyond Shirley
MacLaine and the kids—he is, after all, a politician whose Americans
for Democratic Action liberal voting index dropped from 94 to 43 in
1968, a re-election year in which he faced conservative opposition in
South Dakota.

• *Organization*—In 1971, McGovern student organizers received a
50-page mimeographed manual, touching just about every nit-picking
detail of registering college students to vote, with hints like: "*Important:* Emphasize in all dealings with the election board that you plan
across-the-board youth voter registration, that you will not turn down
non-McGovern supporters who wish to register. (This does not prevent you from concentrating on supporters in your follow-up
efforts.)"

The candidate is the greatest name-collector in politics—he had
40,000 listed in South Dakota; he had something like 600,000 overall.
And each of those people had done something with or for McGovern
at some time, many of them filling out one of millions of cards that
say: "Would you like to . . . Work at headquarters? . . . Recruit on
campus? . . . Canvass? . . . Organize your town or neighborhood?
. . . Drive your car for the campaign? Are you experienced in . . .
Statistical analysis? . . . Press and publicity? . . . Fundraising? . . .
Clerical skills, typing, key-punching?"

The organization was as decentralized as the nation's P.T.A.s. Each
one, in a neighborhood or small town, ran its own show, raising its
own money, doing whatever it wanted with an occasional visit from
a paid ($30 to $50 a week) area coordinator who delivered some
literature and checked to see whether extra help was needed. Usually
it was not. People were doing their own thing, like Susan Fiorentini,
a 25-year-old nurse, who handed out literature and telephoned voters
in Quincy, Massachusetts, answering questions about the candidate—
as far as she knew, Frank Mankiewicz might have been a linebacker
in the National Football League.

Mankiewicz, who was Robert Kennedy's last press secretary, was the senior political coordinator, or something like that, and he was at the center of the operation with three other men, boy wonders Gary Hart and Rick Stearns and an old pol named George McGovern. (Despite publicized women's lib support, the women who got close to the candidate were the pleasant-company type.) Hart, the field operations manager, was a 34-year-old Denver lawyer who looks more like Warren Beatty than Warren Beatty, the actor who hung around the campaign and raised money; Stearns was a 27-year-old Rhodes scholar from the '68 McCarthy campaign who organized non-primary states and did things like busing in students to delegate-selection meetings so that McGovern suddenly showed up winning a few precious delegates in unlikely places like Vermont and Louisiana. But essentially The Man ran his own show—one night about midnight, in the Statler-Hilton Hotel in Boston, a young staffer walked up to Kirby Jones, the traveling press secretary, and said, "You better forget about Saturday's schedule; he just said he thought maybe we should go to California for that fund-raising concert."

These are the highlights of twenty minutes in Mankiewicz's cluttered Washington office one week (the quotes are usually his secretary's voice): "Congressman Rangle is calling" . . . "It's Jimmy Breslin again" . . . "Shirley MacLaine, Pete Hamill, and José Torres just flew in to National Airport and they say they have to see you" . . . Charles Guggenheim, their television man, calls to say he can get Ruth Jones, an almost legendary media time-buyer, who had been working for Lindsay . . . One young man comes in with a press-release draft using the phrase "year of the people" and Mankiewicz changes it to "year of change" because the first phrase was used by McCarthy in '68 . . . Another young man appears with proposed media budgets for primary states—Ohio, $170,000; Nebraska, $30,000; Oregon, $46,000; South Dakota, $17,000; New Mexico, $15,000; California, $460,000; New York, $400,000 . . . Finally, the candidate calls and says he wants to talk for a few minutes about busing because he is speaking at a lunch of the American Society of Newspaper Editors and expects questions from Southern editors.

(McGovern does support busing but there are geographical degrees to that support. An editor in Florida heard different McGovern rhetoric on busing than, say, a Massachusetts editor heard. On Channel 10 in Miami it began: "Frankly, I don't like busing. It's expensive, it's wasteful, it's a nuisance, it's an inconvenience for parents and children . . ." At Boston State College, it began: "I support the Supreme Court.")

• *Imagery*—"McGovern on the Issues" was a 66-page magazine-size booklet with print about the size of the Manhattan telephone book's. It was a formidable and brilliant piece of work that immediately got across the impression that the candidate has researched and pondered everything from H-bombs to boll weevils.

But reading the book—and I'll bet no one did—gave you a different impression: George McGovern is a Senator who talks a lot, which is what the U.S. Senate is about, and co-sponsors a lot of high-minded and unpassed resolutions and bills. Only in a few areas—Vietnam, agriculture, nutrition, and, to a certain extent, conversion of industry from defense to domestic production—do you get the feel of work, of commitment. The rest of it has the feel of an anecdote in McGovern's authorized biography about a day in 1969 when he rushed back to his Senate office from lunch with a newsman, exclaiming, "Sandy Vanocur says the economy is going to be a hot issue. We're going to have to do something about the economy." "What?" an aide asked. "Something," McGovern answered.

In the urban policy section of "McGovern on the Issues," there were lines like, "McGovern proposals include: Decent housing for every family . . . Encouragement of resident participation in the planning and implementation of renewal programs." But the words were not as important as that first impression that McGovern was decidedly deeper and more specific than other politicians. (I was surprised in interviews to find that Senators and their staffs who worked with both men generally considered Ed Muskie more intelligent than McGovern.)

McGovern has said somewhat more than Muskie and a great deal more than Humphrey, but the impression that he alone was seeking and speaking the truth was exaggerated. Those things don't happen in political campaigns; the American political system doesn't produce anti-politicians, even if the best campaigns produce the illusion of anti-politics.

What campaigns generally produce is superficial and simplified distortions—pace and pressure of eighteen-hour days guarantee that. So McGovern was cheered each time he said that he would take care of the 40 percent of American corporations that pay no income tax. That statistic was wrong and it may be ridiculous. According to the Internal Revenue Service, where McGovern's staff got the figures, 40 percent of the country's 1.67 million corporations had either no income or lost money and thus paid no taxes. Another 16 percent did make some kind of profit and paid no taxes. And almost half of the nonpayers were corporations with total assets of from $1 to $50,000, the lowest I.R.S. category. The point is not that the corporate tax structure is any good—it undoubtedly stinks—but that McGovern and every other politician often spend a lot of time talking about things they don't know very much about.

• *Strategy*—"George McGovern, of course, can't be nominated, and even if he is, it doesn't make any difference, since the Democrats are tearing themselves apart in the primaries and Nixon is going to walk in"—that was the conventional wisdom of the day. And I thought then it was probably nonsense. The Democrats, particularly McGovern—with significant help from the other George, Wallace— seemed to have stumbled into a winning strategy: hitting the money issues, playing to people who are convinced they're being screwed and ignored, people who hate the war and feel a need to be part of something meaningful like the great pyramid-club organization that had come together for McGovern.

McGovern had been building a constituency body by body, and that was a grueling, discouraging labor. He started with some kids— the ones who weren't turned off by 1968—and with the smuggest of liberals, the kind of people who clapped self-righteously at a town house in Philadelphia when their host, Joseph Miller, a financier, said: "Finally we have a man who represents us, the principled, thinking people."

However, there aren't enough principled, thinking people or students to win many elections, and McGovern coolly went after the middle of the country, the white ethnics and all that. Like the old days in South Dakota, it was one-on-one, the only way McGovern could do it with his Liberace voice and his cheap-false-teeth delivery (actually he has expensively capped teeth). But he did it very well, walking through one gloomy factory after another—"It's like a Clifford Odets set," said John Austin of *Time* in a Lawrence shoe factory.

James Volis operates the toe-last machine in another Massachusetts factory, the Lowell Shoe Co., and he gets 98 cents for forming the toes of 36 pairs of shoes—"I'm like an athlete, I have to be in shape to make money"—and he makes $160 in a good week. He was for McGovern because "he's for the poor people, and that's us." My guess is that four years ago Volis thought of himself as middle class, and wasn't sure that McGovern could hold him and others if the Republicans started calling the Democrat a socialist and reminding people in Lowell that there are poorer people, black people, at their backs—but at the time McGovern had a hunk of Middle America.

McGovern had to reach out for black and brown hands, and that was not so easy for him. He's from a different world, and even there, in South Dakota, the Oglala Sioux on the Pine Ridge Reservation described McGovern to a reporter as "the man who came here with Bobby Kennedy." He probably deserved just that—this month he visited the reservation and talked about the killing of Raymond Yellow Feather by drunken white men and later told an Easterner: "About all you can do is listen, try to give them a sympathetic ear. There's a great deal of tension but it quiets down until the next incident."

"I had the feeling that McGovern and his people thought the solution to Indian problems was just keeping them happy, giving them a little whiskey," the Easterner said later.

And in West Philadelphia, at 52nd and Market Streets, he was worse, almost dazed by the urban black lifestyle, led around by local black politicians and asking them if one mumbling dude is "really stoned." The people to whom he was introduced ask, "Governor who?" and a block away a black Humphrey operator with the unlikely name of Edward Dasilvio chants into a loudspeaker: "Who is this McGovern? You get off the bus in South Dakota and you might get yourself hung!"

At that point, in May, 1972, you'd have to book McGovern as the favorite in California and Oregon—and if he won there, how could "they" deny him the nomination and give it to Hubert? Perhaps "they" couldn't—they, the old party leaders and George Meany's friends, might not even be at the Democratic convention in Miami Beach. The party's commission to reform delegate selection procedures—the commission chairman was what's-his-name, the junior Senator from South Dakota—did its job so well that there would probably be something close to a complete turnover of delegates from the 1968 show.

The candidate hoped to go to Miami Beach with 1,200 of the 1,500 delegates needed for the nomination. His delegates were people like Caroline Rees of Andover, Massachusetts, assistant professor of Asian history at Bradford College and vice president of the Women's National League for Peace and Freedom, who said, "I didn't vote in 1968, I couldn't vote for one of them. I don't know what I'll do if McGovern is not nominated. I won't compromise my conscience— that's all I'm answerable to."

Even if "they" could hold control of the convention hall, they had to live with the threat of the McGovern organization playing third party, and they would have to remember that George might be a little radical but that he was a regular guy—not a nut like Gene McCarthy. Remember McGovern was up on stage with his arm around Hubert in '68, he's playing games with guys like Meade Esposito, and he sort of came out for Bob Byrd for the Supreme Court. He's a politician and some of that ideological stuff will be chipped away by his ambition —George would rather be President than right.

As nice a guy as he is, George McGovern's ambition, self-righteousness, and vanity have always gotten to people. The official story is that he first seriously thought about being President of the United States when he outpointed Humphrey and McCarthy in a 1968 debate before the California delegation to the national convention. But when I asked him that question, he laughed and said it was when he saw the returns coming in during his first election to the House of Representatives in 1956. I believed him.

The minister's son was a little heavy with lines like, "I will never advocate any position except what I believe to be the truth." He is also the only professional I've ever seen who tries to consistently cut off applause by snapping his hands and trying to speak his next line—it seemed a new level of political egocentricity, as if what the audience wanted to do was unimportant and only his words mattered.

Then there was the business with the comb. He's cursed with disappearing hair and was constantly pulling out a long comb to rearrange what's left. For larger crowds, he ducked down and pulled out a powdery little compact to examine himself in the mirror.

But he's a politician—throbbing veins of ambition, self-righteousness, and vanity are what keep politicians going. That's the way it has to be, said former Senator Charles E. Goodell, who has played power games with McGovern over the years. First, Goodell finessed McGovern by getting out in front on the war issue, introducing the first legislation cutting off military funds; then McGovern refused to support Goodell's bill but rewrote it and slipped it in as Hatfield-McGovern; then they got together as co-sponsors of the final bill, agreeing, among other things, that all the sponsors would get copies of the computer print-outs of the names of the 200,000 people who responded to their financial appeals for the anti-war movement. McGovern's staff volunteered to compile the tapes and a funny thing happened: Goodell and the other sponsors never got them for their campaigns, but they became part of the magnificent lists on which McGovern is basing his run for the White House.

"There are two things worth saying about George McGovern," Goodell said later. "He's a very sincere guy and a politician who knows exactly what he's doing. I'd be much more concerned if George believed what he believes and wasn't a consummate politician."

11 | Richard Nixon, Inc.

There was plenty of time to read in Miami Beach during the week of the 1972 Republican National Convention. One of the things I looked at was *The New Industrial State* by John Kenneth Galbraith, a book written in 1967 which managed to give a pretty fair description of the stockholders' meeting of Nixon, Incorporated:

> With even greater unction although less plausibility, corporate ceremony seeks also to give the stockholders an impression of power . . . As stockholders cease to have influence, however, efforts are made to disguise this nullity. Their convenience is considered in selecting the place of meeting. They are presented with handsomely printed reports . . . During the proceedings, as in the report, there are repetitive references to *your* company . . . Votes of thanks from women shareholders in print dresses owning ten shares "for the excellent skill with which you run *our* company" are received by the management with well-simulated gratitude. All present show stern disapproval of critics . . . No decisions are taken. The annual meeting of the large American corporation is, perhaps, our most elaborate exercise in popular illusion.

It would be an illusion to view what happened in Miami Beach during the third week in August, 1972, in strictly political terms. The delegates themselves were almost irrelevant, small stockholders bustling busily from hotels to Convention Hall with stacks of red, white, and blue literature complementing tri-colored dresses and decorations, rarely mentioning politics, chattering instead the endless small talk of their endless suburb—"Where are you from? . . . Oh, we visited

153

there in . . . We have two children living near . . . George is with
. . . We had a friend who raised German shepherds when we lived
in . . ."

The convention was not a political event. It was an elaborate cere-
mony of a mature corporation, celebrating remarkable sales and better projections, the merchandising and marketing skills of its faceless
managers—what does Bob Haldeman look like?—and above all, celebrating the American corporate values: loyalty, autonomy of the
organization, controlled growth, pragmatism. When elections or candidates did intrude, they were usually discussed within the framework
of that value system. At a pleasant and mannerly reception of the
Republican National Committee, Mrs. Carla Coray, the Republican
Chairman of Hawaii, said sadly to a committeeman from Oklahoma:
"Poor Pete McCloskey. He had so much potential. *Why* did he have
to do this to himself?"

The Republicans aren't a political party anymore, at least not in the
sense that they have any commitment to anything but their own
organization (the corporation) or winning (sales). There is no ideology
left in what used to be the party of Lincoln and Chiang Kai-shek, the
party of isolating godless Communism, balancing budgets, and keeping government's controlling hand off the free enterprise system. The
mature corporation is now solidly in the grip of the managers (there
is also no giant anymore at Ford or General Motors, no Henry Ford
or Alfred P. Sloan). Nixon, Inc. is what James MacGregor Burns once
forecast the Republican party would become:

"Their main base is in the suburbs, with all the advantages and
disadvantages appertaining thereto. During the middle run, at least,
they are far more likely to follow a tactic of opportunism, living off
the errors of the Democrats, than to take direction either toward the
principled left or the principled right."

Pity the poor delegates, particularly the delegates of the principled
right—52 percent of those surveyed by *The Miami Herald* described
themselves as "fairly conservative" or "very conservative." With their
enameled manicures and lapel pins, they tended to look confused,
even a bit ill, as Barry Goldwater beamingly spoke of "opening doors"

to Mao Tse-tung. "These people are being had and some of them know it," said Martin Nolan of *The Boston Globe* as he came off the convention floor just as Goldwater brightened the crowd up by reminding them that Americans are 6 percent of the world's population but consume "over 52 percent of everything of material worth in the world."

The 1,348 men and women who were delegates consume and sell at a pretty fair rate. If there was an average delegate in Miami Beach, he was a small-businessman from the Middle West, a merchant or an automobile dealer, earning more than $25,000 a year.

What brought the 1,348 together was probably a middle-aged, middle-class, Protestant sense of shared responsibility. Galbraith, in Miami Beach as a television commentator, called the whole thing "a grand conclave of public respectability." Like any group securely within a corporation, the delegates were also pretty sure of what they were against: Disloyalty and attacks on the autonomy of their organization. That meant that the bad guys were not so much the Democrats and George McGovern as they were disloyalists like Congressman Paul McCloskey and outsiders like "The Media."

McCloskey was in Miami Beach but couldn't get his name placed in nomination as a symbolic challenge to Richard Nixon's renomination—the delegates, like any responsible stockholders, followed the advice of their management and changed the rules to prevent a McCloskey appearance. Another Republican dissident, Congressman Donald Riegle, a liberal from Flint, Michigan, didn't even get to the Beach as a delegate or party official. And Riegle, a former executive of IBM with a Harvard Ph.D. in management, and the congressman from a district dominated by General Motors, was well qualified to understand what had happened.

"You're on to something when you compare the party with a corporation," he told me before the convention. "In big business today, there are no owners, just managers. There is no moral force, no one stands for anything except loyalty and uniformity. That's why Nixon people can go any way on any question. That's what management is supposed to be—thoughtful, cool, rational decision-making.

The only problem is that the Nixon types aren't very good—they're poor managers. What were they before they came to the White House? Narrow-gauge types, public relations men, marketing guys ... I'd respect them if they were good or had long-range goals—GM does. I had more freedom at IBM than I do in the party. At IBM if you played by the rules and you were right, you'd win one every once in a while."

The media are to the Republican party what Ralph Nader is to the party's merchandisers. Nixon, Incorporated's basic attitude was that what the corporation does, even in the White House, was usually nobody else's business. If it was, then the public relations department would let something out, maybe releases on promotions which didn't mention why the predecessor is being canned. The poison between press and party was stunning for those few days in Miami Beach. "I can't speak to them without remembering that I hate them," said a middle-aged *New York Times* reporter noted for his fairness and Clark Kent mild-mannerisms. "They're so goddamned self-satisfied." I picked him at random—at least half the reporters I met were saying the same thing several times a day. Delegates and reporters had trouble looking at each other, as if both had scars too horrible to look at. There was one lady, however, who looked very much like my mother and who did meet my eyes in the elevator of the Fontainebleau Hotel one morning at 2 A.M. "If I wasn't a good Republican," she announced, "I'd go home right now. Dirty stinking reporters are everywhere in this town."

The autonomy of the party and the corporate right to pick its own members (employees) were also at the core of the only real disputes of convention week. It was significant that those little aberrations were over party rules and not over issues or platforms or candidates. The debates over changing the rules for delegate selection in 1976 should be considered in the light of this comment by a Senate staff member working within the Rules Committee: "The fact is that most of our people want to restrict membership. The argument is that why should blacks and women's-liberation types be brought in to disrupt things? The committee members are saying that the outsiders believe different things and don't belong in our party."

Ironically, Nixon, Incorporated was in the process of recruiting new people, mainly middle-class Catholics and Jews. But that expansion of the party's Protestant base could be interpreted as an indication that many more Catholics and Jews are now eligible for membership—they're pretty much like "us" now. Welcome to America! Welcome to our company.

(One of the uniquely Republican events of the week was a Worship Service on the Sunday morning before the convention began, and a couple of moments there were interesting. A rabbi named Irving Lehrman said, "The Judeo-Christian tradition made possible the American Dream." Republicans used to talk about the Christian or Western traditions. Afterwards, Frank Borman, the former astronaut who had begun the service with his famous moon-reading from Genesis, was approached by an admiring couple who said they were from Minneapolis. "Oh, yes," Borman said, "Minneapolis-Honeywell really helped with the space program.")

The sales literature of Minneapolis-Honeywell—or of Ingersoll-Rand, a corporation I once worked for as an engineer and copy writer —isn't much different from the stuff that was neatly piled around Miami Beach lobbies. The film strips, visual displays, and smiling hostesses in the corners were familiar, too. If sales were down in your district, you could pick up the official looseleaf book of the training and education division of the Republican National Committee and find suggested organization charts and such hints as: "The Special Events Chairman should report to the Scheduler . . . Be sure realistic cost estimates are included . . . While your candidate should stay on the high road, other members of the campaign organization can sometimes take a lower road and actively attack the opponent regarding these same weaknesses . . . Each fund raiser should receive a kit of supplies containing such aids as a script giving a suggested sales pitch for use by inexperienced fund raisers . . . In short, we are simply saying that you will win more elections if you *plan your work,* then *work your plan.*"

The Republicans have been enlarging their corporate vocabulary since 1966 when their national chairman Ray Bliss (now vice chairman) issued a statement after congressional and local elections without mentioning a word about issues or philosophy. He stuck to the jargon of a district manager boosting the morale of his salesmen, saying: "Victories across the nation resulted from the teamwork and dedicated effort on the part of our candidates and party leaders at every level."

By 1968, Nixon, Incorporated was being formed, and the candidate announced his political staff with a classic press release that said: "A strength of the policy group is that it telescopes time and activity. Pivotal decisions, which in a corporate executive committee would be considered weekly or monthly, are acted on daily. Ideas are synthesized, summarized, digested and abstracted; decisions are then made quickly by the policy group with full-fledged dedication to the main task of electing Richard Nixon President. All personal whims and emotional frills are subordinated to this task."

The convention itself worked a plan that included detailed scripts of each public session—the first night's was 50 pages long—telling chairmen which delegates to call on for "spontaneous resolutions," what each person would say and how long each "applause break" and "music break" could be. The music breaks were especially important to the party's strategy to manipulate network television coverage of the proceedings—the band played on for precisely the number of minutes the networks needed to get in commercials. (The Republicans also used only a couple of sentences to introduce important speakers because they had figured out that network anchormen usually do their commentary and analysis during introductions, and convention managers wanted to keep Cronkite's and Brinkley's words at a minimum and the party line at a maximum.)

Shutting off outside voices is a sensible, businesslike thing to do, and the Republicans are still the party of business even if business has changed. It's fashionable these days to say that there is no real difference between the Republican and Democratic parties, but that's much too quick. If the Republicans can be characterized as the corporate party, the Democrats are the academic party. When John F. Kennedy wanted a manager, he turned to a Republican, Robert McNamara of Ford; when Richard Nixon wanted ideas, he turned to a Democrat, Daniel Patrick Moynihan of Harvard.

You can usually tell involved Republicans and Democrats apart when you meet them, and not just by their haircuts. In Washington today, the Republican assistant secretary, or whatever, is a corporate man with attendant habits, disciplines, strengths, and weaknesses. His government service is an interlude. His life is back there in Los Angeles, at Union Oil. (Bob Haldeman, for instance, was a vice president of J. Walter Thompson.) He talks about going home and "making some money," and if he says he's from *The Chicago Daily News* —as one did—it turns out that he wasn't a reporter, he was in charge of merchandising the newspaper's syndicated columns and comics. The Democrat ex-assistant is still in Washington, too, and he sees his exile as an interlude. Government—that is, changing things—is what he thinks he does, and he's biding his time right now at the Urban Coalition, with a trade association or at a foundation.

The Republicans have effectively adapted corporate techniques to politics: market research, computerization, scientific product selection, adequate financing. The Republicans are still No. 2 (in voter registration, at least) and they try harder. They don't waste much energy on internal squabbles—primaries and noisy conventions cost money and they don't count in the annual report—and, except for their vocal right-wingers, they don't get hung up on ideology. Or on prejudice—I don't think it's an accident that the only black man in the U.S. Senate is a Republican, Edward Brooke of Massachusetts, one of the convention's keynote speakers. Probably no white Republican could be elected in that state. That's what market research is all about—if Democrats will buy a black toothpaste, give them a black toothpaste; if they want fluoride, give them fluoride. If they want it striped with liberalism, stripe it.

The corporate party is, understandably, five to ten years ahead of its academic rivals in the application of business know-how to politics. (That doesn't mean they always run better campaigns; the Democrats tend to be much more creative, and that works, too.) In his 1969 study of political technology, James M. Perry of *The National Observer* concluded: "It is a fact that the Republicans have pre-empted the new technology . . . I am sure the Democrats will ultimately catch on and that the balance will be restored. Meanwhile, however, the Republicans will continue to win elections they should, by rights, be losing."

There is also one corporate practice with technological input that's not discussed outside the company—industrial espionage. I haven't the vaguest idea how much of it actually goes on—most companies avoid the questionable publicity of prosecuting competitors if they find a bug in their board room—but it's a fair conclusion that the Republicans would also be ahead in a field like that, which may or may not have any relation to the bugging of the offices of the Democratic National Committee in the Watergate complex.

The interesting questions about private espionage, however, aren't technical. They are moral. If the XYZ Corporation found out it could eavesdrop on its biggest competitor, would its managers sit down and talk about right and wrong? Or would they do a cost analysis? My own experience answers cost analysis: how much is the information worth and how much will it cost us to get it?

Corporations, as far as I can tell, are amoral by definition. That is the bottom line. That's what the Republican party was about in Miami Beach in 1972.

Politics, of course, is sometimes immoral. But at least politics and political debate tend to focus, however blurredly, on questions of right and wrong, good and evil, justice and injustice. One of the statements in Charles Reich's *The Greening of America* that I agreed with was: "Administration seeks to remove decision making from the area of politics to the area of 'science.' It does not accept democratic or popular choice; this is rejected in favor of professionals and experts and a rational weighing of all the factors."

Reich, however, is hardly the man to talk to about corporations; he seems to think they're going to fade away in a cloud of flowers. Reading in Miami Beach while the Republicans gave their vote of confidence to the present management, I came across three thoughts from other sources:

Galbraith in *The New Industrial State:* "The men who now run the large corporations own no appreciable share of the enterprise. They are selected not by the stockholders but by a board of directors which narcissistically they selected themselves."

Antony Jay in *Management and Machiavelli:* "Large states and large corporations have an interest in the *status quo.* They make accommodations with each other, they have gentlemen's agreements, they settle for a fair return on capital and an easy life . . . [They have] no judiciary which is independent of the executive."

Peter F. Drucker in *The New Society:* "[The corporation's] governmental authority over men must always be subordinated to its economic performance and responsibility . . . The first concern of the enterprise must be for profitability and productivity, not for the welfare of its members. The members are not the citizens for whose benefit the institution exists."

Taken together, Galbraith, Jay, and Drucker are describing a rational, well-managed system. The frightening thing to me is that they could be describing the Republican National Convention with the managers smiling down at the stockholders, the ladies in print dresses, and their husbands from the insurance agencies. Very few of the delegates, as it happened, were actually employees of large corporations. But somewhere, in some way, they had absorbed corporate basic training, and that somewhere was probably in the suburbs where they live door-to-door-to-door with the organization men. The corporate families are the interchangeable solid citizens of an endless suburb—when an office manager at Allied Chemical in Wayne, New Jersey, is transferred, his house is filled by a new district sales manager for Dayton Rubber whose old house in Clayton, Missouri, is filled by an engineer at General Dynamics. The suburbs, I suspect, have become a kind of decentralized national company town.

The verbal coin of the national company town has to be small talk because in the end the people next door never really know each other —they only know they are the same. And that was the language of Miami Beach when the Republicans came together for their prearranged vote of confidence in the current management.

There really was nothing to talk about, and it was disconcerting to them to occasionally find a neighbor who shouted a lot or whose kids ran wild. Don Riegle, the discontented young congressman from Flint, was in Miami an afternoon before the convention opened to talk to a platform subcommittee about Vietnam, trying to relate his opposition to the war and bombing to the Republican heritage as the "party of individual human rights." He remembered looking up during his statement into smiling, polite and blank faces and thinking, "They don't know what I'm talking about. What the hell am I doing here?"*

*Riegle left the Republican party after the 1972 election and was re-elected as a Democrat in 1974.

Three

The Big Apple

12 | Abraham Beame

Fifty years ago, Mary Ingerman was *the* girl at the Saturday night dances at the University Settlement House at Rivington and Eldridge Streets on the Lower East Side. "She was the belle of the ball," recalled an old man. "The prettiest, the most popular, the best dancer, the girl all of us wanted to be with. Abe didn't have a chance."

Abe Beame couldn't dance. He was the smartest boy at the High School of Commerce, and he was a tough kid—"Spunky" was his nickname—who sometimes led his own gang into the rock-and-bottle-throwing "block fights" of the Jewish ghetto. But he was just about five feet tall and he couldn't dance. He would sit against the wall of the gymnasium of the settlement house all night and watch Mary dance with others. Then he would ask to walk home with her, and she sometimes said yes—for seven years it was their ritual. Mary Ingerman and Abe Beame were married four days after he got his accounting degree from the night school at City College.

Twelve years ago, Abe Beame, a tiny, self-contained package of caution and calculation, began watching the dances that pick the Mayor of New York. He even went onto the floor and stumbled into a tall WASP named John Lindsay. He still couldn't dance. Jean Kerr, who can talk the way she writes, came into the city room of the *Herald Tribune* one night in 1965 and saw Beame trying hard on television news, then said: "It's embarrassing. Watching Abe Beame campaign is like watching your father get drunk at a party."

But times and dances change—and Abe Beame waited. Perhaps New York would walk home with little Abe. He is a man of numbers

—the Controller, the Budget Director, the Certified Public Accountant, the high school bookkeeping teacher, the Brooklyn precinct captain who could count votes—and most of the numbers looked very good for him at the beginning of 1973.

He might not be getting his name in the papers very much, but Beame began his campaign for Mayor with a real head start: a positive image and a true constituency—elderly Jews living outside Manhattan. These are some of his numbers, culled from past election returns and various public and private polls: more than 85 percent of enrolled Democrats know who Beame is; more than 40 percent of Democrats believe he has done an "excellent" or "pretty good" job as Controller; he is the first choice of between 20 and 30 percent of the Democrats who have voted in past primary elections and the second choice of over 15 percent more; more than 40 percent of the Democratic primary votes will be cast by Jews, and Jewish voters gave Beame two thirds of their primary votes in 1965; a third of the primary votes will be cast by people 50 and over, and Beame is far and away the first choice of older city Democrats; the longer a Democratic voter has lived in the city the more favorably he views Beame, and more than 70 percent of Democratic primary votes will be cast by people who have lived here for more than twenty years.

Pretty dull stuff, but so is Beame—color him gray, his hair, his clothes, his skin. He's not very quotable and he is a reactive politician who does not initiate proposals or issues but, instead, will absorb anything that sounds good or pick apart things that don't. At any rate, the 1973 New York style was to spend as much time as possible defining and deploring problems and as little time as possible specifying solutions. It was a perfect year for gray.

Beame, as described by his 1965 campaign manager, Edward Costikyan, is "unexciting . . . deliberate . . . careful . . . meticulous . . . methodical." Some of that boredom, though, is calculated; it's Beame's basic defense against a larger world. Richard Aurelio, who negotiated with Beame for three years as Lindsay's Deputy Mayor, said: "He is the most guarded man I've ever met. He never once answered a question directly. It was always, 'Let me think about it'

... 'We'll see what we can do.' " Over the years, Mary Ingerman Beame's complaints to friends have been that her husband never, never gives anything of himself, never lets another person know what he is really thinking.

A man is what he is. Beame is known inside the Municipal Building as "grandmother" and inside City Hall as "that little nit-picker," and he can't be changed, certainly not this late in life. Beame, under pressure from both the enemy, John Lindsay, and a new friend, Robert Kennedy, tried to change into "Fighting Abe" in 1965—and it was a disaster.

During the taping of a television commercial, Kennedy needled, "Abe, look at me. Get mad. Show you care." Then Bobby explained that when the camera rolled he would point his finger at Beame and say, "All right, Abe Beame, tell us why you deserve to be Mayor of New York." "That's great," Beame said. "Then what do I say?"

Kennedy and his bright young men also prepped Beame for debates with Lindsay, urging him to get tough, to get mad. He did—and made a fool of himself. After the last debate at WNBC-TV, Beame chased Lindsay into the hall, screaming, "You're a faker . . . you . . . you . . . demagogue," as cameras and reporters took it all in. "Calm down, Mr. Beame," Lindsay said over and over again, looking down soothingly at his opponent.

It wouldn't happen again. The 1973 campaign presented Beame as he really is: dull and competent. The banner this time might have been a comic strip titled *Lolly* which was taped on the wall of his press office on the fifth floor of the Municipal Building. The strip showed a secretary talking to her boss, and this was the dialogue:

"Here you are, sir. I typed your speech."

"About time. What took you so long?"

"I kept dozing off."

There was a Nixonian quality to the Beame campaign, which meant the candidate was hard to find. In the two weeks that I followed him, Beame never made more than one public appearance a day, and sometimes that appearance was nothing more than a bow from a dais in Staten Island or a few inspirational words to Boy Scouts in Queens.

"I don't care for standing up and making the speech," said the candidate, whose public voice is like a badly tuned radio with a squeaky treble that takes over as he gets excited or tired.

Beame didn't expose any new ideas, and not many old ones, either. His rhetoric reflected the tone of his opponents' campaigns. On crime, for instance, Beame's major statements were on the periphery of the issue, like this: "There is just too much bickering and quarreling among those who should be united in the war on crime . . . The Governor disagrees with the Mayor . . . The Mayor quarrels with the Governor and the courts . . . The police brass is at odds with the police rank and file . . . I think the time has come for reconciliation."

Even if he had no more than that to say, the candidate had to get out more before the primary because, in his own words, he had to prove his "vim, vigor, and vitality." He was 67 years old, and that would be an issue. In fact, his managers had certified copies of a physical examination he took earlier in the year, just in case.

The man, of course, never looked like a Wheaties advertisement, but he did put in ten or twelve hours a day at the office, stopped at an official dinner or two, and then squinted over budgets and things at home—a four-room apartment near Prospect Park in Brooklyn—before getting the four or five hours' sleep he's always said was enough. I've been with him well past midnight on tough days and he was hanging in, although at the end he had a mild spastic tendency to suck in air on the right side of his mouth. I remember that from my grandfather who lived past 80; and Beame looked as good as he ever does at eight o'clock the next morning.

The campaign demonstrated how much energy Beame had for the job he wants; he already had enough campaign money to get it. His campaign opened with full-page newspaper advertisements placed by the Committee of 112, featuring affluent and interesting names like William Shea of the stadium; Charles Bassine of Korvettes, a political buff who in 1970 circulated a letter implying that Arthur Goldberg was an anti-Jewish candidate; and Henry Garfinkle, a Lower East Side product who controls a significant part of the country's newspaper and magazine distribution, a business reportedly linked with organized crime. There were also names that don't appear: Abraham Feinberg, the chairman of American Bank & Trust Co., who is one of the nation's most formidable and anonymous political fund-raisers and who gave Beame an $80,000-a-year job at American Bank & Trust after he lost to Lindsay; and Abraham (Bunny) Lindenbaum, who was bounced from the City Planning Commission twelve years ago for raising money a little too enthusiastically for Robert Wagner. Beame denied that Lindenbaum was involved in his campaign, but other politicians reported that Bunny was indeed doing Beame's thing around town.

In fact, any man who had been Controller for seven years (and Budget Director for ten before that) should have developed the connections to finance a couple of campaigns. In *Governing New York City,* Wallace S. Sayre and Herbert Kaufman have this to say about Beame's office:

> He combines in his fiscal powers most of those exercised on a national level by the Secretary of the Treasury, the Controller General, the Council of Economic Advisers and some others . . . He can also, and usually does, draw to his support the real-estate and banking groups of the city.

The city's chief auditor, chief accountant, and investor of $6.4 billion in pension and trust funds was good at what he does. The office, which is supposed to scrutinize and pay the city's bills and check the books of other city agencies, was not as good, but it was a lot better than it was under Beame's successor, predecessor, and 1965 running mate, Mario Procaccino. "Beame himself is a professional—very, very competent. He could handle the books of any corporation or operation in the country," said the chief fiscal officer of a governmental agency who has held similar positions in industry. "But he can't do too much about his people. They're old, tired, and lazy civil servants who often miss the big picture. You get what you pay for, and the city doesn't pay enough to get good accountants."

No Controller had ever before become Mayor, just as chief accountants rarely become corporate presidents—and the reason was that "big picture" problem. Beame issued 250 press releases a year on his

activities—he edited them personally, line-by-line—and they tended
to be like the one showing that he saved $23,063 in frankfurter pur-
chases by the Board of Education. The Beame audit of the Off Track
Betting Corporation was an impressive document by weight, but its
substance concentrated on the $29.37 to $1,337.89 that O.T.B. vice
presidents spent in a year on business lunches, and on recommenda-
tions like these: "Careful consideration should be given to the best use
of computer equipment . . . Care should be exercised in the prepara-
tion of betting transmissions to limit errors . . . New branches should
not be opened in close proximity to existing branches."

The stories about bookkeepers, it seems, were true. "He drove me
up the wall," said one city official with a key role in budget prepara-
tion. "He'd sit through meeting after meeting, saying nothing, just
holding trump cards. He had the information on revenue flow and
special funds, on everything, but he'd hold it back, waiting to embarrass someone or to get what he wanted. And what he wanted was to
keep us from spending money. He knew we'd want new programs if
we knew how much money was available."

"I would try to be La Guardia without the frills," said Beame
himself. "City Hall would be clean, honest, and efficient. People trust
me, I think. I'd like to leave office with that."

The candidate said he would staff his administration with people
"who know how to use the subways." They would be mainly career
people, "the ones who've been skipped over." The best indicator of
his style was probably the First Deputy Controller he chose after he
was elected in 1969—he called out of retirement James Carroll, an old
associate in the Budget Bureau.

Beame was going to have to run as the candidate of the "bosses"
—he would be supported by the Democratic county leaders of Brooklyn, Manhattan, the Bronx, and Staten Island, too—and they were
going to get their pound of patronage if he won. But, in fairness, the
Controller, who has only fifteen personal appointees among his office's
1,200 Civil Service employees, had always been meticulously selective
about what he gave away—he used only the best the organizations
have offered. Beame is a product of the old Brooklyn politics-real-

estate-banking axis but he's not even a buddy of his own county leader, Brooklyn's Meade Esposito. In 1969 Beame was elected without the support of any county leaders, running a cheap, independent campaign that cashed in on the "guilt vote" of people who felt bad about voting against him in 1965.

Esposito and Beame were together in a Park Avenue apartment three years ago with a prominent group of Democrats discussing possibilities for the 1970 gubernatorial election. "I just want a guy I can sell," Esposito blustered. Those closest to Beame heard him snap, "You mean a guy you can buy." For once, someone knew what Abe Beame was really thinking.

John McCooey and Irwin Steingut would spin in their graves if they heard stories like that. Little Abe, a teacher at Richmond Hill High School, first came to them at the Madison Democratic Club in Crown Heights in 1932 when McCooey was still running Brooklyn. He idolized Herbert H. Lehman, who was running for Governor that year, and he wanted to make "contacts" for the tiny accounting firm he had set up at 1440 Broadway with his boyhood friend, B. Bernard Greidinger.

After three years of running errands, Beame asked the club leader, Irwin Steingut, an Assemblyman and the father of Stanley Steingut, the present Assembly minority leader, whether he could be an election district captain. "They laughed at me at first," said Beame, whose E. D. was bordered by Utica and Schenectady Avenues and Montgomery and Crown Streets, "but I was the best captain in Brooklyn. I'd just walk the streets, knocking on doors. I set a quota of twenty calls a night. It paid off. I loved it." Beame would sometimes carry his district for the organization by votes like 390-to-4, and he kept the captain's job even when he was Budget Director of the city from 1952 through 1961. The people of the district are still among his closest friends, dropping over for a night of canasta with Mary.

The elder Steingut and Beame grew closer and closer over the years, working together at home on politics and Steingut's tax returns and in Albany, where Beame served a dual role as a Steingut aide and a legislative representative for the Joint Committee of Teachers Organizations, the forerunner of the United Federation of Teachers. (Doing Steingut's taxes must have been interesting because the Assembly Speaker was once convicted of contempt of court for "evasive" answers on about $184,000 in unexplained income over a ten-year period. The conviction was later reversed.)

In 1946, when William O'Dwyer became Mayor and when bosses were bosses, Steingut installed Beame as Assistant Budget Director, and within six years he had moved up to Budget Director, one of the city's most powerful positions.

Beame's life has been a series of small, careful steps—teacher to Certified Public Accountant, assistant to director. When he became Budget Director, his ambition was to become Deputy Mayor or run for Borough President of Brooklyn. Then Wagner offered him the chance to run for Controller and he won easily. For the first time, he says, he realized he could become Mayor.

Carrying the rather heavy load of Wagner's record even though he had attacked his former benefactor in the 1965 Democratic primary, Beame just couldn't stand up to what seemed to be the inevitability of John Lindsay. The final vote was 1,149,106 to 1,046,699, and Beame went to the bank and to disappointment, boredom, and remarkably self-contained bitterness. The only thing that gives him away is that Abe Beame, who has a tidy little sense of humor, cannot joke in Lindsay's presence; sometimes he is barely able to speak coherently.

It has been a satisfying climb for Philip Birnbaum's son—the family name was changed shortly after Abraham David was born. Birnbaum barely escaped from Warsaw in 1906 during a police roundup of socialists, and he reached the United States, while his wife went to London, where Abraham was born that year. The boy was in New York before his first birthday and his mother died when he was very young. After that he was pretty much on his own while his father desperately tried to make it with a series of small restaurants, sometimes taking his sons to hear the American socialist heroes of the day, Eugene V. Debs and Morris Hillquit.

Beame, whose father was a Liberal party captain in Coney Island until he died in 1965, came from a special time and place. Richard Hofstadter in *The Age of Reform* provides an insight into the boyhoods of the Abe Beames:

> The same Progressive periodicals, and even the Socialist periodicals, that pilloried the evils of American society, tore into its established ideas, and offered blueprints for progress and reform, were full of little individualistic advertisements intended to tell clerks how they could improve themselves and "get ahead"—so that simply by moving one's eye from left to right, from one column to the next, one could pass from the world in which the Beef Trust or Standard Oil was being exposed and denounced, to the world in which "You Too Can Be a Certified Public Accountant."

"We wanted the economic stability and security that was denied our parents," recalls Bernard Greidinger, now Dr. Greidinger of the New York University Graduate School of Business Administration, who has known Beame since they were both seven years old. "We talked about nothing but finding 'a certainty' that was vital to us, a permanent job. We started with bookkeeping and then realized with a degree we could be teachers and that was security. In college we learned about accounting, that was a profession . . . Abe never had anyone to open doors for him. No family."

Young Abe went to work in grammar school. The story may be familiar, but that doesn't make it any less impressive: he worked six hours a day at the machines in a stationery plant, reeled off 100 after 100 on his Regents' examinations, enrolled simultaneously in two divisions of City College at night ("It was against the rules, but they never checked"), getting his degree *cum laude* in three years, played basketball and recited "Gunga Din" at the settlement house, got a scar under his left eye in a bottle fight, and painfully courted his Mary.

When Beame talks about his courtship, he uses the old-fashioned phrase "keeping company." He is from other generations, a survivor. I keep imagining that he was always there, that he was the small guy standing behind Peter Minuit, saying, "No. No, not $24. It's only worth $19.95."

*　　　*　　　*

Abe Beame as Mayor was even smaller than I imagined when he ran in 1973. The man who campaigned on the slogan, "If You Don't Know The Buck, You Don't Know The Job!" turned out to know neither. By early 1975, New York City was on the edge of bankruptcy —it could not pay back money it had borrowed, probably illegally, during Beame's tenure as Controller and Mayor.

For seven pathetic months, the Empire City reeled as its mayor first said there was no crisis, then announced more than once that the crisis was over, promised employee layoffs to cut expenses and then could not prove that anyone had actually been laid off, and, finally, turned political control of his city over to committees of bankers, Governor Hugh Carey, and the federal government. If a New Yorker had left town on the day Beame was elected and returned two years later, he could only conclude that there had been a *coup d'état.* New York, in 1975, was being run by people named Felix Rohatyn, an investment banker, and William Ellinghaus, the president of New York Telephone Company. Beame, a lonely figure in a lonely City Hall, was reduced to ribbon-cuttings at shopping centers—and to being booed at a "Save the City" rally in Times Square.

What had happened to New York was not all Beame's fault—John Lindsay deserved a major share of that credit, too—but the former budget director and controller had been a major contributor to municipal policy based on political cowardice and dependent on what could only be called fraud. For years, the city had been knowingly and illegally unbalancing its budget with tricks like "rolling over" expenses into future fiscal years and listing as anticipated revenues fictional taxes such as property levies on parks and embassies—all to keep a high level of local services and high electability for officials like Beame.

In the end, the city avoided outright default through a series of emergency plans mandated by the state-appointed Municipal Assistance Corporation, headed by Rohatyn, and the Financial Control Board, headed by Ellinghaus, and federal loans totalling $2.3 billion —loans grudgingly approved by Congress and President Ford, who was forced to reverse a personal pledge to let New York default.

Still, little Abe Beame survived in a way. Governor Carey decided against advisers who wanted Beame removed from office for cause—and, in the new privacy of City Hall, Beame sometimes talked about running again in 1977.

13 | Hugh Carey
Nelson Rockefeller

Jimmy's is a restaurant on West 52nd Street that specializes in lousy food, good drinks, and better conversation, if you like better political conversation. People do say the damnedest things there. One night— it was March 18, 1973—a bunch of overaged adolescents who practice or observe the political arts were there laughing about Nelson Rockefeller's latest, his attempt to resurrect Robert F. Wagner as Mayor of New York City. One guy even cracked up everyone by saying, "He's already planned the next election for Governor—Malcolm Wilson against Hugh Carey."

One thing has to be remembered about the recent politics of the Empire State: Nelson A. Rockefeller. Political New York could be viewed as a circle with Rockefeller at its center. The web radiating from Rockefeller is tangled, bipartisan, and sometimes barely visible, but it is there, woven through the fiber of the state's four parties— Republican, Democratic, Liberal, and Conservative—and their public minions. "People will think someday it was an exaggeration to say Nelson Rockefeller owned New York," said Russell Hemenway, the national director of the National Committee for an Effective Congress and a very sophisticated practitioner and observer of state politics. "But he owned the Republican party and he owned the Democratic party. You simply could not touch the man in New York."

The outsiders might not think it's an exaggeration. Consider what has happened to the six most dangerous politicians outside the Rockefeller circle since the death of Robert F. Kennedy in 1968: Mayor John Lindsay was replaced by Abe Beame, a regular Democrat elected with undisguised Rockefeller help; State Senator John Marchi, the official Republican candidate for Mayor in 1973, was demolished by the Beame alliance; Senator Charles Goodell, the Republican-Liberal candidate for the Senate in 1970, was jettisoned for an unofficial Rockefeller-James Buckley ticket in 1970; Representative Mario Biaggi, a one-time Rockefeller aide, had a real shot at the Democratic nomination for Mayor in 1973, before grand jury testimony about his personal finances mysteriously began appearing on the front pages of city newspapers; Assembly Speaker Perry Duryea, a potentially strong candidate for the Republican gubernatorial nomination, was indicted for violation of a state law that had twice been declared unconstitutional; Howard Samuels, an erratic and untrusted Democrat who seemed close to the Democratic gubernatorial nomination, was wiped out by Carey, who had been Rockefeller's favorite congressman for ten years.

So, the 1974 New York election seemed to be fought well within the Rockefeller orbit, not an inner circle by any means, but a loose system of radially distributed power and favors developed over fifteen years, a prosperous balance of people and institutions that sometimes looked as if they were fighting a lot harder than they actually were —Rocky's trained Republican leaders and Democratic "bosses," the big banks and the big unions, men who seemed as far apart as Alex Rose of the Liberal party and James Buckley of the Conservative party.

The center was holding. Not that it didn't make a difference who won in 1974—Hugh Carey, the Democratic-Liberal candidate, and Governor Malcolm Wilson, the Republican-Conservative, were very different men. Among other things, Wilson was dull beyond description, the Lamont Cranston of politics with power to cloud men's minds, and Carey was a lively piece of proof that only the Irish should be allowed in politics.

Wilson was elected Lieutenant Governor with Rockefeller back in 1958, which gives him the distinction, in the words of Albany Mayor Erastus Corning, "of spending fifteen years playing second fiddle in a one-man band." The Rockefeller-Wilson ticket was consciously

designed as a moderate-conservative duplicate of the successful Ei-
senhower-Nixon team. Some state Republicans, however, thought
"reactionary" was a better description for Wilson, who in the State
Assembly had earned a reputation as a superb legislative technician,
debater, and representative of Francis Cardinal Spellman.

Wilson, who became Governor when Rockefeller resigned in
December, 1973, described himself as "a fiscal conservative and a
human-rights liberal." He is also boring—when you ask him what
time it is, he not only tells you how to build a watch but also recites
the history of chronology—and one recent night in Lake Placid he
greeted a friendly crowd with: "It's been a very interesting day for me.
Under the felicitous concatenation of circumstances I've had a day
where I've seen the microcosm of all New York State—what makes
the state tick."

My favorite Wilson campaign stop came that same day at the 41st
annual convention of the New York State Conservation Council—a
euphemism for the state organization of 250,000 rod and gun club
members—at the Stevensville Country Club hotel, 100 miles north of
New York City. The Governor spent two hours there demonstrating
why he probably would not be the Governor after January 1, 1975.

First, he spent ten minutes in the hotel lobby chatting and whispering—he whispers a lot—with two aides. Then it was on to the Carni-
val Lounge, where Wilson began by saying, "I know most of the
people in this room"—which was apparently true, because he introduced or reminisced about almost every one of the 150 people there.
He took six minutes introducing the seven council officers and legislators sitting at the head table. He saw someone from Shirburne and
told about the time "Janet Hill Gordon took me up to see Mr. Gaines
and the factory where he makes 'Burger Bits.' " Then he talked about
how Mike Petruska had died, and how, in memory, he had held up
appointing a replacement for Mike on the New England Interstate
Water Pollution Control Commission for five months, but today he
was naming "one of your own, he's right here, Stan Spisiak." Then
he began a roll call of "those who aren't with us today" . . . "gone
on to his reward" . . . "left us" . . . "called away" . . . "on to another

and, we hope, better world than this vale of tears in which we live."

"Malcolm Wilson sure is close to a lot of dead people," said Jack Kole of *The Milwaukee Journal,* as Wilson got down to the business of saying he would reduce the minimum age for free senior-citizen hunting and fishing licenses from 70 to 62, and he would never make sportsmen line up to register their rifles and shotguns like common criminals. It was smoky and surreal in the lounge, and things seemed to happen in slow motion, but finally the Governor accepted a gold medal, spoke a couple of minutes about it, and went on to a press conference under the heads of the state record black bear (469 pounds) and white-tailed deer (248 pounds).

It was not a happy meeting of candidate and reporters—Wilson does not enjoy the game, and he avoided eye contact with his questioners. He was testy when pressed and took up a good part of the 45 minutes rummaging through his pockets for three-by-five file cards noting things like the fact that the state's share of Federal jobs decreased from 8.1 to 6.6 percent during the fourteen years Hugh Carey had been in Congress. "It's all right; we believe you," said Judith Michaelson of *The New York Post,* as he flipped through the cards for a number. "No," Wilson said, "it's important that you get it right."

Carey, as fate would have it, visited the Conservation Council the next day. For him, the hunters and fishermen were unmoved, a Grant Wood group picture. The man from Brooklyn was desperate to make some connection with these people—he is essentially a small-time Hubert Humphrey, very anxious to please—but he never had a chance after telling some bad duck-hunting stories and ending, gamely and lamely, with, "I'll tell you, nothing compares to being in this state in the autumn . . . Smokey the Bear can't do it all himself, he needs your help."

The Democrat was more in his element, and more himself, a few nights earlier at a party rally in Tonawanda, near Buffalo. There were only a hundred people in Carey headquarters, a storefront on South Main Street, but five of them were "The Tamburitzan Boys—Music for all Occasions" pounding out "Happy Days Are Here Again" and "The Sidewalks of New York." With "Matt Murphy for Assembly"

balloons dancing over his head, town Democratic chairman George
Hanratty exuberantly kicked off the festivities by introducing candi-
date Robert Abrams as "the next Attorney Gentleman of the state of
New York."

Carey was introduced by Assemblyman John LaFalce, a candidate
for Congress with a perpetual Jaycee grin and a habit of greeting
people with "H-e-e-e-y!" and leaving them with "O-k-a-a-a-y!" "A
guy named Carey," LaFalce began in a hushed tone which quickly
escalated into hysteria. "Names. When you read the history books
certain names make you tingle. Put chills in your spine. Goosepim-
ples. Al Smith. Herbert Lehman. Franklin Roosevelt. Bobby
Kennedy . . . We have got it back again! We have a great man! Hugh
Carey!"

"I came in here tonight wondering whether it was the appropriate
time to endorse John LaFalce," Carey began. "I've decided. I'll endorse him. I'll endorse his mother. His uncles. Anyone who has
anything to do with John LaFalce, I'll endorse."

The guy's a pro, and he has a sense of humor. The rest of the speech
was nonsense, of course, but politicians and political reporters are
among the chosen few who spend their adult years going to pep rallies.
Later on in the Tonawanda speech, Carey showed that he had mastered a basic Humphreyism—realizing that you've gone too far or said
the wrong thing, then turning a thought around and loading it with
hyperbole to try to bury the original sin. This time Carey began
talking about Ramsey Clark, his Senate running mate, by saying, "He
came to New York from another state"—oh, oh, shouldn't say that!
—"He lives here with his wife and child. He has a sister in Amherst.
He's a real New Yorker in heart and spirit. Remember the only
original New Yorker was the brother of the king, the Duke of York."

Carey's links to Rockefeller are more complex and more illustrative
and more vulnerable than Wilson's. He is, after all, a *Democrat* and,
toward the end of the campaign, he finally stopped saying that he
thought Rockefeller was "a good, if not great Governor." He said, as
Frank Skeffington might have, that all along he meant "all human
beings are good."

Hugh Leo Carey was a good congressman who was also smart enough to be bored in Washington—"It was drudgery, and I wasn't about to sit there and vegetate for the rest of my life"—and he became the "independent" candidate for Governor in a rather traditional and fortuitous way: He was rejected by "the bosses." The Democratic leaders of New York City's four largest counties endorsed the unpredictable Howard Samuels because they miscalculated—they thought Samuels's visibility ("Howie the Horse") as the city's Off Track Betting chief made him unbeatable in the Democratic primary.

In many ways, the bosses are a pathetic bunch who for fifteen years have done more following than leading, more guessing than bossing. The seemingly Byzantine patterns of New York politics have often been nothing more than their twisting efforts to keep their small duchies within the Rockefeller empire while trying to appear to be part of potential rebellions. Anyway, Carey did want their shaky anointment, and before Samuels got it, the congressman consulted daily with Brooklyn leader Meade Esposito, Bronx leader Patrick Cunningham, and even with the old Tammany Hall boss, Carmine De Sapio, whose public bossing was cut short by a term in the Federal penitentiary at Lewisburg, Pennsylvania. (New York reform Democrats, the kind who believed George McGovern was right from the start, are institutional outsiders who can be charmed by a Carey and ignored by a Rockefeller.)

Not enough people outside Bay Ridge and environs really knew much about Carey. At least professionals didn't know enough—their evaluation of him might have gone something like this a year ago: a smart, lace-curtain Irishman who was the "class" of the New York congressional delegation, which isn't saying much; a buddy of House Ways and Means Chairman Wilbur Mills who got along with Rockefeller; a Kennedy liberal who had to hide it sometimes to survive in redneck Brooklyn; a quitter who dropped out of the 1969 mayoral race to support Robert F. Wagner and ended up losing his own primary for City Council president; and something of a dirty fighter. In sum, he was categorized as a talented regular who might end up as borough president of Brooklyn or a senior congressman. "Portly"

was *The New York Times*'s favorite adjective for him—words like that
don't attach to statesmen or comers.

All of that was true, but there was obviously much more. Most
important, the "pros" didn't know that "Hughie" was very, very
ambitious or that the Careys were Kennedy-rich. Carey politicked his
way onto the House Ways and Means Committee, but once he had
been blocked from the leadership ladder by the rise of another Eastern
Catholic, Tip O'Neill of Massachusetts, he realized there was more
to life than kissing Wilbur Mills's amendments—he was in a hurry,
and when Rocky stepped out of Albany, Carey began looking into it.

Politicians were vaguely aware that the Careys were not poor—
"they have an oil business, you know, delivery trucks." It's an oil
business, all right. Edward M. Carey, Hugh's brother, is the sole
owner of New England Petroleum Corp., one of the largest private
companies in the world, grossing more than $800 million a year—and
that's only one of his seventeen companies. Because NEPCO is not
publicly owned, relatively little is known about it except for information required by Massachusetts corporate laws and Edward Carey's
testimony before the Senate Foreign Relations Committee in 1974
after State Department objections to a $40-million cash deal between
NEPCO and the Libyan Government during the Arab oil embargo.
(Edward Carey refused to be interviewed about his business or his
brother. Calls to his New York office—he is officially a resident of
Puerto Rico—were accepted by a Mr. O'Hara, who said he had been
authorized to say only: "We are a private company and it is our policy
not to grant interviews.")

Brother Ed does own trucks, the Burns fleet that fills a lot of the
fuel oil tanks in New York, and he owns ships, 30 tankers. NEPCO
is an integrated oil company controlling crude oil from Arabian well-
heads to its own refineries and on to its own gas stations, at least 250
in Canada alone, and to customers like Long Island Lighting Company, of which it is the sole oil supplier, and Consolidated Edison,
which gets 45 percent of its oil from NEPCO. Keeping things in the
family, brother Hugh was on the NEPCO payroll for years as a
consultant, and his Brooklyn law firm was NEPCO's counsel.

Whatever it all added up to, Edward Carey met in the spring of 1974 with David Garth, perhaps the best political media consultant in the country, to talk about making Hughie Governor. Garth asked how much money was available and Ed Carey answered, according to a witness: "Whatever it takes."

It took $1,297,500 of Ed's money—and that figure may be on the low side. The brothers Carey drove their oil trucks around, under, and through New York State's shiny new "campaign reform" law. Ed started by lending his brother's campaign $950,000 before the law took effect on June 1. The money kept flowing after that until Samuels —whose biggest blunder was taking Carey lightly because he believed the Brooklyn congressman could not raise enough money for a major campaign—began screaming that Ed Carey's post-June 1 contributions and loans were exceeding the law's $105,000 limit on family contributions. O.K.—Hugh began paying back his brother with loans from his brother's business associates—$250,000 worth miraculously came in one day. The new lender-contributors were such concerned New Yorkers as Pierre Senecal ($31,500) of Chambly, Quebec, and the Quebec Oil Co., a unit of the Carey Energy Corp., and K. K. Tse ($10,000) of Hong Kong.

It was a joke, but Samuels was never really able to make it an issue, partly because he had put a lot of his own money ($261,000) into his campaign and partly because Carey could talk circles around him. Samuels tried to make it "oil interests" and Carey said, "Stop picking on my family." When Samuels pointed out that Edward Carey was trying to build an oil pipeline across New York to carry foreign oil picked up in Rhode Island, Hugh Carey answered that was because "my brother so loves the state of New York that he's built the first refinery here in fifteen years." Yeah, like Aristotle Onassis so loved the state of New Hampshire that he wanted to build a competing Northeastern refinery there—that's what Samuels should have answered, but he didn't and, anyway, polls indicated that New York Democratic voters generally believe brothers should help each other. "What's a brother for?" was an answer regularly received by both Samuels and Carey pollsters. Perhaps New Yorkers have been condi-

tioned by the way the Rockefellers financed campaigns for brother
Nelson.

(Did Hugh Carey favor family oil interests as a congressman? Hard
to say. Until recent months, the interests of foreign oil importers and
"good government" liberals were roughly the same. When Representative Carey voted to end the oil-depletion allowance for domestic
producers, a "good" vote, he was also voting to improve the competi-
tive position of his brother, a dealer in foreign oil. The same is true
of "good" air pollution votes—clean air requires low-sulfur oil, which
means Arab oil, which is what Ed Carey distributes. The one issue the
congressman may be vulnerable on is water pollution control—he has
voted against controls, which might be interpreted as voting for oil
slicks, an occupational hazard for tanker owners and offshore oil well
advocates, and Ed Carey is both. But Hugh Carey personally opposes
offshore drilling—advocating it on Long Island would be political
death.)

Even with NEPCO employees working at his headquarters as
"volunteers," candidate Carey seemed to have turned his campaign
financing into a rhetorical asset: "New Yorkers have seen enough of
the influence of private money over public policy—an influence that
forces every major candidate, including myself, to reach out to sources
of campaign financing . . . This will be the last campaign fought with
private campaign funds. New York will have public financing of
campaigns."

But this time, anyway, he could afford Garth—and Garth is both
expensive and good. Carey paid him a $10,000-a-month retainer for
nine months, plus a 15 percent agency commission on media buys,
which totaled $687,668 in the primary alone, plus 17.62 percent of
production fees, plus two Garth employees on the Carey staff at more
than $1,000 a week.

He got his money's worth. He even looked better: Garth persuaded
him to lose 30 pounds and a "new" Carey suddenly appeared around
town with dyed hair, contact lenses, a Dunhill wardrobe, and no
drinking except for a little wine with meals. He learned to walk with
his chin up—hide the folds, good for lighting—and in eight brisk,

newsy commercials, he was anything but portly. He was a vigorous 54-year-old man, an ex-war hero striding along with his twelve children.

"This year, before they tell you what they want to do . . . make them show you what they've done," was the message, and it got across as Carey outspent Samuels 8-to-1 on television. Maybe it got across too well—you sometimes think Dave Garth could take any of us (with a rich brother) off the streets and win a Democratic primary, especially since New York television news has downplayed political coverage because their viewer surveys tell them people prefer light news programs with teams of cute little Dick-and-Jane reporters. *Newsday* on Long Island quoted a voter, a Republican woman from Elmont who obviously gets her political news from Garth commercials: "Carey's on television a lot. He's a man—so masculine and sincere. I don't know much about Wilson. I saw Carey working in his district, helping people. The publicity he gets is why I guess I like him."

When he's winning, as he has with John Tunney in California and Dan Walker in Illinois, Garth plays down his influence. He emphasized that Carey was a good congressman and a good personal campaigner and that Samuels blew it. All true, although it was also true that Carey ran just as well in parts of the state he never visited as in the parts where he campaigned heavily. "Television isn't that important," Garth said over and over again, but, then, finally, he said, "Remember, Malcolm Wilson could still win this." How? "If we're off the tube another ten days!"

Carey *was* good, not quite the combination of Henry Clay and Sam Rayburn that appeared in the commercials, but head and shoulders above most city congressmen. He is bright and quick, glib and scatter-mouthed—"He's an encyclopedia without an index," one friend said —and he never, never stops talking, thinking, free-associating, insisting on dominating any conversational group that doesn't include Wilbur Mills or other senior congressmen. "I finally figured it out," said Clay Felker, the publisher of *New York* magazine after a lunch with Carey. "He's reciting for the nuns; he has to get it all in before they call on someone else."

With Mills and others who have outlived congressional anonymity, Carey was deferential to the edge of obsequiousness. He was also deferential when it counted—he voted against every effort to reform the House of Representatives by upsetting its hallowed seniority system. But that's the way Congress works, and Carey was effective because he played the game and worked for Hale Boggs and with worse men to angle his way from the Interior Committee up to the Education and Labor Committee and finally, in 1971, up to Ways and Means, the Mills Committee that passes on all money matters and assigns House members to other committees.

Congressmen who have worked with Carey describe him as "well informed, a guy who knew what was going on" or "influential." There is a world of difference in those terms—friends use the latter, but both friends and enemies agreed that Carey was the fourth or fifth most effective member of Education and Labor, where he spent most of his Washington time. He was a principal author of the Elementary and Secondary School Act of 1965 and chaired the Subcommittee on Education for the Handicapped, which he practically created and which was responsible for a dozen laws making it possible, for instance, for deaf people to get the education and training to become working, productive citizens.

All of that was proclaimed by the Garth commercials. They also announced that Carey "got" the Brooklyn Navy Yard reopened as an industrial park—he didn't do that, but he was one of the key New York figures fighting for the yard as far back as 1964. That was when he and Rockefeller began a relationship that sometimes included daily phone calls and meetings, especially when they worked effectively as a team to push for Federal Revenue Sharing with states and localities. It became law in 1972. (Rockefeller has said from the beginning that the original revenue-sharing idea came from Malcolm Wilson.)

The Rockefeller-Carey relationship was rarely publicized but was well known in their offices, and staff people on both sides characterized Carey as an important, if secret, adviser who would talk by telephone with Rockefeller or Rocky's political agent, James Cannon, on an almost daily basis over long periods of time. "It was a rather useful relationship on both sides," Carey says now. "I had a sense of the Congress and they had something I wanted: access to the White House. And, up until the end of 1972, Rockefeller wanted people to look upon him as much as a Roosevelt as a Rockefeller."

Except for their occasional mutual admiration, only one instance of Rockefeller help for Carey has ever been overt enough to be obvious. And that incident, shrouded to the point that it may be shady, was supposed to be covert.

In the 1972 election, Carey was in trouble in his own district against John Gangemi, who had the Republican nomination for Congress and whose name was already printed on Conservative party nominating petitions. But Gangemi never got the Conservative nomination— somebody named Jones was put on the ballot at the last minute, and Carey was re-elected with 52 percent of the vote.

What happened? William Wells, then the Brooklyn Conservative leader, says his party got "certain promises" from Rockefeller's man Cannon, and from Carey. George Clark, then the local Republican leader and now the county chairman, was publicly backing Gangemi. But he says he agreed to set up a meeting between Carey and Wells, at Carey's request, and: "They met in my real-estate office and I was there. Carey told Wells that he wanted him to pull the Conservative backing of Gangemi . . . 'We can't do that. We can't back a liberal so-and-so like you,' Wells said. Carey said he didn't want support, just another candidate to cut Gangemi's vote. 'Let's talk absolute specifics,' Carey said, and I knew they were going to talk money and I didn't want to be there. Carey came out smiling later and said Wells was 'reasonable.' . . . Wells told me later that Carey gave him $10,000."

Wells, who supported Carey for the governorship, said that Clark, who was close to Wilson, was lying. "I didn't get a dime," he said. "Rockefeller and Carey got what they wanted and I just don't want to say any more." Carey said that it's true that Rockefeller helped him through Cannon and that Wells did ask him for money or for legal advertising for small newspapers Wells owned. "I gave him nothing," Carey said, "I don't handle money in my campaigns."

Stories and denials like that are the plasma of Brooklyn politics, and Hugh Carey was in Brooklyn a long time. Phil Tracy, a *Village Voice* political writer who once worked for Carey, described his ex-boss as: "A mean bastard who plays politics as dirty as anyone I've ever met in the profession, but don't deny Carey his streak of idealism. It's there and he honestly believes it." Carey charges in 1969 about New York Fire Department inefficiency—charges that the congressman knew were untrue—particularly got to Tracy. According to Tracy, Carey told him: "What harm did it do? Who knows? Maybe the city really is burning up. Lindsay would never tell us. In the meantime, we get some publicity, and that's what counts in this game."

What counts most to Hugh Carey, I think, is the game itself. He loved running for Governor but gave absolutely no indication of having thought much about being Governor. The Carey primary campaign against Samuels, in which Carey rolled up 61 percent of the vote, consisted of little more than the quick candidate, the rich brother, the sage Wagner, and the talented Garth. While Samuels ground out reams of detailed position papers and deployed hundreds of field workers, Carey went on television proclaiming "independence . . . independence . . . independence."

"I'll admit that I don't have an intimate knowledge of state government," Carey said. "I think I have a better grasp of how it *should* run than of how it *does* run."

Was he just trying to get into the national game in 1976, as candidate or power broker? "I'm going to have a voice in 1976," he answered. "But mainly I'm going to work, to lead and stay close to my family. I'm not a Kennedy. I'm a guy who worked his way from the freshman team to the junior varsity to the scrubs. *This* is my big play."

Maybe. But what happens when Carey reads that he might be the stuff of the '76 All American team? There are two ways he could actually become "independent." He could go national, leaving New York power within the circle that hardened during the Rockefeller years. Or, he could plug away at home, an ingrate insider remembering something that Fiorello La Guardia once said: "The best guarantee of independence is monumental ingratitude."

On paper at least, there are great similarities in the lives of Hugh

Carey and Malcolm Wilson, the loser. Both are the products of middle-class Irish homes a few miles from Manhattan in the World War
I era; both were educated only in Roman Catholic schools. Carey is
from St. John's University and St. John's Law and Wilson is from
Fordham and Fordham Law. (Both, incidentally, have spent a lot of
their time amending bills to channel government money to nonpublic
schools.) Carey's father was in the coal and oil business in Brooklyn,
and his mother was once Nellie Bly's secretary. Wilson's father was
a patent attorney in Yonkers, and his mother was something of a
power in local politics: She got her son his first Assembly nomination
when he was just 24. Carey was a major in the infantry in Europe
during World War II. Navy Lieutenant Wilson commanded a gun
crew during the Normandy invasion.

The difference, according to men who know both of them, may be
greater than the similarity. Both are serious Roman Catholics, but
Carey is an anti-clerical Irish Catholic. The Democrat, something of
a Kennedy worshipper, has also had his share of tragedy—two of his
fourteen children, his oldest sons, were killed in an automobile accident in 1969, and his wife, Helen, died of cancer early in 1974 at the
age of 49.

Wilson, who is half Irish, has boasted that he has never tasted
whiskey, wine, or beer. Maybe he grew up too fast. He was a prodigy,
graduating from college at 19 and going to Albany at 24. His religion
and his politics have always been mixed—at least in the eyes of
beholders—and in 1948 he was pushing legislation to ban "obscene
movie advertising." Although he tells it differently now, he was often
ignored, even forgotten, during his years as Lieutenant Governor, and
Rockefeller affectionately called him "my hack." After Rockefeller
prepared his first inaugural speech in 1959, someone remembered that
no one had consulted Wilson. He was shown the speech just before
Rockefeller gave it and panicked the second floor of the State Capitol
by intoning: "The Governor cannot give this speech." What? "There
is no mention of the Deity in this speech."

An "under God" was written in, and Wilson pronounced himself
satisfied.

When executives at WINS radio in New York City asked him about the major problems facing the community, he listed inflation, jobs, and crime, then added: "A society that condones anything will soon believe in nothing. I'm talking about dirty pictures . . . I really get uptight . . . pornography . . . Forcing a school or a Boy Scout camp to hire sex deviates. I'm against that."

If he was invisible as Lieutenant Governor, he seemed visibly indecisive after Rockefeller resigned on December 15, 1973. His stewardship and election prospects got stuck almost immediately in the long gasoline station lines that clogged the grand roads Rockefeller had built all over the state. One of the reasons for the lines, a reason that never became public, was that Wilson did not understand that he had control over releasing and distributing millions of gallons of emergency state allocations held at refineries, awaiting his order. It waited twenty days until Federal officials asked him why he was letting the gas sit there.

What was public was that the new Governor wasn't doing anything, in fact had no intention of doing anything, even anything symbolic. Pressure mounted on him to institute mandatory odd-even days for gasoline sales, especially after Governor Brendan Byrne instituted that system in New Jersey and it seemed to make life a little easier for drivers. Wilson's response: "I have a visceral reaction against Government directing people what to do."

Finally, *The New York Daily News,* the state's largest newspaper, published short profiles of Byrne and Wilson on the same page under the headlines: BITE THE BULLET BYRNE; WAIT AND SEE WILSON.

Wilson is a modest man, loyal and thoughtful to friends, but he is no campaigner. On the surface, his effort looked something like a Rockefeller campaign with familiar faces like state campaign director R. Burdell Bixby and press secretary Harry O'Donnell—capable men who began their careers with Thomas E. Dewey—and city campaign director Fiorvante Perrotta, who handled the five boroughs for both Rockefeller and Richard Nixon. But the difference was that there was no super-metabolic campaigner out front—"Let's cut this short, I want a nap," Wilson whispered to O'Donnell one 11 A.M.—and Wil-

son makes the decisions in the back room as well. There was also no
$7.2 million, the amount Rockefeller reported spending on his 1970
campaign, and many people believe the report fell about $5 million
short of what was actually spent. The former Governor, however,
contributed the legal individual limit of $46,000 to his successor's
campaign.

Wilson is a very conservative man, and his conservatism goes much
deeper than his teetotaling and the narrow, twenty-year-old ties he
wears with puritan determination. Before World War II, he was the
favored speaker at Young Republican conventions that passed resolutions saying things like: "We shall fight with every means at our
disposal the efforts of foreign agents to destroy our American way of
life . . . but we are aware that the greatest threat to our liberties comes
not from without but from the New Deal trend toward dictatorship."

Several years ago Wilson told me: "This is a conservative state.
New York is a conservative city, except for some parts of Manhattan,
that is . . . People have been going along with programs they didn't
really like for a long time. They were only talking about their true
feelings in the golf club locker rooms, or on the street—wherever they
talk. The conservative feeling broke into the open about June of 1970
—you could almost feel it—people could see what was happening in
their own lives . . . Public housing was supposed to be 'pass-through'
housing—a place for the deserving poor until they earned enough to
afford someplace else—but exemptions after exemptions were put in
until working people could come and see the new cars around public
housing projects. I think we need public housing, but for the *deserving*
poor."

In 1974, of course, the deserving poor and a lot of the working class
in New York were on unemployment insurance. Even though Wilson
did raise those benefits that year, unemployment, inflation, and Watergate made it just about the worst time for a Republican like Wilson
to face the electorate. Each day, Carey and his Democratic running
mates pounded away at the fact that 250,000 manufacturing jobs in
New York had disappeared during the Rockefeller years. Wilson
could only counter: Yes, but those jobs were all lost in New York City

and crime is the reason—he favors phrases like "urban jungle."

But Carey wasn't the easiest guy to run a law-and-order campaign against because, in the words of Frank Russo, a Democratic leader on the Lower East Side of Manhattan, "My people will never believe Carey is soft for a very simple reason: He looks like an Irish cop." In fact, Wilson never believed he would have to run against Carey—like almost everyone else he thought he would be facing Howard Samuels, and had planned a campaign labeling him soft, permissive, and a bit radical.

The depression and panic of Republicans, when they realized Carey would probably win, was reflected in an editorial in a Massena newspaper that Carey carried in his wallet—the newspaper warned that unless Wilson won, Democrats would shift $2 billion of state money from upstate to New York City and that in St. Lawrence County "not a highway will be repaired, snow-plowing will be suspended."

With visions of Massena abandoned under three feet of snow, the faithful followed their Malcolm. It turned out like a scene at the state A.F.L.-C.I.O. convention in Kiamesha Lake: 50 leaders of construction unions, which support Wilson, closed ranks behind their candidate to escort him to the podium, then marched through the corridors of the Concord Hotel as Wilson confidently led the front ranks into a Men's Room.

For the Democrats, there were euphoric visions of state jobs and judgeships. At a party rally in Buffalo, Carey's running mate for Lieutenant Governor, State Senator Mary Anne Krupsak, straightened 200 spines with one oblique reference to what politics is often about: "I'm thrilled when I look out and see the talent in this room."

Miss Krupsak, the first woman to run for statewide office since a female Secretary of State went to jail for misuse of public funds 40 years ago, is a serious, all-work-and-no-play liberal from the Schenectady area. She knocked off two male opponents in the Democratic primary and got inordinate media attention for a candidate for an office with few duties and less power. Wilson's Wilson was Ralph Caso, the county executive of Nassau County, who is noted for total loyalty to the powerful Nassau Republican organization and for wearing white, patent-leather boots. (Lieutenant Governors, like Vice Presidents, cannot be voted for separately in New York, and their primary function is to succeed the Governor in case of resignation, disability, or death.) Lieutenant Governors, and even U.S. Senators, have very little to do with power in New York. The two centers of political power in the state are the corner offices on the second floor of the State Capitol in Albany and the ground floor of City Hall in New York—the Governor and the Mayor.

Nelson Rockefeller made his first attempt to bond the two offices inside his circle in 1965 when he put up $500,000 of his own money to start the campaign of a young Republican congressman for Mayor. The congressman, of course, was named John Lindsay, and he was so monumentally ungrateful as to deny that he ever got the money from Rockefeller—so the Governor lost a half million dollars and eight feuding years.

By 1973, Rockefeller was ready to try again, and by then he had solidified his ties to regular Democratic leaders like Meade Esposito of Brooklyn and Patrick Cunningham of the Bronx, the "boss" closest to Carey. Esposito, particularly, was proud of his relationship with Rockefeller, bragging about judgeships, clerkships, and a Picasso etching the Governor had given him while Brooklyn Democrats were providing critical votes in the Legislature for the Governor's bills.

Suddenly, while Esposito was talking about a "one-shot Mayor," Rockefeller proposed the same thing under a different name: a "fusion Mayor." Esposito's choice for a one-term Mayor was Abe Beame—the Brooklyn leader has always had personal problems with Hugh Carey, who was the Governor's first choice for a save-the-city Mayor. Rockefeller, who realized a fusion Mayor would have to be a Democrat, let it be known that two other Democrats were acceptable to him —Beame and former Mayor Robert F. Wagner, who became a Rockefeller consultant on governmental relations.

"Saving the city" (and getting rid of Lindsay) was very much the mood of insiders in that spring of 1973. Leaders of the new Association for a Better New York, basically a coalition of the city's biggest landlords, were calling for a "four-year Mayor" to clean up crime and protect their investments—as business moved out of the city, the vacancy rate kept climbing in the city's commercial towers, including Rockefeller Center. In fact, the president of Rockefeller Center, Alton Marshall, former secretary to Governor Rockefeller, was a leading voice in A.B.N.Y. along with former Mayor Wagner and Howard Rubenstein, a public-relations man who became the *de facto* manager of the Beame mayoral campaign.

Although events—including pressure on John Marchi not to run and the discrediting of Mario Biaggi—seemed to be leading inevitably to a Beame victory in November, 1973, Rockefeller made one more startling move: He proposed Bob Wagner, his one-time Democratic foe, for the Republican nomination for Mayor. If he had pulled that one off—Wagner backed out when conservative Republicans like George Clark rebelled—the Governor would have had the pleasure of sitting back and watching two friendly insiders contest for mayoral power: Wagner vs. Beame.

It didn't happen, of course. Marchi, with the support of Clark and the Conservative party, won the Republican nomination without opposition. But without Rockefeller's support, Marchi was broke and hopeless—"I got nothing, absolutely nothing from the party," Marchi said. "It was very lonely." Beame was elected and he and Rockefeller immediately and publicly proclaimed an era of good feeling between Albany and City Hall.

The emergence of Al Marshall, whom many people think is Rockefeller's most capable lieutenant, as a factor in city politics seemed to be a signal of just how concerned the Rockefellers were about the future of Manhattan Island—and their substantial investments from Hell Gate to the Battery. Marshall, with $306,867, was the second biggest recipient on the Nelson Rockefeller gift list released by the Senate Rules Committee in November, 1974, when Rockefeller was awaiting congressional confirmation as Gerald Ford's appointed vice president. William Ronan, chairman of the Port Authority of New York and New Jersey, who topped the list at $625,000, is also directly involved in Manhattan development as landlord of the new World Trade Center, which happily dovetailed with David Rockefeller's master plan for the development of Lower Manhattan.

There is more to the gifts than meets the eye—money may not buy happiness, but it can buy silence. One reason Nelson Rockefeller's public reputation was so pretty was that no one who has ever served him has ever turned and attacked him or even provided unflattering anecdotes to nosy reporters.

The power of the money can be irresistible—in Charles Goodell's case, for instance, Rockefeller was able to cut off Republican contributors during the 1970 campaign, and soon enough Goodell was out of the Senate and out of the way. And, after James Buckley had won, Rockefeller arranged the paying off of hundreds of thousands of dollars of Goodell campaign debts.

Whether or not there really are conspiracies behind my theories, Wilson vs. Carey (with Wagner in the background) was the succession race that realized Rockefeller's best fantasies. Duryea vs. Samuels, for instance, would have been a disaster for Nelson A. And the fact is that in New York, Rockefeller fantasies had a way of becoming reality for the rest of us.

"Hugh Carey was Nelson Rockefeller's man in Washington," said Russell Hemenway. Would he be a Rockefeller man in Albany? The answer is no, but . . . he is a man that the Rockefellers are comfortable with. It is not every Democrat who can go through a campaign for Governor without saying more than ten bad words about a Republican who has just totally dominated a state for fifteen years. (The ten bad words Carey occasionally used, by the way, were "Rockefeller spent our money as if we had his money.")

Instead, Carey happily beat the drums of change, singing slogans: "The process of Government has been run behind closed doors; the people have been shut out, and behind those closed doors the forces of private wealth and political power have spun a web of privilege and are immune from accountability or challenge . . . I want the word to be heard loud and clear . . . New York's Government is not for sale."

New York's Government hadn't been for sale for sixteen years— it had been owned by Nelson Aldrich Rockefeller. And Hugh Carey was well within the web of privilege and influence. It all reminds me of a slogan I once heard: "This year, before they tell you what they want to do . . . make them show you what they've done."

*   *   *

In December, 1975, New York, city and state, were a financial shambles and Governor Carey had broken most of his campaign promises—he was proposing tax increase after tax increase to try to close the state and city gaps between revenues and expenses—and he told me: "I didn't know the true condition of the state. Perhaps I should have, but I was misled like everyone else."

In fact, in crisis, Hugh Carey turned out to be a more forceful and effective leader than anyone could have expected. After a couple of months of trying to disassociate the state and himself from New York City's fiscal problems—he was almost literally in hiding in early 1975 —Carey made himself the *de facto* mayor of the city. In the agonizing battle for Federal aid to New York and to convince Washington and private investment markets that the city was sincerely attempting to put its finances in order, Carey emerged as the most credible and effective spokesman for the city.

State government suffered as the Governor concentrated on the city —major positions were unfilled for months—but he had no choice and did what he had to, and did it rather well. Still, with Dave Garth's capable assistance, Carey found time to encourage the organizations of uncommitted delegate slates—known as "the Carey slates"—for the 1976 New York Presidential Primary. Then, after a December 15, 1975, lunch with Garth, Alex Rose, and Bob Wagner, the Governor announced that he would not be a candidate for President because he would be devoting himself full time to state problems. *The New York Times* noted: "Thus, politically, the statement tended to blur any identification with the uncommitted slates, particularly if they lost in the April 6 Presidential primary, and also to present Mr. Carey as a dedicated officeholder too busy for active Presidential politicking, which, even his advisers concede, would probably be unproductive anyway . . . There is general agreement among those closest to the governor that, unlike Mr. Rockefeller and Mr. Lindsay, he is not panting after the Presidency, although he certainly would be receptive 'if lightning strikes.' "

14 | Matthew J. Troy

Matty Troy is the biggest liar and the most honest man in New York politics. He is the George Washington Plunkitt of our time.

Plunkitt, as serious students of politics know, was a Tammany Hall district leader and sometime State Senator and Magistrate from the West Side of Manhattan whose wit and wisdom were immortalized in a 1905 book titled *A Series of Very Plain Talks on Very Practical Politics.** The little volume contained such enduring truths as these:

> Politics is as much a regular business as the grocery or the drygoods or the drug business. You've got to be trained up to it or you're sure to fail . . . There's only one way to hold a district: you must study human nature and act accordin' . . . You can't keep an organization together without patronage. Men ain't in politics for nothin'. They want to get somethin' out of it . . . I might sum up the whole thing by sayin': "I seen my opportunities and I took 'em."

Like Plunkitt, Matthew Joseph Troy, Jr., City Councilman from the 16th District and Democratic Chairman of Queens County, is a plain-spoken Irishman who started training up to the business at the age of twelve. And someday there will probably be a book of truths from Troy.

> There are so many legitimate ways to make money in politics that I can never understand why anyone steals . . . Reformers are strange people.

*Plunkitt's philosophy, delivered for 30 years from a shoeshine stand in the old New York County Courthouse, was recorded and published by a *New York Evening Post* reporter named William L. Riordon. The book was re-issued by E. P. Dutton in 1963 under the title *Plunkitt of Tammany Hall.*

They think they're interested in good government until they get what they want, then they're the worst regulars who ever lived . . . The media is 99 percent of a political career in this town. You get them by being controversial. You've got to tell them the truth, but it helps to embellish it a little . . . Lying is an essential part of the political process. You do it to feel out the other guy's strengths and weaknesses . . . It's not how much power you have, it's how much power the other guy *thinks* you have . . . Only egomaniacs are in politics. I love the guys who talk about serving the public. This business is about men kissing your ass and girls who ----.

Troy, who is 45 now, started young because of Matthew Troy, Sr., who was Fiorello La Guardia's personal attorney and a maverick Brooklyn politician who regularly lost elections and just as regularly was appointed to jobs by his friend the Mayor. "Young Matt," as many people still know him, first got his name in the newspapers when he was arrested during a fistfight while poll-watching for his father. The swinging started when the kid spotted an election inspector marking paper ballots with a tiny piece of lead jammed into his thumbnail —and the guy wasn't putting the Xs next to Troy Sr.'s name. Years later, after Troy graduated from Fordham Law School, the arrest delayed his admission to the New York Bar when a "character and fitness" committee chairman challenged him with the question: "Pretty handy with your fists, aren't you, son?" Troy remembers answering: "No, sir. The other guy damned near killed me."

If fighting wasn't his game, politics was. Troy turned out to be a handy guy with a quote after being elected to the City Council from Queens Village in 1954. And if the quote, or Troy's version of a closed meeting, turned out to be a little embellished, so what? If a bruised reporter later challenged Troy, the laughing answer would be: "You should never trust politicians."

"The people who thought Troy was some kind of clown were sadly mistaken," said Murray Schumach, the City Hall bureau chief of *The New York Times*. "He's different, very special. He's smart and tough, and a very shrewd judge of people. He's like DiMaggio was in center field, a natural."

So he was. Smart enough to stand apart in the Council, which may not be saying very much, and, in 1973, to take over one of its islets of power, the Finance Committee. Tough enough to take over the Queens Democratic Executive Committee in 1971. Shrewd enough to keep his enemies and colleagues perpetually off balance ("I'm not an opinionated man, I swing with the tide"), sometimes by telling the truth, sometimes by embellishing it, always by being unpredictable—unpredictable enough to endorse and campaign for George McGovern when it suited his purposes.

Matty Troy knows what he's doing. The words and anecdotes that follow show that—A Series of Very Plain Talks and Little Stories on Very Practical Politics, Delivered by Matthew Joseph Troy, Jr., the Queens Philosopher.

EGO

"My ego is immense or I wouldn't be in politics. There is nothing I like more than going into a room and knowing that the people there are waiting for me to say 'Yes' or 'No' . . . A lot of ego satisfaction is what I've gotten from politics. You also meet a lot of nice people."

POWER

"I worked all my life to get into a position of power and I'm not about to play it down . . . The one thing more important than power is fear of power. I get things because people are afraid of what I might do. I lived for weeks off a picture of me on the front page of *The Daily News* with McGovern and Ted Kennedy at the airport. What no one knows is that all I said to them that day is, 'The car's over here.'

"When I called on Tom Eagleton to resign as the Vice Presidential candidate last year, I got this call right away from Gary Hart. 'What do you think you're doing, Matty?' he said, and started hollering at me. I was on the spot, so I said, real tough, 'Do you think I'd do something like this without talking to McGovern first?' Hart got humility right away and I never heard from him for the rest of the campaign. I found out he wasn't talking to McGovern, either—and he was supposed to be the campaign manager. I did anything I wanted to after that . . . I've learned that you can get away with anything with bluff and saber-rattling."

FUN

"I have a good time. I want to have fun every day. One of my problems with the other county leaders—the four gravediggers—is they take themselves so damn seriously. Especially Meade Esposito. Everybody gets quiet when he talks, and I love to keep talking. If he says anything about it, I say, 'Meade, I listened to your bullshit for three years and you still haven't said anything' . . . When we get together, you'd think a grand jury was after us with everyone whispering and looking over his shoulder. The first thing we always do is make a pledge that no one will speak to the press. Then, when it's over, we all race like hell for the nearest telephone to call reporters and get our side into the papers."

PATRONAGE

"Patronage is why people love me so much. Most of what I have goes to lawyers, the big things anyway—that's the way it is. I pick the law secretaries and clerks to the judges in Queens County. They have the right to turn down my people, but then I send over someone different until they're satisfied. I have five of the 50 Assistant District Attorneys—I should have more, but you know Mackell [Queens District Attorney Thomas Mackell] and I don't get along. I have a lot of jobs at Borough Hall, but not as many as in the past because Donnie [Queens Borough President Donald Manes] likes to look independent —part of that's a charade, but part of it's true. With Rockefeller, the state patronage I get is all part of deals, usually for votes he needs in the Legislature."

MAKING DEALS

"Making deals is what a leader does. I make twenty small ones a year —trading votes in the Legislature for a job or two—and a big one every two years. But the first big one shattered all my illusions about dark rooms. Sid Hein [the late Republican leader of Queens] and I met in a diner on Queens Boulevard for two hours and divided up the county for the next couple of years. I insisted that we put it in writing, and I wanted him and Rockefeller to sign it—they wouldn't sign anything, but we agreed to write it out."

Troy still carries the agreement, dated May 17, 1971. It reads, in part:

> Five new Supreme Court judgeships. Repubs to get three—Dems to get two (plus Dems to get replacement for Tony Livoti)—all on a bipartisanship basis . . . If legislators go to Civil Court vacancies, then the special election for legis. vacancy will have no Repub. opponent . . . Repubs agree to give bipartisan endorsement to Boro. Pres., District Attorney and Surrogate . . . Repubs and Dems will split (half-each) Counsel to Public Administrator replacement for Lou Laurino . . . Repub to expedite appointment of Queens Democrat to State Investigation Commission (except no to Murphy and Tessler) . . . Repub to permit MJT to appoint reapportionment head, once Repub seats are protected . . . MJT to receive bipartisan councilman endorsement in 1973.

"Rockefeller has such a great reputation as a square dealer, but that's not what I found out. He keeps wanting to renegotiate. I gave him Queens votes in the Legislature to put a jetport in Newburgh— what did we care about Newburgh?—in return for the right to pick a Supreme Court replacement if Seymour Thaler went to jail. Well, Sy's been convicted and I haven't heard from the Governor. When I do, you can bet he'll want something else thrown in. Lindsay's better. I agreed to lay off him if he got the Urban Task Force out of Queens and I haven't heard a peep out of those task force jerks since."

REFORMERS

"I don't even talk to reformers anymore. They can't deliver anyone, they always have to go back and talk to a thousand people . . . I know what they think of me. In the McGovern campaign, they thought I was a hick from Queens Village . . . I could take elocution lessons and sound like lace-curtain Irish like them."

MONEY

"Money is not that important to me. I just want enough to educate my children. But politics has certainly helped me. Before I was elected to the Council, I was handling criminal law, maybe 100, 125 cases a year, and was making $20,000 or $25,000 a year. Now I handle two hotels in Queens, some negligence cases, and a couple of estates. I gross a little better than $50,000 from the practice, and my partners do almost all the work. I get $34,000 from the Council with everything. I don't get paid as the chairman, but the county Executive Council gives me a car [a 1973 Lincoln Continental] and a driver and an unlimited expense account.

"People come to me all the time asking me to handle zoning variances or other city business. They usually say something like, 'This is very important to me and if you can take care of it, it will be well worth your while.' It's lucky I'm a councilman because it's against the law for me to handle city business as a lawyer—if I was just county leader, I'm not sure I'd resist the temptations. A builder came to me the other day and he said he wanted a road opened and I said I'd see what I could do. 'Thanks,' he said and slid an envelope across the desk. I knew I shouldn't, but I wanted to see how much was in the envelope. There was a stack two inches thick and the bills on the top and bottom were hundreds. Maybe it was $5,000. I gave it back and he said, 'But we've been doing business in the city this way for 50 years.' "

THE CITY COUNCIL

"The Council is a zero. The city should thank God it has no power . . . The only things wrong are the membership and the rules."

THE MEDIA

"I get along with reporters. Maybe they think I'm a clown, but I like them and I go out with them—that's what counts . . . You need them, that's how the game is played. I used to go to them all the time. A couple of reporters in City Hall offered to 'take care' of me in those days for $300 a week. But now they come to me . . . One thing I learned in the McGovern campaign was that the national reporters are cream puffs—they'll write any press release you hand them. The New York guys are much tougher even if they're not above manufacturing a few things."

LYING

"You have to lie. Lying is part of the dueling process when politicians are feeling each other out. It's like bluffing in poker. I don't like it, but I certainly do it . . . If I've got $15,000 to run a campaign, I'll say I've got $100,000. The other guy may say he's got $50,000 when he doesn't have the price of a postage stamp. I'll say I've got this or that county leader when I haven't really talked to them, but who knows whether I'm lying or they're lying when they deny it. The leaders never trust each other anyway."

KEEPING YOUR WORD

"Keeping your word is important in politics, and I always keep my word. Except when I can't."

One time Troy didn't keep his word was last year when he promised to support Dominic Baranello, Democratic chairman of Suffolk County, for a spot on the Democratic National Committee. When the voting started, Queens votes began going to Jack English of Nassau County, and Baranello raced over to Troy, and witnesses remember this conversation:

BARANELLO: What are you doing? You said you were with me.

TROY: I know, but I also said I was with Jack.

BARANELLO: You gave your word.

TROY: I also gave my mother my word that I'd never have anything to do with women.

GEORGE McGOVERN

"I never thought George McGovern was a savior or anything. I supported him because I thought it would help my image. And it did. I'm the same schmuck I've always been, but now people know I've been in a national campaign and they can't dismiss me as a Queens conservative . . . He's a very decent man and I respect him personally, but, God, I'd hate the thought of him as President. He was in over his head. I remember this night in Wisconsin or someplace. It was a quarter to five in the morning and a bunch of us were drinking and laughing, you know, in a hotel room. A guy from *The Times* was standing on a table singing dirty songs and there's this little tap on the door. It's McGovern, and he says, 'Excuse me. I don't mean to disturb you and I don't want you to stop. But I wondered if you knew how long you were going on so I could plan when to go to bed.' The *Times* guy leaped off the table and slammed the door in his face. Could you imagine anyone slamming a door in Nixon's face?"

EDWARD KENNEDY

"He's like me. A put-on artist. He knows it's all bullshit. We were in basic training together during the Korean War, at Fort Gordon in Georgia. We had bunks next to each other. I was the squad leader, and he was the assistant squad leader. His father fixed it up so that we would be assigned as M.P.s to Supreme NATO Headquarters in Paris and then we took physicals and I lost out because I was an inch under six feet. You had to be six feet to be on the honor guard. So he went to Paris and I went to Korea. Then I worked for him in the 1960 campaign.

"Jimmy Breslin talked me into calling this press conference at City Hall last year to say Teddy should run for Vice President. The idea was, I was supposed to be close to McGovern and I was a friend of Teddy's so people would think it was kind of official. Only Teddy heard about it and he called me that morning. It went something like this:

" 'What are you trying to do, you son of a bitch? You're putting me in a corner.'

" 'Well, somebody should make you put up or shut up. You've been diddling with the whole country for a year.'

" 'I want you to call off that conference.'

" 'The reporters are there. What am I going to tell them?'

" 'Tell them you just stopped by to make a horse's ass of yourself. If you don't, I'm going to tell them you're a self-serving son of a bitch who's always using my name.'

"I said 'Up yours' or something like that and hung up. Of course I couldn't go ahead with the Vice Presidency thing, and I did make an ass of myself."

DUMMY CANDIDATES

A standard technique in New York Democratic primaries is to try to split your opponent's vote by putting up a dummy candidate from the same ethnic group to try to cut his vote. Troy's candidate this year for Councilman-at-Large in Queens is Eugene Mastropieri, the incumbent, an Italian. The reform challenger will probably be Arnold Feinblatt, a Jew. This is Troy's embellished scenario for what will happen:

"They'll put another Italian in the race to cut Gene's vote and I'll find a guy named Abe Schwartz and get his name on the ballot to cut Feinblatt. Soon there'll be fourteen Italians and fourteen Jews running. The only difference is that the reformers will get people to run by telling them that they're doing their bit for good government, and I have to get jobs for the losers I put up."

THE FUTURE

"Loyalty is everything in politics. There is nothing second. That's what we had with the old-fashioned bosses and that's what we need now to make the city work again. I want to be that boss—I could be right now if I were in Meade Esposito's position, but I'm too young and Queens isn't a strong enough Democratic county . . . That's what I'm after and it would work for everybody. If there was a Democratic Mayor and I was in charge, people would stay in line and do their jobs. God help them if they didn't—they wouldn't get a streetlight fixed unless they stayed in line and did their job for the party and the city."

*   *   *

Matty Troy's future was not too bright after this article appeared in *New York* magazine in May, 1973. His openness made him a marked man in New York politics—"I liked it, but your piece was the beginning of the end," he told me later—and after backing two losers, Mario Biaggi for mayor in 1973 and Howard Samuels for governor in 1974, Troy was deposed as county chairman in a coup engineered by Mayor Beame.

15 Jacob Javits

Jacob Javits has always reminded me of the ball that comes down at Times Square on New Year's Eve. When he lights up, you know it's already happened.

The senior senator from New York is one of the best men in the United States Senate. He is smarter, harder working, and more effective by half than most of the men hiding behind "Honorables" in Washington. An outsider in the minority party, he has left small but significant marks on most of the major federal legislation of the last twenty years by the sheer force of his own energy and intellect.

Like a string collector, he has been building up bits of political credit for 30 years. But for what? He wouldn't cash it in on Vietnam. He wouldn't cash it in on Watergate. He is 72 years old, and if he isn't careful—or, rather, if he isn't less careful—he will be remembered as a man who once marked up a thousand bills, never lost an election, and was around a long time.

Javits, to say the least, did not light up on Watergate and what Richard Nixon did to America. The senator's action and rhetoric after the nation's most famous burglary would make a long chapter if anyone decides to write a book called *Profiles in Caution.*

The complete politician is a master of creative caution. He has postured and pontificated brilliantly since June 17, 1972, without ever committing himself to anything until just after it has happened and without ever being sidetracked by complicating issues, like right and wrong. His most spectacular day was April 3, 1974, two weeks after his junior colleague, James Buckley, called on President Nixon to resign for the good of the country.

Javits called a press conference to say the President might like to consider resigning—for a while. He emphasized that he wasn't urging Nixon to do anything, just pointing out that under the Twenty-fifth Amendment the President had the option of temporarily stepping down and letting Vice President Gerald Ford act as President for a while, perhaps during an impeachment trial or summit conference. He then added that Buckley's action was "sterile" because no senator can force a President to resign. One man's courage, it seems, is another man's sterility.

Watching Javits do his thing—*survive*—is a casebook study in clever followership, in minimum-risk politics. It is instructive to look at the senator's doings over the two-week period from April 27 to May 10, 1974, the period before and after the release of the President's grubby and edited transcripts.

• *April 27*—Javits ponders the future, which is always a lot safer than dealing with the present, in a long speech to the Ripon Society titled "Building National Institutions for the Future"—a speech that is played as front-page news by *The New York Times.*

In the speech, he postures as a risk-taker—"Congress, unwilling to accept risk-taking responsibility, has been much too weak . . ."—and proposes that Presidents be required to present annual reports to Congress and submit once a year to British-style parliamentary questioning. It's a smart stance, similar to Javits's War Powers bill, pushed and passed *after* Vietnam, requiring Presidents to receive specific congressional authorization to engage American troops anywhere for more than 60 days.

From now on, Javits can take the statesmanlike view that he is dealing with permanent institutional reform—the controversy of the day is, after all, too petty for a statesman.

• *April 28*—Sure enough, on *Face the Nation,* Javits touches the theme: "I've been hitting that very hard in terms of beefing up the Congress so that it will assert its authority . . ." He also responds to a question about impeachment and the House Judiciary Committee by saying, "If I were the committee . . ."

• *May 1*—An hour after *Face the Nation,* a New York jury acquitted John Mitchell and Maurice Stans of some Watergate-related charges. Javits, according to friends, immediately began reassessing his position and today he says: "I am not a member of the Judiciary Committee, so I can't postulate what I would do if I were a member."

In his regularly scheduled biweekly news conference—conferences he began only after Jim Buckley began holding his own as soon as he got to Washington—Javits refuses to respond to questions on the transcripts released by the President the day before. "I do not intend in any way to comment on the substantive nature of the publication. I will be a judge or a juror . . . if it ends with the issue of impeachment in the House . . . I cannot characterize my attitude, belief or disbelief, toward the evidence or its substantive nature . . . it would compromise my role as a possible judge."

When asked whether the President was wrong in giving edited transcripts instead of the tapes subpoenaed by the Judiciary Committee, Javits answers: "No, sir. I will not say—there is no right or wrong. That's what he feels he wants to give them. But we have a right . . . to say that 'we're going to hold him responsible for whatever assumption we make from the fact that [he] didn't give us what we asked for.' "

When asked whether the President or the Judiciary Committee was responsible for "dragging out Watergate," Javits answers, "I think it would be pointless of me to blame that on anybody. The point is to look forward . . ."

• *May 7*—Javits tells Roger Mudd of CBS News that he has nothing to say about the transcripts: "I may well be one of the 100 judges. When I comment, I'll be prepared."

The Javits statement looks a little ridiculous on *The CBS Evening News* when it appears after strong comments—"shabby" . . . "immoral" . . . "shocking"—from other Republican senators. Javits's staff explains that Mudd pulled Javits off the Senate floor and the senator didn't know that his Republican colleagues thought the time had come to unload on Nixon. Javits, in other words, didn't know it was safe to have an opinion.

• *May 8*—It's safe now, and apparently Javits feels prepared to comment. He tells *The Washington Star-News* that the general tone of the transcripts is "dismaying." (On the same day, New York's other elder statesman, Nelson Rockefeller, makes his first comment 1,000 miles away in Kansas City. He says the transcripts are "dismaying.")

In a television taping for broadcast in New York, Javits adds that the tapes "are not decisive either way." He also says that as a lawyer he can't call on the President to resign. "I believe it is unprofessional for me . . . the President has said 'I will not resign because I am innocent.' Therefore, if I call on him to resign, that is, in my judgment, tantamount to a finding of guilty."

A lawyer, not a leader. I suppose a man has a right to cast himself in any role he chooses. Javits sometimes makes another choice. "What you have to understand," he once told a news staff member, "is that I am more than a senator, I am an institution."

I talked with Javits a week later about institutions, leadership, and morality after he had taped a television show called *Crisis in the Capital* with the four senators from New Jersey and Connecticut— Jim Buckley went to a Public Works Committee meeting, telling CBS that people knew where he stood on the President.

"You know," Javits said as we walked to his car, "I have to admire Buckley sometimes. He really does what he wants. I've been around for a lot longer than him and I'd never have the guts to turn down CBS."

Part of my conversation with Javits went like this:

Is the impeachment process primarily judicial, political, or moral?

"I'd say it's a third each—a third political, a third moral, and a third judicial . . . the judicial part is procedural—due process—and we [the Senate] are a jury."

Then does a senator have any obligation to provide political leadership and moral leadership to his constituents? Should he stand up and say, "Look, this is wrong!"?

"I've given moral leadership in the insistence that the President tell all he knows . . . but if I have to trade off the moral leadership I could give in denouncing the President for prejudging the case—if people want that moral leadership, I can't give it to them. I can't, in conscience, pass on my views on the substantive issues involved here."

Do you have strong personal, private views on the right and wrong of this thing?

Javits hesitated for a long moment, then said, "I suppose I do." After another hesitation, he added, "I'd be less than human if I didn't."

Javits, in case you haven't guessed over the years, is not exactly a man of passion. To me, at that moment, he sounded like a burnt-out case—but then lawyers often sound that way to me.

Burnt-out is a terrible phrase to apply to any man, but I have heard Javits's own staff using it after his *Face the Nation* appearance. That Sunday he was asked about the alleged anti-Semitic remarks in the Presidential tapes. This, in part, was his reply:

"I think they're irrelevant . . . I think the public can understand those things . . . I'm Jewish, and I can understand them. I don't approve of them; I don't tolerate them; I don't feel that—you know, I feel that they indicate a kind of state of mind that I feel very seriously against. But nonetheless, in the running conversation of a man in high office, with a lot of things on his mind, and sometimes expressing a passionate feeling if someone's annoying him—it's not admirable—but I think it will be understood."

Well, I don't understand that coming from Javits, a man who once told me about the dozens of congressmen who would never talk to him, never shake his hand because he was a Jew. That was in 1947 when he first came to the House of Representatives. But it was in the mid-1960s that Senator James Eastland, the old Mississippi bigot, turned to him at a Judiciary Committee meeting and said: "Javits, I don't like you, and I don't like your kind."

There are things in this world to be passionate about. Whether or not Nixon is found guilty after due process, what went on in his White House is wrong! It is not "dismaying." It is wrong, wrong, *wrong*—and if we don't know that and don't do something about it, we are in deep trouble. We can forget all that sixth-grade stuff about Wash-

ington and Jefferson and Lincoln—we won't have anything to do with
those people.

I guess I wanted Javits to sound something like William Cohen, the
33-year-old freshman congressman from Maine who is the only
Republican on the Judiciary Committee who voted to send the President a letter gently reminding him that he had not complied with the
committee subpoena of Watergate tapes. I had asked Cohen the same
questions I asked Javits, and part of his answer was: "This is an issue
that transcends—it's just more important than my political survival."

(Cohen won his district, the woods and villages of the northeast
corner of the United States, with 54 percent of the vote in 1972. In
1974, after taking a strong Watergate stand and after Nixon's resignation, he won 72 percent of the vote against Mark Gartley, a former
Navy lieutenant who was one of the first prisoners of war to return
from Hanoi. At the same time, Javits was being re-elected with just
46 percent of the vote against Democrat Ramsey Clark and Conservative Barbara Keating.)

Cohen, a lawyer and a not-so-liberal Republican, is a very amateur
poet. But he likes to quote professionals and this time he chose T. S.
Eliot and lines from *Murder in the Cathedral:*

> The last temptation is the greatest treason:
> To do the right deed for the wrong reason.

Jacob Javits, I have no doubt, will do the right deed in the end, most
times, on most issues. And he will do it for the wrong reason—because
it had already happened, the ball was down on Times Square. Happy
New Year!

16 | James Buckley

James Buckley is an honest politician. He is a man of conscience. He may be the strangest, or worst, senator New Yorkers have ever elected —and the odds are they won't do it again.

Buckley's conscience, to borrow the title of a small book by Barry Goldwater, is the conscience of a conservative. In 1970, he was elected a U.S. Senator by accident and he had to choose either to represent a national conservative constituency synonymous with the name Buckley or to represent New York and the state's gritty, often grubby, political self-interest as interpreted by more traditional representatives.

It was an easy choice for a man of conscience. Among the things he told his staff at the beginning were: "I want to be a U.S. Senator, not a politician or a candidate for re-election . . . I'll tell you what I believe. Tell me the political implications later."

It is now later. The political implications are that it will take another accident or divine intervention, something on that order, for James Lane Buckley to be elected to a second term in the Senate in 1976. "I suppose I have made it difficult for myself in '76," said Buckley, who very much wants to be re-elected. "I remember one two-week period where I voted against motherhood twelve times. But the voters can spot a phony, and if I start waffling, I'll destroy my greatest asset—voters think of me as a non-politician. I like that image. It enables me to do what I want to do anyway."

Leaving aside the question of whether the voters can spot phonies, the Senator has not actually voted on motherhood—if he did, Buckley, one of ten brothers and sisters and the father of six, could be counted as a defender. What he has done is speak out against emergency federal aid to New York City and vote against Social Security, the minimum wage, mass transit, vocational rehabilitation for the handicapped, child care, seat belts, price controls, business taxes, and almost everything else that he has interpreted as government intervention into the free market or individual liberty. "Each one of us is accountable for ourselves," he said. "Ultimate freedom is based on self-discipline . . . that includes the freedom for each of us to make mistakes."

Buckley's *Principia* as outlined to me include:

"To preserve a society where an individual has maximum control over his own destiny within a framework that holds the society together.

"There are no problems to which you cannot apply the experience of 2,000 years of Western society. There is a reservoir of wisdom, of understanding human behavior and motivation—as an example, when you have an option, it is wiser to choose a non-governmental option over a governmental option.

"My philosophical touchstone—I think it comes from Plato or Aquinas—is the rule of subsidiary: no government should be exercised at a higher level than the lowest competent authority."

Those principles have led Buckley on some interesting crusades— interesting, that is, for a junior senator from New York. He spent hundreds of hard hours in his "effort to free the American farmer from government paternalism," a floor fight to eliminate federal subsidies to wheat, feed grain, and cotton farmers. He spent even more time in a quixotically courageous fight to eliminate "pork barrel" from public works legislation—until his peeved colleagues reacted by eliminating New York's pork: $14 million to clean up New York harbor and an unspecified amount to correct beach erosion on Long Island from Fire Island to Montauk.

The great pork crusade was pure Buckley: great morality, good conservatism, and lousy politics—at least lousy politics under the old rules. "Pork" is the goodies that are added to every public works bill for no other reason than that influential members of Congress want that road or dam in their home town. It's not that the projects are necessarily bad—most are badly needed—it's just that they benefit only one area; they are not part of any established national policy.

Well, Buckley, a member of the Water Resources Subcommittee of the Senate Public Works Committee, started speaking the unspeakable. He moved to eliminate 44 "special interest" projects totaling $109 million of the $1.2 billion harbors and rivers bill of 1973. He was, as some of his worst enemies admitted to me in private, absolutely right on the merits. He was so right his colleagues thought he must be kidding; subcommittee chairman Mike Gravel of Alaska accused him of being "childish." Buckley wasn't kidding, so other committee members asked him to list the special-interest projects, one by one—they overruled him consistently until he came to New York projects, and then voted to kill those. Buckley continued his anti-pork fight on the Senate floor and, very predictably, lost 71 to 9.

Buckley, like Paul Douglas, the Illinois liberal who was the last pork-fighter in the 1950s, is not the slightest bit self-conscious about going it alone. When he's not going it alone, he usually isn't going New York's way—if the safe New York way can be judged by Senator Jacob Javits, who has a well-deserved reputation for keeping a clever wet finger in the winds from home. In one ten-month period through 1972, Buckley voted with Javits 85 times and against him 88 times. In the same period, Buckley voted with Senator Strom Thurmond of South Carolina 156 times and against him 29 times. In *Congressional Quarterly* ratings, Buckley voted with Republicans on 83 percent of all roll calls, with President Nixon 80 percent of the time, and with the Conservative Coalition of Republicans and Southern Democrats 79 percent of the time. When I asked him which of his colleagues he most admired, he started on the right—Goldwater, Jesse Helms of North Carolina, and Harry Byrd of Virginia.

In fact, although Buckley is popular and respected in the Senate— he was the only freshman to receive significant mention as "bright" and "hard-working" last year in the Ralph Nader survey of legislative assistants' attitudes toward senators—he is hardly even a minor force in the Congress. "He is just too far right," said a well-placed Senate aide. "His positions are so rigid, he can't get in the game."

What Buckley appears to be representing best in Washington is The American Right—in order, the Buckley family, *National Review,* the American Conservative Union, Young Americans for Freedom, and *Human Events.* That is a demanding constituency, particularly when your brother is William F. Buckley, Jr., editor of *National Review* and a founder of Y.A.F. (55,000 members), which features "Free Non-Union Lettuce" stands at its meetings and lists Anna Chennault, John Wayne, and Herbert Philbrick as "national advisers." The A.C.U. (70,000 members) is a kind of Y.A.F. alumni association, and *Human Events* is a sometimes perceptive right-wing weekly with leads like "In a new effort to strangle free enterprise, the Senate last week . . ."

They are a strange and vital breed: Social Darwinists, convinced they are the fittest. They assembled, about 500 of them, in January, 1974, in Washington for a three-day American Conservative Political Action conference. They are certainly not the hard-hats, or white ethnics, or Catholic working class, or conservative Democrats who did so much for Jim Buckley in 1970 and Richard Nixon in 1972. They are, in general, committed, young, upwardly mobile, middle class, determinedly intellectual, institutionally paranoid Christian gentlemen. Much of what they are about was projected in the conference's closing event in an address by Senator James L. Buckley:

> We have to present a common front against the great heresies that still dominate our times. I want to quote Frank Meyer [a late *National Review* editor who like many dedicated conservatives was a former Communist]: "In opposition to this image of man as neither free nor inspired by a transcendent destiny, the differences between libertarian and traditionalist are thrown into their true perspective" . . . The time has come for conservatives to assert what is rightfully theirs, the intellectual leadership of this country, in the schools, in the media, wherever ideas are promulgated and discussed.
>
> I am convinced that the missionary field has never been so ready to hear

the Conservative gospel . . . Americans are hungry for a sense of commitment to an ideal higher than the satisfaction of their appetites . . . Any political party that forthrightly builds its platform on the bedrock of Conservative principle and insight will be the majority party of the 1980s . . . If no party so bases itself . . . then we will see a continuing erosion of our freedoms and vitality that in time will spell the end of the American nation as we have known and loved it.

There it is: God and Man in Washington.

Some of his words refer to the internal politics of conservatism, the split between traditionalists and libertarians. The dialogue of the split is sometimes as incomprehensible as left-wing dialogues of the 1930s, but it seems to come down to this: traditionalism is crusading, very Catholic enforcement of virtue in the society and usually manifests itself in almost fanatic anti-Communism; libertarianism verges on anarchy, with each individual having almost total freedom of choice. Libertarians would translate Adam Smith's free-market theories of business into all social interaction—drugs and sex, for instance, would be a matter of individual choice. In one ultimate example—proposed by their antecedents, nineteenth-century laissez-faire liberals—government would not build lighthouses because shipping and insurance companies could build them if they wanted them.

Jim Buckley describes himself as "somewhere between" traditionalism and libertarianism. He is certainly a traditionalist on abortion, devoting a good part of his life to ending "the slaughter of the innocents" with a Constitutional amendment. He is, however, a libertarian on seat belts and has introduced legislation to allow drivers to disconnect the gadgetry that makes it impossible to start a car without buckling the seat belts—we, he believes, should have the freedom to be "idiots," and government has no duty or right "to take all the risk out of life."

Most Buckley voters in Queens would have been as out of place at an A.C.P.A. conference as at an A.C.L.U. rally. They didn't know who Jim Buckley was when they voted for him. In fact, if you remember that campaign and "Join the March for America," they didn't really vote for Buckley, they voted for patriotism and against the liberalism of Charles Goodell and Richard Ottinger, the Republican-Liberal and Democratic candidates in the three-way race that split: Buckley 39 percent, Ottinger 37, and Goodell 24.

The Buckleys, in fact, are a hell of a lot more radical than Dick Ottinger or Charlie Goodell—the true conservatives *really* do want to change America. Jim Buckley never claimed otherwise in 1970. But no one listened to him because the focus was on the twin liberals. In 1976, the focus will be on him. "The numbers are coming our way, people are moving right," said F. Clifton White, who managed the 1970 campaign and will be Buckley's main man again in 1976. That may be true, but there will also be questions coming the senator's way from his "average citizen." Like this one: Are you representing us, or are you telling us what's good for us, or maybe what's good for our souls? The U.S. Senate, after all, is not the church.

When Buckley first announced in 1968 that he wanted to be a senator—he received more than a million votes as a Conservative party protest candidate that year against Javits—his knees were shaking as he read through his prepared text. "He reminded me afterwards," said Bill Buckley, "that that was the first time he'd spoken in public in seventeen years—since he spoke before the ornithological club of Millbrook, New York."

His knees don't shake anymore, but the junior senator hardly has the egocentric instincts, habits, and lifestyles of a professional politician, a perpetual candidate. The first time he was invited to appear on *Face the Nation,* Buckley asked his press secretary: "Do I have to do it? I planned to spend Sunday with the family." He refers to the nightly rounds of receptions, parties, and dinners favored by campaigners-for-all-seasons like Javits as: "Cosmetics . . . It's all a fraud —what I'd like is more time to think."

Buckley wants both the Republican and Conservative nominations in 1976, and the one political exercise that he's done faithfully is courting upstate Republican leaders. He has raised, by his estimate, $250,000 for county G.O.P. organizations with speeches at upstate fund-raising events—for two years many of those events, not incidentally, were on his way home from Washington for weekends with his wife and children in Sharon, Connecticut. (New York's junior senator hopes to avoid being labeled "the third senator from Connecticut." In 1973, he bought a $125,000 home in northwest Washington and moved his family from his six-acre place in Sharon, which he still owns and which cost him $75,000 in 1968. His official residence, his voting address, is an East Side apartment shared with a sister, where he has stayed for years when he was in New York City. The senator's children are all in private schools, the younger ones at St. Alban's, a Washington Episcopalian school—their father added that they receive Catholic training one day a week.)

"Vulnerable" is the pollster's word for Buckley's political status at home. His staff is worried that he's going to be labeled a "do-nothing senator" because he hasn't been particularly visible on New York television or in the city newspapers. (Buckley has a small bet with his press secretary, Leonard Saffir, that he will receive more column inches this year in *The Chicago Tribune* than in *The New York Times;* it was close last year.)

Buckley's vulnerability—polls have shown that his "favorable" job rating ranges from 53 percent in Syracuse to 34 percent in New York City, with most suburban ratings in the 40s—may be more complex than his visibility or his problems within the Republican and Conservative parties. He was elected by a constituency that crossed all party lines, and that constituency, according to one pollster, is "disappointed."

"His people, Queens conservative Democrats, for example, don't know yet what he's been doing in Washington," the pollster said. "The problem is that his slogan in 1970—Isn't It Time *We* Had a Senator?—was too good. They really thought Jim Buckley was going to do something for them. Now they feel that he hasn't made a damn bit of difference."

In 1976, Buckley will try to educate New York voters as to why he thinks increased Social Security is bad for them (government spending is too high); why the minimum wage shouldn't go up (it forces employers to lay off or not hire poorly skilled youths and poor people); why federal child care programs are bad (they will lead to

"thought control"); why abortion must go ("it's murder"), and why
he voted for the supersonic transport prototype when he seemed to
be against it on environmental grounds (we could only determine
environmental damage by testing a prototype SST). Buckley, by the
way, voted against federal loans to bankrupt Lockheed Aircraft, calling the loans "unwise intrusion into the free market mechanism."

"Intrusion" is almost always a bad word to a Buckley, except when
it comes to legalization of abortion—then people should not be "free"
because they're inside the circle of mortal sin. I asked Buckley if he
would cut welfare to the point where people starved. "No," he answered, "but if they did not do such work as is available, they would
have to live in a significant lack of comfort."

Even on environmental issues, his chosen specialty, the senator
thinks the federal government has gone far enough. "There is not
much more to be done by Congress . . . I'm a conservationist, not a
preservationist. My approach is based on a recognition that we have
to restore air and water quality in the context of a highly technical
society, and we can't disrupt it overnight."

Buckley, the 1976 candidate, will also have to be the official local
defender of the Nixon-Ford years and their contribution to the
American spirit. A bit ironic, that, because Buckley has vocally opposed Presidential initiatives many New Yorkers cheered: détente
with Russia, the opening to China, and wage and price controls.
Buckley's operative quotes include phrases like these: "The driving,
disciplined, fanatic force which is Communism" . . . "opposes the
abandonment of Taiwan" . . . "this anti-military binge" . . . "invite
a technological Pearl Harbor."

"My ultimate defense in the campaign will be that I have been
someone who has tried to be honest with the voters," said Buckley in
his rather Spartan office decorated with Revolutionary War and Hudson Valley paintings, Audubon prints, and photographs of his trips to
the Arctic and Antarctica. "I came here from a job that satisfied me
fully and I could go back. This is a dispensable job."

The job that satisfied Jim Buckley was vice president of the
Catawba Corporation, the family business, a corporation organized in

1948 to, according to Securities and Exchange Commission records, "render financial, technical, and other services to corporations primarily engaged in the exploration for, and the production of, petroleum in foreign countries."

Catawba has only eleven employees, including John Buckley, its president. The corporation sells its services to several other small corporations looking for oil, gas, and minerals all over the world. The other corporations, all controlled by Buckley family stock, sound as romantic as the wildcatting and exploration that William F. Buckley, Sr., did to build the family fortune in Mexico: Pantepec, Pancoastal, Canadian Southern, Magellan, United Canso, and Coastal Caribbean oil corporations.

The whole thing sounds a lot more impressive than it apparently is. The Buckleys try to find oil concessions abroad to lease them to the major oil companies—the problem is that they seem to be the dry-hole champions of the Western and Eastern Hemispheres. The Buckleys simply aren't as rich as everyone thinks. Most estimates of their wealth are based on a report that Buckley, Sr., left an estate of $100 million to his ten children in 1958. He didn't. What was worth $100 million was the stock of the subsidiary corporations which was distributed among 100,000 shareholders.

Buckley has told friends, surprised friends, that he is not a millionaire, that his net worth is in the $500,000 range. He wouldn't tell me, and he publicly answered a *New York Times* request for his income tax returns and a net-worth statement by telling the editors it was none of their business and suggesting that *The Times* demonstrate its "good faith" by publishing the financial records of Arthur Ochs Sulzberger and other *Times*men. In late 1975, with re-election on his mind, Buckley reluctantly announced that the total 1974 income of himself and his wife was $165,000, less an unspecified amount deducted for oil-depletion allowances.

"Each of us has to work to maintain the private-school lifestyle we're accustomed to," the senator said of Buckleymen. "We have lived high on the hog on the assumption that our ship will come in one of these days."

Buckley said he could not live on his $42,500 Senate salary and he is eating into capital—the profits of Catawba are equally divided among the children of W.F.B., Sr. He also makes more than $30,000 in speaking honoraria and uses about half that to help pay for his Senate offices in Washington, New York, Albany, and Rochester.

What Buckley, Sr., did leave his family was hard Roman Catholicism, doctrinaire conservative politics, and an extraordinary sense of civilization. Two quotes tell a lot about the Buckleys. The first is from Priscilla Buckley, now managing editor of *National Review:* "There was nothing complicated about father's theory of child rearing. He brought up his sons and daughters with the quite simple objective that they become absolutely perfect."

The second is from James Buckley: "Civilization is a gossamer web. If we loosen the garb of common political traditions, we will destroy it. That's why I'm reluctant to take off my tie, or why the way the British dress for dinner in the jungle is so sensible."

Will Buckley, as W.F.B., Sr., was known to friends, was a hard man. He survived in the rough early days of international oil gambling, and he became an important, controversial foreigner in Mexico. Some of his political thinking came through in testimony before the Senate Foreign Relations Committee in 1919: "The truth is that it does not matter what a great majority of the Mexican people think; the mass of the people have not the ability to think clearly and have not the knowledge on which to base convictions, or the public spirit to act on them."

This founding father's children have the knowledge and the benefit of their father's convictions. The ten young Buckleys received a rigid tutorial education in three languages, traveled extensively, and no matter how young they were, were challenged to compete in the intellectual world of their father.

Young Jimmy, now the third oldest at 50, was always remembered as his mother's favorite, and the quietest in family discussions. He was interested in animals—keeping his own little zoo in Sharon—and in bird-watching. He went to Yale and Yale Law School with time out for World War II and Navy service as a deck officer on a landing craft at places like Okinawa and Leyte.

Back home he practiced law for a while in New Haven, married Ann Frances Cooley, a former Central Intelligence Agency European desk officer from a prominent and wealthy St. Louis family, had five sons and a daughter—and generally went around being known as Bill Buckley's quiet brother.

Bill and Jim Buckley, as far as I can tell, agree on everything except personal style, and Bill's involvement with the Conservative party pulled his shaky-kneed brother into politics. The rest—with the help of $2 million in 1970 contributions, including a $15,000 gift and a $100,000 loan from W. Clement Stone—is history.

I have avoided, until now, saying that Jim Buckley is a nice guy. Everybody says that first—and everybody is right. He is charming, mannered, and modest; all the lines in his face are from smiling and laughing. His engaging attributes are heightened by a slight, almost thoughtful, stammer and a courtly manner—when Jim Buckley greets someone he places his heels together and bows slightly, the degree and length of the bow depending on the sex and age of the person he is honored to meet.

Someone once said that a Buckley is never rude by accident. Senator Buckley is probably just never. Once, on the monthly television show he tapes for showing in New York, a guest called Senator William Fulbright's views "naive and stupid." Buckley immediately dispatched a "Dear Bill" letter: "I was completely caught off guard during my television interview with Bruce Herscheshon of U.S.I.A. . . . I just wanted you to know that the program was totally unrehearsed and that I regret the personal references."

Charm, I suspect, will not be the issue in 1976. James Buckley, the man who has been true to himself, will be. Whatever you think of his views—I think they range from ridiculous to refreshing—you have to admire an honest man. But vote for him?

Buckley never made it in baseball either—instead of touching bases he marched to a different drummer. In a privately published family history, his sister Priscilla said: "He was shy; he loved wandering in the woods; he was impossible on the baseball field. He was always mooning and looking at birds instead of covering third base like he was meant to."

Epilogue

On November 2, 1972, after more than a year of crossing and recrossing the American continent, trying to get his message and vision across, George McGovern, the Democratic candidate for President of the United States, landed in Battle Creek, Michigan. With five days to go before Election Day, McGovern was dragging and his campaign was dragging, but instinct and the dregs of his adrenalin carried him to the airport fence, where a small crowd was cheering him.

Well, most of them were cheering. A big fat kid in a windbreaker, who may have been 20 years old, was shouting, "Go back to South Dakota, ya bum! Nixon's gonna beat you so bad you'll be sorry you left." McGovern leaned over the little fence and beckoned the heckler, saying, "Let me tell you a secret." The kid came to the fence and George McGovern said, "Kiss my ass!"

I thought that was the high point of the McGovern campaign. I remember Artie Schmidt sitting in his living room in Bayside, Queens, a few nights before, saying, "I don't understand politicians and I don't think they understand us." Well, nobody had any trouble understanding McGovern that day.

I don't think American politicians, most of whom are professional candidates—running for office is what they do for a living, not representing or governing—understand their people anymore. Usually, I don't think they even see them—at least McGovern *saw* that kid in Battle Creek, that one individual. What they do see is an endless chain of hands to be shaken, backs to be slapped, questions to be talked about, answers to be avoided. If there is one thing the professional candidate knows, it's that answers, real answers, may make some people mad—and America's perpetual runners are in the business of avoiding getting anyone upset.

Of course, what happened in recent years is that almost everyone is vaguely upset. Apathy has become the 1970s catchword for non-participation in the political process, but, as far as I can tell, many of the non-participating, non-voting Americans are not apathetic at all. They are hostile. They feel they are being had, that national politics is a put-on.

Perhaps I'm a romantic, but my own experience continually indicates that people are not as stupid as politicians think they are. (Political writing could be defined as a polar stuggle between romanticism and cynicism. More often than not it is the voters, if you talk to them long enough, who attract you to hope, and the candidates, if you watch them long enough, who attract you to despair.) In Bayside, the Queens district I wrote about at the beginning of this book, where about half the voters are Roman Catholics and most of those Catholics send their children to parochial schools, candidates for federal and state offices, almost without exception, tried to peddle a single political line: *I'm really personally against abortion and for governmental aid to parochial schools, but there isn't much a poor politician can do.*

Some of those candidates, their records indicated, were lying. But, whether or not individual politicians were truthful, the interesting thing to me was the candidate consensus that this was the way to survive with Catholic voters. And the Catholic voters? Most of those I talked with knew condescension when it hit them; there was something of a consensus that they were being put-on, being kept dumb and happy.

Was that political con and the cynicism it bred on both sides necessary? I hope not and I think not. At least I didn't think it was necessary with people like Artie Schmidt and Patricia Mulfall, the kind of Bayside voters that politicians, from Richard Nixon down, thought they were making happy. On abortion, after hours of thoughtful conversation, Schmidt said: "I personally believe it's murder, but I can't impose my standards on other people." On aid to parochial schools, Pat Mulfall, whose husband was paying tuition for two children at St. Robert's on a $9,000 salary, said: "I don't want Mayor Lindsay telling Bishop Mugavero what to do or vice versa."

Almost four years later, on February 3, 1976, President Gerald Ford offered his definitive position on abortion during an interview with Walter Cronkite of CBS. The President's assistants made it clear that their man expected the question and he was ready. Ford said that he thought the U.S. Supreme Court "went too far" in striking down laws against abortion, but that a Constitutional amendment restoring the laws would also be going "too far." "If there was to be some action in this area," he continued, "it's my judgment that it ought to be on a basis of what each individual state wishes to do under the circumstances." The answer was perfectly circular, since a Constitutional amendment would be required to give states local options on abortion. What Ford had said was identical to, and as meaningless as, what candidates in Bayside told Artie Schmidt and his neighbors in 1972: *I'm personally against abortion, but there isn't much a poor President can do.*

Ford, who has spent his adult life running for office, is a master of the Politics of Un-Responsibility, the art of transferring responsibility (and blame). It's a survival technique used by incumbent politicians, the old faces, just as cosmetics and cosmetic surgery is being used these days to keep their features from showing age as long as possible. As the faces in the nation's corridors of power get older and older beneath powder and surgical tucks, un-responsibility and inevitable disillusionment are eroding what used to be the power of the people, by the people, and for the people. Democracy atrophies as politicians minimize their responsibility in order to maximize their tenure and the people out there, the constituents, turn away from politics and old faces (almost half the adult nation could not be persuaded in 1974 to take the most minimal political action, voting). How many Americans have seen through Washington's most energetic game, the endless baseline rally of responsibility-shifting from the White House to Congress and back?

All the while, much of what used to be the people's business has been shifting to institutions further from public control—corporations, bureaucracies, public-employee unions, the press, and the courts. Politicians in the 1970s find position more comfortable, and safer, than power and responsibility. So bankers took political control of New York City from elected officials incapable of making the most obvious decisions, multinational corporations filled the power vacuum when the United States government could not formulate energies policies, newspapers and the courts conquered a President while Congress debated procedure, and a single federal judge took over the schools and much of the government of Boston as the city's politicians ran for un-responsible cover.

Those actions—a trend, I think—constitute a political crisis. The loss of political power was most dramatic in New York City, where a visitor returning after a few months away in 1975 could have reasonably concluded that he had missed a *coup d'état.* After years of hiding budget deficits with borrowing and lies about the city's economic base and prospects, New York's elected government simply handed policy control of eight million Americans over to state-appointed commissions of bankers and businessmen to avoid immediate bankruptcy. And political things seem to be moving in the same direction across the country: In Boston, elected government could not or would not deal with school integration; in New Jersey, the courts were in the process of dictating tax reform legislation. Professor Samuel P. Huntington of Harvard, for one, saw similar federal portents, and you don't have to agree with the specifics of his argument to understand the point he is making about abdication of power:

> The United States government has given up the authority to draft its citizens into the armed forces and is now committed to providing the monetary incentives to attract volunteers with a stationary or declining percentage of the GNP. At the present time, this would appear to pose no deleterious consequences for national security. The question necessarily arises, however, whether, if a new threat to security should materialize in the future (as it inevitably will at some point), the government will possess the authority to command the resources, as well as the sacrifices, which are necessary to meet that threat.

Whether or not things have gone as far as Huntington thinks, there is something a little ridiculous about the President of the United States traveling the land pleading impotence, as Gerald Ford did in 1975 and 1976. Part of his plea was that "the bureaucracy" would not let him do anything. "Why don't you go back to Washington and do something about it, then?" someone grumbled loudly in a San Francisco audience. "Those people work for you, you know!"

If things are that tough in Washington, then maybe the American people should do poor Jerry Ford and a lot of the other old faces of 1976 a favor and get them the hell out! The one thing I'm sure I've learned in hanging around politics for too many years is that we have to protect ourselves against the old faces (and protect them from themselves): throw the rascals out, at least periodically, the good with the bad, the honest with the dishonest, the competent with the incompetent. No matter how well intentioned most of the people who go into politics are at the beginning, they are almost irresistibly drawn into a process that serves its own internal needs—the most obvious being continuous re-election or election to higher office. More than anything else, I would like to see serious discussion of Constitutional limits on the tenure of public officials. Let a citizen who serves, say, eight years in elected office, follow that with four years in private life before he or she can run for anything again. If Thomas Jefferson could periodically go home to Monticello to check the fields and do painful things like thinking, then so can the rest of us, including those who think they're big enough to take his place.

Index

229

About the Author

Richard Reeves learned politics in his father's house, and in Jersey City where his father was a judge there was plenty to learn. He founded a newspaper, the *Free Press,* in Phillipsburg, New Jersey, two years after graduating from Stevens Institute of Technology as a mechanical engineer. He later joined the *Newark News* as a reporter, moved to the *New York Herald Tribune* where he won several awards for reporting, and then joined *The New York Times* where he was the paper's chief political correspondent until 1971 when he left to free-lance. More than a hundred of his articles have been published in several magazines. His first book was *A Ford, not a Lincoln.* This is his second. He has been host of his own television show, *Sunday,* on WNBC, New York, and is a co-host of *In Conversation,* a nationally syndicated radio program. He has taught political writing at the Columbia School of Journalism and political science at Hunter College.